KINGPINS, HUSTLES AND HOMICIDES
PHILADELPHIA TRUE NOIR

GEORGE ANASTASIA

A *PHILADELPHIA INQUIRER* BOOK

CAMINO BOOKS, INC.
PHILADELPHIA

Manufactured in the United States of America

1 2 3 4 5   13 12 11 10

Library of Congress Cataloging-in-Publication Data

Anastasia, George
Philadelphia true noir: kingpins, hustles and homicides / George Anastasia.
p.cm.
"A Philadelphia Inquirer Book."
ISBN 978–1–933822–26–6 (alk. paper)
1. Crime—Pennsylvania—Philadelphia—Case studies. 2. Criminals—Pennsylvania—Philadelphia—Case studies. I. Title.

HV6795.P5A53 2010
364.109748'11—dc22   201001357

ISBN 978-1-933822-26-6
ISBN 978-1-933822-29-7 (ebook)

Cover and interior design: Jerilyn Bockorick

Photographs on pages 2, 78, 130, 171 and 172 courtesy of *The Philadelphia Inquirer*.
Photograph on page 228 courtesy of Danny Provenzano.

Publisher
Camino Books, Inc.
P.O. Box 59026
Philadelphia, PA 19102

www.caminobooks.com

FOR JULIET AND NICOLAS

CONTENTS

GANGSTAS AND DRUG LORDS

THE TAKEDOWN OF "ACE CAPONE" 130

COSA NOSTRA 2000

REEL TO REAL 229

PROLOGUE

Life isn't always fair. Bad things happen to good people. The world is cold and gritty and dominated by characters who lack compassion, who only care about themselves. Too often, they come out on top.

In fiction, there is a literary genre built around life painted in that dark, cynical motif. It's called *noir*, the French word for black. And it has provided us with some classics.

Novels about hardboiled characters—usually cynical private detectives who have been around too long and who expect to be disappointed—have fueled the noir concept for decades. Think Dashiell Hammett, Raymond Chandler, Mickey Spillane or contemporary writers like Walter Mosley, Elmore Leonard and the late Robert Parker. "Film noir," the cinematic version, has spawned gems like *The Maltese Falcon, The Big Sleep, Body Heat* and *Pulp Fiction*, to cite just four examples.

If serious journalism is, as someone once said, the rough draft of history, then true crime reporting is the foundation for the fictional world known as noir. This book provides a piece of that foundation.

The stories that follow are slices of Philadelphia life taken from an underworld where people don't play by the rules and where the good guys don't always win. These are stories about wiseguys and drug dealers, con men and murderers. They're the people I've been writing about in *The Philadelphia Inquirer* for the past 30 years. A few of the longer pieces that appear in this book were originally featured in *The Inquirer Sunday Magazine*, a showcase for in-depth articles that was discontinued several years ago.

Economy and quality are often at odds in the newspaper business. The magazine was a place where reporters and editors had room to tell stories in narrative form, stylistically and with, when warranted, a touch of attitude. (Or as we say in Philadelphia, "atty-tood.") But the magazine wasn't a money-maker and so it was jettisoned. There's a lot of that going on in the newspaper business today. It's part of our noir.

Once again I want to thank the dozens of editors at *The Inquirer* who had a hand in shaping the stories that are part of this anthology. And a special thanks to Edward Jutkowitz and Brad Fisher at Camino Books, both of whom enthusiastically supported this project.

PHILADELPHIA
TRUE NOIR

Rabbi Fred Neulander

MURDER AND MAYHEM

Journalism is about information and access. In its noblest form, it is the search for the truth. The reality, however, is that day in and day out, what we have are a lot of facts. Very often we don't have a clue about the truth. But at some point you've got an editor who wants to know when the story is going to be ready, and so you write it based on the facts at hand. Two weeks later, you've got more facts and maybe another story that either advances the first story or contradicts it.

The facts, you see, don't always lead you to the truth. Reporting is asking questions and then telling stories based on the answers. Journalism is not brain surgery. We're not finding a cure for cancer. Sometimes we help find the truth. But on most days, when we're good, what we do is enlighten, inform or entertain.

I think that I've done some of that over the years. You start out in this business looking for the four Ws that are supposed to be the building blocks of any article: who, what, where and when. But you quickly learn that the best stories are the ones that try to get at the elusive fifth W: why.

Many of the stories that appear here are built around that question. Some have to do with homicides. Others are about hustlers, including a tale about one of the most daring con men of the 20th century. Naturally, he ended up wheeling and dealing in Atlantic City.

Unfortunately, the most compelling murder stories involve women as victims. Two have been solved. Two remain mysteries, which is all the more tragic for their families. "Closure" is an overused word, but in writing about these investigations and in meeting the families of those who were killed, I think I came away with a better understanding of what that concept entails.

All the stories are sensational in a tabloid sense. Two attracted widespread attention. These would be the Tom Capano and Rabbi Fred Neulander murder cases.

I was asked to go down to Wilmington, Delaware, in the summer of 1997, about a year after Anne Marie Fahey had turned up missing. At that point no one had been charged with a crime, but the supposition was that her former lover, prominent attorney Thomas Capano, had had something to do with her disappearance.

I've been fortunate that *The Inquirer* has had me on a rather long leash. When an editor asked me if I had time to look into the Fahey case, I said I first wanted to make a few phone calls. One person I called was a lawyer tangentially involved in what at that point looked like a stalled investigation. When I asked the lawyer if this was a story worth pursuing, she didn't miss a beat.

"This case," she said, "has every human vice imaginable."

I told my editor I'd be happy to check out the story. I was in Wilmington the next day. And for the next 18 months I spent more time writing and reporting on Capano, Fahey and the provincial world of Wilmington society, politics and business than I did writing about the mob, which was and is my beat at the paper.

The fundamental question behind the story, of course, was why? Why did Tom Capano, a wealthy lawyer with a wife, four young daughters and at least two other willing mistresses, have to kill Anne Marie Fahey? Why would a man who seemingly had everything risk it all over a doomed love affair? Why would a sophisticated and legally savvy individual like Capano think he could get away with murder?

The answer was in Fahey's diary, which was discovered by her family on the night she turned up missing back in June 1996. That's when they first learned that their youngest sister had had an affair with the politically connected lawyer, had broken it off and for several months had been rebuffing his attempts to rekindle the romance.

In her diary, Anne Marie described Capano as a "controlling, manipulative, insecure, jealous maniac." That about said it all.

There were no words from Carol Neulander, the wife of Rabbi Fred Neulander, but her murder was, like Fahey's, a media sensation. So were the two trials that ultimately ended with the prominent Cherry Hill, New Jersey, rabbi sentenced to life in prison.

I was involved in the coverage of both trials. In fact, I was one of four reporters cited for contempt because we had contacted jurors after the first Neulander trial ended with a hung jury. The judge in that case, in a ruling that underscored both her arrogance and condescension, issued an edict banning all the media from making any attempt to talk with the jurors about their deliberations.

This seemed to fly in the face of the tenets of the judicial system, not to mention things like freedom of expression, freedom of speech and a free press. Being a juror is one of the highest callings an American can undertake. Someone once described jurors as "citizen soldiers." I respect what jurors do. I respect the entire legal process. It is, as God knows and as I have seen over the years, hardly perfect. But it is probably the best system going anywhere in the world.

Knocking on doors to try to get jurors to talk about their deliberations after any trial is a journalistic pain in the ass. Most don't want to discuss what went on. And it is their right to decline. But telling reporters they are barred from asking questions seemed un-American. And so four of us set out to locate and question the panel about how and why it had been unable to reach a verdict in the first Neulander case.

A few jurors were happy to discuss the process, although most would not go on the record with their names because of the atmosphere of fear and intimidation the judge had established. We wrote a story saying, in effect, that the jury had deadlocked nine-to-three to convict and that the holdouts had trouble with the credibility of the government's key witnesses, the hired hit men who said the rabbi had paid to have his wife killed.

We were cited for contempt, tried and convicted. We got six-month suspended sentences and shorter terms of community service. We eventually had the convictions overturned on appeal. It was an interesting experience. I'd do exactly the same thing again in a heartbeat.

The second Neulander trial, moved to Freehold, New Jersey, from Camden because of all the publicity, was again a circus. This time *Court TV* provided daily coverage. With basically the same witnesses and the same evidence, the prosecution won a conviction. This time hearing from the jurors wasn't an issue. Shortly after the trial ended, one of them was talking to *Court TV*.

Murder and Mayhem is the title of this section, and the other stories include two unsolved and unsavory murder mysteries that never received the kind of attention that the Capano and Neulander cases did. There's also a story about a bizarre legal donnybrook that pitted Steve Wynn against Donald Trump, heavyweight egos out to show the world which one was bigger.

And finally there are three pieces on the Fort Dix terrorism trial and the people caught up in it. This was a troubling case of murder and mayhem 21st-century style. The trial ended with convictions, but in my mind at least, no clear-cut answers. Like all good stories, the question was why.

THE DREAM MERCHANT OF ATLANTIC CITY

MARCH 13, 1988

The police moved in on the stylish beachfront house before dawn. There were two detectives from the Manhattan District Attorney's Office, an FBI agent, three investigators with the Internal Revenue Service, two detectives from the San Diego Police Department and four sheriff's officers from Del Mar, California.

It was still pitch-dark when one of the New York detectives pushed open a huge wooden door that led into an atrium in the center of the house. Armed with an arrest warrant, the police followed. The sheriff's officers covered the beach in front of the property. Seconds later, John Peter Galanis, 44, the man police had come for, emerged sleepily from one of the bedrooms and casually greeted his visitors.

"Tom, you didn't have to do this," Galanis said, upon recognizing Tom Jackson, one of the New York detectives. "Can I ask you just to wait while I get dressed?"

And with that, John Galanis—"cool as a cucumber," Jackson would later say—began preparing to face criminal charges that he was the mastermind of one of the biggest investment scams in the country.

His arrest last May in his three-million-dollar house along the beach in Del Mar capped a two-year investigation that had taken New York detectives, IRS agents and the FBI from Greenwich, Connecticut to Miami, Florida and from the Boardwalk in Atlantic City to the beach near San Diego. The trail, strewn with tens of millions of dollars, led into and out of the country and through a maze of companies, corporations, affiliates and subsidiaries that are all part of what federal authorities now call the "Galanis organization."

Galanis, who has pleaded not guilty to all the charges against him, remained in the background while friends, family members and associates headed those companies. Through six years of wheeling and dealing, and despite strict Securities and Exchange Commission regulations requiring full disclosure, the name John Peter Galanis did not appear on a single document in any of the more than 100 limited partnership syndication offerings now under investigation.

Yet federal and state indictments in New York now allege that Galanis was the undisclosed principal and hidden director of those deals, deals that involved hundreds of millions of dollars in investor funds, bank loans and tax write-offs, deals that the indictments and more than a dozen civil lawsuits contend were fraudulent. In response, Galanis denies those allegations and says he was only a consultant. He insists he did not defraud anyone.

The deals under investigation involved close to 4,000 wealthy investors: doctors, lawyers, businessmen, professional athletes and celebrities, including a former U.S. congressman from New York, basketball star Reggie Theus, New York Islander hockey player Pat Flatley and actor/comedian Eddie Murphy. Murphy invested $240,000 in the most celebrated of Galanis' now-suspect projects—Atlantic City's failed Boardwalk Marketplace.

In addition, a dozen small banks and lending institutions have been closed or brought to the brink of financial collapse; three mutual funds in Oakland, California have been looted of about four million dollars; a private bank in Texas has been stripped of its assets and is now being liquidated, and a three-block area of Atlantic City has been left in a shambles.

Chandra Galanis, John's wife, was frazzled on the morning of his arrest. "She was screaming," said one of the detectives. "She was very upset. She freaked out." But Galanis was soft-spoken and polite. He retired to a bedroom to dress for his court appearance and, a few minutes later, emerged to ask his arresting officers a question: "Do you think," said the man who some law enforcement officials consider one of the top white-collar criminals in America, "that a business suit would be appropriate?"

At his zenith, John Galanis owned a yacht, crisscrossed the country in a private jet, and maintained a fleet of fancy automobiles. In his younger days, he had displayed a penchant for flashy cars—Lamborghinis and Ferraris. But later he preferred the more sedate yet elegant Mercedes, Rolls-Royce or Cadillac. On one occasion, according to a former associate, he bought an Aston Martin to impress a client in a pending Atlantic City deal. Three days later, after the deal collapsed, he took the car back.

A six-footer who often ballooned to 300 pounds, Galanis fancied himself a gourmet and spent thousands of dollars reinforcing that image while wining and dining business associates at some of his favorite haunts: Lutèce or the Jockey Club in Manhattan; Mille Fleurs or the Fairbanks Ranch Country Club in San Diego; the quaint but fashionable Homestead Inn in Greenwich, where, after dinner, Galanis would sit on the porch, sipping a cognac while holding court for a dozen or more cronies.

"John would always take the liberty of ordering for you," said a former associate. "He'd look over the menu, choose the most expensive dishes and then order several bottles of the best wine."

"And he never, ever let anyone else pick up the check," said another.

John Peter Galanis had style. During his six-year ride on the crest of what may be a half-billion-dollar investment fraud, the rotund, baby-faced financial whiz lived almost a fantasy-world existence where money was no object, where every whim—his and his family's—was satisfied. Of course, two pending indictments and a dozen civil suits allege he did it with other people's money, but no one denies that he did it with a certain panache that at times could be endearing. Neighbors in Greenwich, for example, still talk about the time he hired an entire circus to perform at his son's backyard birthday party. And everyone remembers the "Hawaiian luau" at a Utah ski resort two years ago, where Galanis celebrated his birthday in grand style. On that particular occasion, he rented a local restaurant for the night, had tons of sand trucked in to create a "beach," and treated 100 guests to Maine lobster, roast pig and all they could drink.

"It had to be the most extravagant party of all time," said an Atlantic City businessman who attended. "He had the pigs being roasted right there. All kinds of food. There were bands, booze, broads. It was wild, like a Roman orgy."

Galanis basked in the glory of it all as guests came up to congratulate him and to tell him that, once again, he had outdone himself. The Atlantic City project may have been crumbling as he and his friends partied in Utah, but at that point, in the early spring of 1986, he was already looking for new investment opportunities.

A JOHN GALANIS STORY

There was a salesman named Al Feldman who suffered a heart attack while working for Galanis in New York City. At the time, the man's wife and two children were en route by plane from the West Coast to Boston, the first leg of a planned vacation in Maine. When he heard about the salesman's heart attack, Galanis had an associate fly to Boston to meet the wife and children. He then arranged and paid for their flight back to New York, where he had reserved them a room at the posh Helmsley Palace in Manhattan. He also provided a limousine to take them from the airport to their hotel and from their hotel to the hospital during the two weeks the salesman was hospitalized.

"And the funny thing was, John never really liked [Feldman]," said an associate who recounted the story as an example of Galanis' generosity. "But when he heard about the heart attack and about his wife and family, he was touched and he did everything he could. Money didn't mean anything."

Like almost all Galanis stories, this one has a flip side. Al Feldman died a few years later. Family members and other associates familiar with the incident say Galanis deducted from commissions due the salesman the entire cost of the flights, hotel room and limousine service—a bill of some $30,000.

In a recent interview, John Galanis' face became somber as he was told the first part of the story. "Feldman was a friend of mine," he said solemnly. But when asked about the deductions, Galanis' demeanor became more businesslike. Only the hospital costs were deducted, he said at first; then he said he wasn't sure. Someone else, he said, handled that matter.

"My view is the guy was in trouble and someone had to step forth, help his family," Galanis said. "I think, by the way, the guy had made more than a million dollars that year. So, I think one has to keep it in perspective if there were deductions, which I do not remember them honestly. I do remember the hospital. I don't remember the hotel."

In many ways, John Galanis was a man of his times—the epitome of the new breed of rogue entrepreneur who has turned greed into a virtue and the Wall Street financial community on its ear.

"I would describe him as an unprincipled, manipulative person who found it easier to cheat than to play it straight," says a New York securities law attorney familiar with Galanis' background. "John didn't [care] what anybody thought of him. . . . He was pretty much an amoral guy. If he thought he could make a buck, he would do it, regardless."

Last May, *Time* magazine, in an article on morality and business ethics, described the 1980s this way: "What began as the decade of the entrepreneur is fast becoming the age of the pinstriped outlaw, his prodigal twin." Accompanying the article, stripped across the top of two pages, were the photos of some of today's top Wall Street wheeler-dealers, all of whom have been charged with financial crimes. There were Dennis Levine and Ivan Boesky, of stock-fraud and insider-trading fame; Marc Rich, the fugitive commodities broker; Victor Posner, the corporate raider; and Jacob Butcher, the big-time banker. John Galanis' photo was in the middle of the top row.

Under different circumstances and for different reasons, it might have been quite an accomplishment for this son of hard-working Greek-American parents to have his picture prominently displayed in America's most widely circulated news magazine. But for John Galanis, fame more often came in the form of notoriety, despite a background that seemed to promise a reprise of the American success story.

Galanis grew up in Ipswich, Massachusetts, a quaint and historic New England town about 20 miles north of Boston. He had what appeared to be a typical suburban middle-class upbringing. His father, Peter, owned a local diner and operated a successful motel. His mother, Stella, still sings in the local church choir. Acquaintances describe the Galanises as decent, industrious people who embraced the American work ethic and shared the rewards of their diligence with their only son.

After attending a local high school for two years, John Galanis transferred to Kimball Union Academy, a New Hampshire prep school, where he played lacrosse and football and was active in the debating club, the French club and the drama club. From there, he went to Syracuse University, where he majored in international relations and talked of a career in the State Department. He graduated in 1965, and after less than a year at Boston University Law School, he moved to New York, giving up dreams of law and diplomacy to focus instead on what some would say soon became his obsession: money.

Galanis plunged with relish into the world of mutual funds and investment counseling. He got a job at Merrill Lynch as a portfolio manager and later moved to an executive post with the Neuwirth Fund. During this time, Galanis got married and had a son, but the marriage soon ended in divorce. Several years later, at a party, he met Chandra, who was teaching in the city at the time. They struck up a conversation and quickly realized they had both gone to Syracuse and knew some of the same people. They began dating, and a few months later, they were married.

By this time, Galanis was an up-and-comer on Wall Street, living in a swanky apartment, driving a Lamborghini and assembling million-dollar investment deals. He had left Neuwirth to become general partner of Takara Partners, a mutual fund management firm set up by a man named Akiyoshi Yamada. Among other people with whom Yamada had business dealings, court records indicate, was another high-flying mutual fund broker named Robert Vesco.

By 1971, according to federal court documents, Galanis and Yamada were the focus of a federal investigation into stock manipulation and offshore mutual fund fraud. Authorities alleged that Galanis and Takara used bribes and payoffs to artificially inflate the prices of stock in which they were dealing. When the prices reached an optimum level, they would dump their shares, taking huge profits while leaving their investors holding what quickly became worthless securities.

A federal appeals judge later compared one of those fraudulent deals to a "Byzantine plot" in which, the judge said, Galanis "proceeded to weave a tangled web of falsity." In total, the deals involved some $12 million, and their complex, convoluted nature set the pattern for future Galanis projects. In 1973, Galanis was sentenced to six months in prison and five years' probation after pleading guilty to a conspiracy charge.

One of the stipulations of his probation was that he not serve "as an officer, director, agent or other fiduciary in the discretionary investment or management of the funds or assets of others." He was also enjoined by the SEC from engaging in fraudulent stock offerings, the first of two such injunctions.

After Galanis was released from the federal prison in Danbury, Connecticut, he shifted from mutual funds to limited-partnership tax shelters. And for the next 15 years, he moved virtually unmolested through the world of high finance, keeping various investigative and regulatory agencies at bay.

"It's an almost farcical commentary on the financial community," says New York attorney John Klotz, whose client has been trying to collect a $1.8 million judgment against Galanis stemming from a 1973 mutual fund fraud. As a disgruntled broker who says he lost hundreds of thousands in Galanis deals puts it: "You go rob a bank with a gun and they put you in jail. He did it with a pen, and nobody did a thing about it."

The current investigations focus on oil- and gas-drilling ventures sold by a company called Transpac between 1981 and 1983; luxury condominium syndications sold by two companies—Madison Realty & Development and Consolidated Mortgage—in 1984; and the NATCO (Nashua Trust Company) Boardwalk Marketplace project in Atlantic City in 1985.

"Galanis appears to have engaged in one fraudulent enterprise after another since the 1970s," said Deputy Manhattan District Attorney Clinton Calhoun 3rd in a brief filed last summer opposing Galanis' request for reduced bail. Calling Galanis "nothing less than a career criminal," Calhoun summarized the Atlantic City scam: "Galanis and his accomplices raised more than $75 million from investors and then, by means of a lengthy series of transactions, stole the investors' money."

A picture that hung in one of the NATCO offices shows Galanis during a visit to Atlantic City. He is standing on Kentucky Avenue next to one of the motels that were part of the Boardwalk Marketplace project. He is wearing a blue blazer, gray slacks and penny loafers, his moon-shaped face creased with a smile as he stands on the sun-drenched sidewalk with the wind blowing his stylishly thick brown hair.

"He was a gentleman," said Alicia Brown, an interior designer who worked for NATCO in Atlantic City. "Just the most quiet . . . always very understated.

"I liked him. I don't like what he did, but that's big business. He got away with it. . . . He is a genius, a rogue. He's something books are written about."

Atlantic City and John Peter Galanis were a perfect match. Casino gambling, the city's lifeblood, is an industry where success is measured by a company's ability to take a bettor's money and give him nothing in return. Galanis came to town in 1985 after a series of tax-shelter deals that worked on that same principle, according to the pending indictments. And despite the heat of growing FBI and IRS investigations into the Transpac and Madison/Consolidated deals, he decided to roll the dice one more time. Always working behind the scenes—but, according to the indictment, clearly the man in charge—he launched Boardwalk Marketplace, a bold plan to turn a decaying section of the city into a commercial and tourist attraction that would rival New York's South Street Seaport or Baltimore's Inner Harbor.

Nashua Trust Company, a firm in Greenwich, Connecticut, that shared the same offices, the same corporate parent and some of the same corporate officers as Transpac, Madison and Consolidated, showed up with fancy brochures, grandiose plans and what appeared to be a potful of money. Using dozens of subsidiary companies, NATCO began buying up old hotels, motels, vacant lots and buildings along a three-block area near the Sands, Bally and Claridge casino-hotels. NATCO pushed all the right buttons. It hired two well-connected Atlantic City law firms. It put out lengthy, detailed and highly sophisticated investment offering sheets. It even produced a 15-minute videocassette narrated by the same pinstripe-suited actor who does the television commercials for the *Wall Street Journal.*

The city rushed to embrace the plan. Investors from across the country quickly followed. "They played off the emotions of the city," recalled Michael Mooney, chairman of the Atlantic City Planning Board and an early supporter of the project. "They played the same game with investors, I'm sure. . . . They were very calculating individuals and they took a shot at the most vulnerable spot in the city. . . . It was all a shell game."

Boardwalk Marketplace promised to deliver what Atlantic City still sorely needs: hotel and commercial development unrelated to casinos. Anyone who has spent more than a day in the resort knows that if you take away the 12 lavish casinos, Atlantic City has fewer attractions than it did 10 years ago, when Resorts International opened the town's first gambling hall. There are no movie theaters, few bars and restaurants, none of the quaint shops and stores that are so common in other seashore towns.

NATCO wowed the city fathers with its plan to take a dozen old hotels and motels and use them as the anchor of a new commercial and tourist district. The hotels, most of them built in the 1920s, would be restored, and around them NATCO would construct boutiques, restaurants, art galleries, theaters and bookstores. There was even talk of an aquarium.

The concept was a city planner's dream. Finally, after 10 years of false starts and missed opportunities, here was a chance for Atlantic City to become more than just Las Vegas with a beach. That was the package, or "the product," as they say in the tax shelter game.

Galanis succeeded, the government alleges, because he offered investors something for nothing. He gave them glitz and glitter and a chance to beat the IRS. But in reality, his Atlantic City deal was the last in a series of Ponzi schemes that left investors, the IRS and Atlantic City itself holding an empty bag. Never mind that most of the buildings NATCO purchased were overpriced and beyond restoration. So what if the specific renovation plans were unrealistic. This was a deal that had to look good, had to sound good. It wasn't necessary for it to actually work. Slick brochures, fancy artist's renderings and inflated financial projections were offered to investors. It was like the cotton candy they used to sell on the Boardwalk: all sugar and fluff, no substance.

In 1985, NATCO put together nine limited-partnership offerings that were designed to finance the start-up of Boardwalk Marketplace. Then, teams of salesmen, who had sold Galanis' oil- and gas-drilling tax shelter ventures and his luxury condominium offerings, went to the well one more time. In some cases, these salesmen returned to the same investors. Although the IRS and FBI were already sniffing around the earlier projects, none of the investors was yet aware of any problems.

Units in each partnership sold for about $100,000. Investors, as in the earlier tax shelter deals, were promised write-offs of two to three times their investment in the first few years of the project and substantial profits down the road, once the hotels were up and operating and the revenues were flowing in instead of out.

NATCO did, in fact, use investors' money to renovate three motels and gut half a dozen larger hotels in the summer of 1985. But the money—diverted illegally into other ventures, the government alleges—dried up as winter came, and today those stripped and boarded-up hotels preside over a bleak wasteland.

Not surpirsingly, there never were significant revenues, a pattern characteristic of earlier Galanis deals. To this day, no one is certain how many wells were drilled in the Transpac ventures; little, if any, of the projected revenue ended up in investors' pockets. Virtually all of the luxury condominiums purchased in the Madison/Consolidated offerings have been lost in foreclosures. Some that were listed in the deals that investors bought were never purchased to begin with. And Boardwalk Marketplace collapsed as NATCO retreated into bankruptcy in June 1986. Only then did people begin to track millions of dollars ostensibly earmarked for this grand Atlantic City redevelopment plan to the doorstep of companies, corporations and individuals linked to John Peter Galanis.

"I figured it was real estate in Atlantic City, how could you go wrong?" said one investor from Long Island.

Interviews with dozens of investors from around the country indicate that before NATCO's collapse, most were aware of only two things: Boardwalk Marketplace was in Atlantic City, and Atlantic City is the East Coast gambling capital of the United States.

"It was basically a tax shelter deal," recalled Jim Smith, a businessman from Winona, Minnesota, who invested $97,500 in a unit of the Columbus Hotel Limited Partnership, one of the nine Boardwalk Marketplace syndications. "My accountant called me about it. He thought I'd fit in nicely."

When the deal collapsed, Smith's reaction was typical, and in many ways explained how and why seemingly sophisticated investors were so easily separated from their money. "There is a Columbus Hotel, isn't there?" he asked.

Galanis was arraigned in San Diego on May 12, the day of his arrest. He waived extradition and one day later was flown to New York. He remained in jail—part of the time at Riker's Island, a dungeon-like New York City prison—until the first week in August. He was freed after family members, including his wife, mother and sister, posted property, jewelry and other security to satisfy a $10 million bail requirement.

Manhattan authorities, in seeking the high bail, said they feared Galanis might flee the country rather than face the charges against him. Privately, investigators have compared Galanis to fugitive financier Robert Vesco. Like Vesco, Galanis has links to offshore and European companies and bank accounts, they say.

Galanis and nine associates have been charged, in a 105-count New York state indictment, with grand larceny, fraud and conspiracy in connection with the Boardwalk Marketplace and Madison/Consolidated deals. "During the time covered by the indictment," the District Attorney's office said in announcing Galanis' arrest, "over six million dollars was paid directly to Galanis or members of his family from NATCO and partnership assets; substantially more was paid for the benefit of him and his family, such as to cover American Express charges and bills to Tiffany's for his wife, Chandra Galanis." The DA's office later upped that estimate to eight million.

Galanis and seven associates, including three of those charged in the Atlantic City scam, also face a 57-count federal indictment charging them with racketeering, tax fraud and securities fraud in connection with the sale of the Transpac oil- and gas-drilling limited partnerships. Galanis and two of those named in the federal indictment have also been charged with bribing officials of a now-defunct New York state bank and with the fraudulent takeover of a Salt Lake City bank. Additional charges allege the fraudulent takeover of a Connecticut bank and a company that managed three Oakland, California mutual funds.

Transpac involved about $50 million in investor funds and $172 million in phony tax write-offs, according to Vincent L. Briccetti, an Assistant U.S. Attorney who has been tracking Galanis with bulldog tenacity for more than two years. The Madison/Consolidated and Boardwalk Marketplace deals each involved about $75 million in investor funds. Those deals also included the alleged takeover of several small banks that were brought close to financial ruin after providing millions of dollars in financing for the projects through first- or second-mortgage loans. For example, more than $10 million in losses at Tri-County Savings and Loan, of Maple Shade, New Jersey, were directly linked to its involvement with Consolidated, according to federal banking authorities who eventually ordered that the small thrift be sold.

Galanis has pleaded not guilty, as have most of those indicted with him. Seven former associates, including his brother-in-law Thomas Williams and onetime close friend John Lewis, have pleaded guilty to related charges and have agreed to cooperate with investigators. The Transpac case is set for a federal trial this spring in White Plains, New York. A New York state trial on the other charges is likely next fall.

ANOTHER JOHN GALANIS STORY

In 1983, Jason Galanis decided that he wanted to attend Burke Mountain Academy, an exclusive Vermont prep school where the tuition, room and board amounted to $11,000 a year. His father willingly obliged. Even though Jason spent less than a semester at the school, where top-flight ski training is combined with strict academics, John Peter Galanis became something of a patron of the academy, contributing $50,000 to a drive to finance a $100,000 refurbishing of the school's science center and donating the use of an $80,000 home near the campus that he purchased just before Jason enrolled.

"Whenever we wanted anything, he was very quick to be helpful," recalls Warren Witherell, the founder and former headmaster of Burke. The science center project, Witherell said, would not have been completed without Galanis' anonymous gift. And even though the house is now being lost to the school in a mortgage foreclosure, Witherell has nothing but kind words for John Peter Galanis. "He was extremely generous," he said. "As it turns out, it may have been with other people's money as well as his own. But I found him to be a gentleman, a kind sort, who was always willing to help people."

"He's very manipulative," said Cindy Williams, Galanis' estranged sister-in-law, as she sat in the high-ceilinged living room of her home in Greenwich, Connecticut, just down the road from Galanis' estate. "He's very good at finding a person's weakness and using it, whether it's money, women . . . or whatever."

Cindy Williams is the younger sister of Chandra Galanis and the wife of Thomas Williams. Thomas Williams declined to comment publicly about the Galanis case because of the pending criminal charges and a civil suit brought by Chandra that alleges he defrauded a trust fund set up for Galanis' children. Cindy Williams shakes her head in dismay while discussing her sister and brother-in-law.

"It's a game to both of them," she said. "They use people. People are like inanimate objects on a board that they move around." Both John and Chandra Galanis equate wealth with power, Cindy Williams believes, and they have traveled through life buying whatever they want or feel they need, including friends. "Five hundred dollars to her was like $10 to you or me," she said of her sister.

Chandra Galanis—her given name was Carol, but she began using the more exotic Chandra shortly after graduating from college in 1965—would go on legendary shopping sprees at only the finest women's stores, returning, friends recalled, with bags full of clothes that she might wear only once or twice before discarding. She was equally extravagant with her four sons, spending literally thousands at local toy stores.

Cindy Williams described a Christmas morning at the Galanis estate when the boys left dozens of presents unopened, such was the magnitude and quantity of the gifts that were stacked under and around the Christmas tree. Months later, Williams recalls finding many of the presents, still wrapped, stored in a closet. Her own two small children also received lavish gifts from the Galanises, Cindy Williams recalled. "But you know, I can't ever remember my sister picking up my children to hug or kiss them," she said.

Chandra Galanis said she has heard most of this before. Jealousy and vindictiveness, she claims, have caused her sister to twist reality. If she has a fault, Chandra said of herself, it is that often she has been too kind and generous, going out of her way to help family members with financial and personal problems. She acknowledged that she has spent money, sometimes lavishly, but seldom, she said, on herself. "I went on three shopping sprees with my husband in 19 years, and those are the three times I got some nice clothes," she recalled, adding that she prefers to wear jeans. "I never went out and bought a fur coat. I had my hair done twice a year. But I did spend money on other people—in fact, mostly on her."

If there were wrapped gifts around the house after Christmas, she said, they were presents for other people's children, gifts that had not yet been given. And if there were closets full of expensive clothes, they were in the Williams' home, not hers.

The Galanises lived with their four sons on a lavish estate that John built near a small lake in Greenwich. There were servants, cooks and chauffeurs, and the well-maintained grounds included a tennis court and an expensive jungle gym set. Parked on the grounds, along with the Rolls-Royce and the Cadillac, were two motorized golf carts that the boys used to get around the huge property.

Later, in part to escape the growing negative publicity surrounding the collapsed Atlantic City deal, the Galanises moved to Southern California, where Chandra, according to property records, purchased two homes, one in Rancho Santa Fe, worth an estimated $1.8 million, and the other on the beach in Del Mar, valued at three million. The Del Mar property was once featured in *Fine Homes* magazine, which called the Del Mar coastline "the most expensive real estate in the world."

Both California properties were purchased in 1985, at the time Nashua Trust Company was raising $75 million from investors for the Atlantic City project. NATCO's court-appointed bankruptcy trustee has since alleged that the Del Mar property was purchased with funds illegally funneled out of the Boardwalk Marketplace deal. In addition, bankruptcy records show the flow of tens of thousands of dollars out of the company to something called the "C. Chandra Galanis household account." Company records also indicate that John Galanis routinely ran up bills of $30,000 to $40,000 on company-issued credit cards.

The Galanises have said that the funds represented either the repayment of loans they made to the company or compensation for John's consulting work. Prosecutors, investors and a New York state grand jury allege the payments were part of a multi-million-dollar fraud.

"There are certainly two sides to him," says Richard Enright, an attorney and longtime acquaintance who was corporate secretary for many of the companies linked to Galanis in the current investment fraud investigations. Enright says that Galanis was sometimes volatile and often "brilliant." He cared deeply for his family and would think nothing of interrupting an important business meeting to play with one of his sons, Enright said. "I'm convinced it wasn't his intention to defraud anybody."

Others say Galanis is a master at seduction, that his charm and personality, indeed his entire lifestyle, were tools that he used to seduce people into doing what he wanted. "He was like Fagin," says Michael Lerner, a lawyer from Newark, New Jersey, whose firm is handling the NATCO bankruptcy. There is no other way, Lerner said, to describe how and why so many business associates went along with Galanis and his deals.

"If somebody told me John Galanis was behind a deal," added John Lowe, a New York lawyer and former federal prosecutor, "I'd assume it was a crooked deal and I wouldn't want any part of it. . . . I wouldn't touch anything involved in it because I'd figure either I'd lose my money or wind up in jail."

Wearing a conservative gray business suit and black penny loafers, a 270-pound John Peter Galanis maneuvered easily through the lunchtime crowd jamming Madison Avenue in midtown Manhattan. It was a crisp weekday afternoon in January, and the sun, making its first appearance in a week, seemed to lift the spirits of everyone in the city. Galanis, reflecting that mood, was optimistic, predicting that he would be vindicated, that the indictments were without merit, that he was a victim of overzealous prosecutors, disgruntled former associates and his own personality.

He was broke, he said. He and his wife had borrowed money and sold their assets—jewelry and the like—to live on. If he had money, if he had, as some investors and investigators believe, stashed millions away in secret bank accounts, he'd be able to mount an unbeatable legal defense and would win his trials easily. "It would be a slam dunk," he said, as he sat in a health-food delicatessen eating a bowl of beef barley soup and a salad.

Sure, Galanis admitted, some of the things he did seemed larger than life. He dined at expensive restaurants from time to time, treated his family to certain extravagances, generally lived well. But, he said time and again, over lunch and during a five-hour interview in his lawyer's Madison Avenue office, he did not steal anyone's money.

"There was no intent to defraud. I have not entered a deal in the last 15 years with intent to defraud anybody, at any time. . . . Every nickel can be accounted for."

Former associates who are now testifying against him, he said, have either been pressured by the government or have made a deal to get a light sentence and shift blame for their own crimes. Prosecutors and investigators—and the news media—have gone off on a wild goose chase, he added, finding crime and conspiracy where there were none, using him as a target. "They wanted to break me," he claimed over lunch.

Later, as Galanis sat in his lawyer's office 21 floors above the bustling streets of midtown Manhattan, he was even more expansive. "I don't believe the government wants me to go to trial, because I don't believe they can prove their case. . . ."

Fielding an array of questions, displaying a full range of emotions, Galanis was, by turns, charming and angry, arrogant and emotional. He teased and joked with the female photographer taking his picture. He bemoaned the 50 pounds he had put on since his release from jail. He praised his wife for her support and spoke fondly of his four sons, the oldest of whom, he said, hopes to attend Stanford University.

Galanis insisted that he was not a hidden principal behind the various investment deals. He was a financial and marketing consultant, and anyone who did business with the companies knew of his involvement and his past criminal activities. All he did was give advice, make recommendations. He was not the man in charge.

His brother-in-law, Thomas Williams, lied to investigators and basically undermined the operations of several of the companies, Galanis charged. Williams and John Lewis, once a close friend and head of the Atlantic City operation, along with their wives, had plotted "the destruction of John Galanis' businesses," he said. "It is, I believe, an indication of juvenile envy . . . a true Cain and Abel type story."

Angry investors and government investigators have another view. To them, the two former top aides have come clean and, most important, provided a road map through the maze of Galanis' companies, affiliates and subsidiaries. Without that type of insider information, authorities say, tracking Galanis was like peeling the skin away from an onion. Piece by translucent piece, the onion begins to disappear. And when you are done, there is no core. There's just a pile of onion skins. Lewis and Williams make the connections, help trace the money and expose the patterns that show, according to the indictments, a grand scheme to defraud both investors and the IRS.

Lewis, like Williams, has pleaded guilty to state and federal charges in connection with the Transpac and Boardwalk Marketplace deals. In announcing his guilty plea and agreement to cooperate last year, the Manhattan DA's office said Lewis had disclosed that "John Peter Galanis was the true originator and the control person of the entire [Atlantic City] project" and that "virtually all funds would be channeled to people and entities controlled by Mr. Galanis."

Shortly after his release from prison on bail in August, John Peter Galanis checked into the Ritz-Carlton Hotel in New York, where he and his wife stayed for more than a week. Rooms at the hotel cost about $200 a night. From the Ritz, Galanis moved to an apartment in New York City. Under the terms of his bail, he is not permitted to leave New York without government permission. His wife returned to California, where she remains with their four sons.

Rumors abound about the pending cases and the ongoing investigations by an alphabet-soup conglomeration of agencies, including the FBI, IRS, SEC and the Manhattan DA's office. More than a dozen civil suits continue to wind slowly through the federal courts in New Jersey, New York and Connecticut. The bankruptcy proceeding plods apace in U.S. Bankruptcy Court in Camden.

Galanis' lawyer, Brian Barrett, told a New York Supreme Court judge at a bail hearing in January that the charges revolve around "a technical and complicated series of transactions that the district attorney is never going to be able to prove were fraudulent."

But John Klotz, the feisty New York City attorney who has been trying to collect a judgment against Galanis that dates back to 1973, says the issues are not complicated at all. "For all the so-called sophistication of these deals," says Klotz, "all he did was stuff other people's money in his pocket."

IN THEIR OWN WORDS:
THE SURREAL RELATIONSHIP OF ANNE MARIE FAHEY AND TOM CAPANO

OCTOBER 4, 1998

The couple didn't look happy. That's what the waitress told the FBI agent who interviewed her about a month later.

They came in around seven o'clock. It was a Thursday in late June 1996. Anne Marie Fahey wore a light-colored print dress and a frown. Tom Capano was unremarkable. The waitress struggled for the word. Finally she settled on unfashionable, not the kind of customer she was used to seeing in Old City's Ristorante Panorama. It is a place where movers and shakers come for lunch, where lovers come for dinner. It is a restaurant that prides itself on its wine list and menu, that boasts of being a piece of Rome set down in the heart of the City of Brotherly Love.

Anne Marie Fahey and Thomas J. Capano were memorable, the waitress said, because she couldn't fit them into any niche. When an FBI agent showed her a picture of Fahey, she recognized her right away. But she also remarked that the photo made her look "much healthier" than she appeared that night at dinner. That night, the waitress noted, Fahey looked "frail, sallow and washed out." Her hair looked "disheveled and flyaway." She seemed "sad and uncomfortable."

They had cocktails—a vodka sea breeze for Fahey, a rum and tonic for Capano. And then a bottle of white wine. The waitress recommended the fish, which Anne Marie ordered. Capano asked for one of the chicken entrees. They also shared two appetizers, maybe the fried calamari and the bruschetta. Neither ate much and when the waitress asked if everything was all right, Capano shooed her away.

That's one of the reasons she remembered the couple. The other was Capano himself. His look wasn't right for the restaurant, the young waitress said. His large, horn-rim eyeglasses, his barbershop haircut, his conservative sports jacket "all seemed outdated compared to the regular clientele."

Fahey seemed "extremely solemn." She didn't say very much during dinner, which lasted nearly two hours, "barely touched her food," and spent much of the time toying with her wine glass. Capano was "definitely very dominating"; Fahey was "very meek."

They passed on dessert, but Capano ordered a "very cold" glass of white wine for Fahey and a sambuca for himself. When the waitress brought the check, Capano took out a credit card and slid it and the bill across the table to Fahey. The waitress said they left a few minutes later without saying much else. She remembers that Fahey, who had tabulated the bill and signed Capano's name on the credit receipt, "left a very good tip."

Usually, the waitress noted, she is able to tell whether a couple is having a business meeting or is out on a date. But she told the FBI agent she could not figure out "why this couple was there." She recalled "absolutely no joviality or conversation."

Fahey and Capano left Panorama about nine that night. Two hours later, investigators believe, Anne Marie Fahey was dead. The waitress may have been the last person, other than Tom Capano, to see her alive.

This month in Wilmington—absent a last-minute plea bargain or an unexpected scheduling change—jury selection will begin in the case against Thomas J. Capano, the wealthy lawyer and former political power broker accused of killing Fahey on the night of June 27, 1996.

It is a surreal story, a soap opera, an outlandish script from a made-for-television movie: Rich, powerful and secretly obsessive lawyer carries on clandestine, two-and-a-half-year extramarital affair with beautiful, young anorexic secretary to the Governor of Delaware. Racked with guilt linked in no small degree to her Irish-Catholic background, she tries to end the affair. In a rage, he kills her and then dumps her body in the Atlantic Ocean, 60 to 70 miles off the coast of southern New Jersey. That is the prosecution's theory of the case. That is what will be presented to the jury. There is no body. There is no murder weapon. There is no cause of death. Capano, 48, has pleaded not guilty. He has been held without bail since his arrest last November.

Anne Marie Fahey was killed, prosecutors believe, shortly after Capano drove her back to his home in Wilmington following their dinner at Panorama. The next morning, they contend, he and his younger brother Gerard—who is now cooperating with authorities and is expected to testify at the trial—took Fahey's body far out to sea off Stone Harbor and threw it overboard inside a large trunk.

Only Tom Capano knows the details of Anne Marie Fahey's final minutes, prosecutors say. It is the crucial blank spot in the middle of a troubling, sensational saga that could provide a month's worth of fodder for the likes of Jerry Springer or Oprah Winfrey.

The story has it all: power and politics, betrayal and wealth, sex and obsession. But the most haunting twist is the echo of the voices of Fahey and Capano, captured in more than 50 e-mail messages sent between them in the six months leading up to Fahey's disappearance, including one sent the day before she was allegedly killed.

The messages, better than any witness or other piece of evidence, provide an account of the troubled relationship that prosecutors say ended in murder.

E-mail from Fahey to Capano, January 29, 1996, 7:50 a.m.:

> Tom,
>
> First let me start off by saying that I'm sorry for the pain I have caused you over the weekend. I spent a good part of yesterday morning/afternoon at Valley Green Park thinking about a lot of stuff: Us, girls, eating disorder, my family, etc. I desperately want to talk to you, but I'm too afraid to place the call. I do love you Tommy and no matter what happens—I will always love you.
>
> Annie

From Capano to Fahey, next day, 10:59 a.m.:

> Annie,
>
> Our system was down yesterday so I just got your e-mail. . . . I desperately want to talk to you, too, and I'll go out of my mind if I don't soon. Please don't be afraid to place the call. I need to hear your voice. . . . Not hearing from you since Saturday afternoon is making me crazy. And you know how much I love you and need you. I'll wait for your call. Te amo [I love you].

Tom Capano was a highly respected and politically connected former state prosecutor and the scion of one of the richest families in Delaware. Fahey was the youngest of six siblings in an up-by-their-bootstraps, Irish-American clan that moved in many of the same political—although not economic and social—circles as Capano.

Only her closest friends knew of the relationship, which Fahey had gone to great lengths to keep secret from her family and boyfriend. Notes in her diary, which her sister read on the night she reported Anne Marie missing, were the first hint to family members and investigators. More details came from letters and the e-mail messages between Fahey's computer at the governor's office and Capano's at the Wilmington office of the Philadelphia law firm of Saul, Ewing, Remick & Saul. The friends in whom Fahey confided filled in the rest.

What emerged is a confusing and sometimes contradictory tale of guilt, anxiety and infidelity that shocked many who knew Fahey and

Capano. That Capano might be capable of murder seemed improbable, even to those who thought him smug and arrogant. He had a reputation and a history of political and public service that, on the surface at least, left him above reproach. Beneath that surface, however, investigators say they found a "control freak" who had been manipulating women for a decade and a half.

In 1980, according to an FBI affidavit that is now part of the case, Capano is believed to have hired a thug to harass and threaten a legal secretary who had spurned his sexual advances. Eventually, she quit her job and left Wilmington to avoid Capano. After Fahey disappeared, the thug told the FBI that Capano had told him he wanted him to "hurt the bitch," had boasted about his power and influence in Wilmington, and claimed that "this is his town, this is his state" and that no woman could turn him down.

Capano and his younger brothers, Louis Jr., Joseph and Gerard, were part of the city's nouveau riche. They moved along the second tier of wealth and power in a city steeped in tradition and proud of its provincialism. There are the duPonts and a half-dozen other families whose roots stretch back to colonial times. And then there are the new arrivals—the bankers, lawyers, developers and politicos who make things happen and get things done.

Successful in varying degrees in their own right, all four Capano brothers and an older sister benefited from the wealth and financial clout accumulated by their late father, Louis J. Capano, one of Delaware's premier builders and construction contractors in the 1960s and '70s.

Over the years, Louis Sr. amassed a fortune in real estate holdings that at different times included office buildings, apartment complexes, hotels, restaurants and shopping centers. Louis J. Capano & Sons was also responsible for building more than a dozen middle- and upper-middle-class housing developments. Nearly everyone who has lived in the Wilmington area has heard of or, more likely, had some contact with a Capano or a Capano-connected business enterprise.

The Capano boys were spoiled, self-centered and for years did pretty much whatever they pleased. But until Anne Marie Fahey's disappearance and the murder investigation in which he quickly became the prime suspect, Thomas Capano had been known as the "good brother."

A graduate of Archmere Academy, a private Catholic boys school, Boston College and Boston College Law School, Thomas was the brother who helped smooth over the problems of his younger siblings even as he moved up the ladder in Wilmington's political and social circles.

"Any time there was a problem in the family, Tommy was the one who would straighten things out," Kevin Freel, a member of one of Wilmington's most active political families, said one night as he sat at a table in O'Friel's, his popular pub.

"He was the good guy. Then this business with Anne Marie happened. You hear about how he was manipulative and controlling and taking advantage. We were sitting here in the bar one night talking about it and saying how unbelievable it was. Then somebody said, 'Yeah, he's acting just like a Capano.'"

E-mail from Fahey to Capano, February 7, 1996, 7:51 a.m.:

> Good Morning Tommy,
>
> I'm sorry yesterday was so bad. . . . Sorry I did not call you back last night . . . wanted to see the last part of NYPD Blue and, of course, I fell asleep and woke up around 1:30. . . . Tommy, I meant what I said on Sunday night about right now only being able to offer you my friendship, and if you cannot deal with that then I understand. I'm still very much confused, and I am trying to work out a lot of personal things on my own. I would like to talk to you about what happened yesterday . . . but again it is up to you.
>
> Annie

From Capano to Fahey, same day, 9:50 a.m.:

> Good Morning Annie,
>
> Thank you for the e-mail. . . . I also watched NYPD Blue and wanted to call you at the end. . . . but thought you might be asleep. . . . I'd like to have dinner with you Saturday night. . . . I understand that you're confused and want to limit our relationship now to friendship. I love you enough to accept that and ask only that we treat each other kindly and honestly. I don't want to lose you. I also think we shouldn't lose the closeness we've developed. If nothing else, you know you can tell me your fears and hopes and rely on me to support you. I still want to be there for you, which, I guess, is the surest sign that I still love you with all my heart. You cannot do all this on your own, Annie. No one can. Let me help. . . . You look like you could use a good meal! And you have to admit I've always fed you well. Te amo.

The Faheys, four brothers and two sisters, had grown up looking out for one another. Their mother died while they were children. Anne Marie, the youngest, had just started grammar school. Their father, an alcoholic, soon fell apart. He died 10 years later. For the most part, the children raised themselves. And it is with pride that they point to the fact that four of them went on to graduate from college, including Annie, the tomboy who grew into a sophisticated but insecure beauty.

The Faheys all knew that their sister's happy-go-lucky exterior was a thin and easily cracked shell, that inside she was an emotionally frail and easily manipulated young woman full of self-doubt that could be traced to her virtually parentless childhood.

As a college student, Anne had spent a year studying in Spain and dreamed of a career in the foreign service. But at the time she disappeared, the closest the 30-year-old Fahey had gotten was the front desk at the governor's office in Dover. She agonized constantly over her inability to live the life she desired on the $31,000-a-year salary of a gubernatorial aide.

Tom Capano could give her that life, albeit secretly. He lavished her with clothes from expensive dress shops, a television, books, appliances and cash for trips. He even offered to buy her a sports car—a Lexus 300 SL—and to set her up in an apartment.

Most of Fahey's casual friends and acquaintances had no clue about either her insecurities or her secret relationship with the wealthy and powerful lawyer. Instead, they talked of the smiling Annie, the woman who loved a good joke or trivia question, the comic with the uncanny ability to mimic even perfect strangers, the dark-haired beauty who could easily slip her conversation between English and Spanish, a language she loved.

And they remembered the laugh.

"It would be the middle of happy hour on a Friday afternoon," Kevin Freel recalled. "The place would be packed. You couldn't hear yourself think. But above it all you would hear this warm, wonderful laugh and you'd know Annie was in the room."

There were times, however, when Anne Marie Fahey wouldn't or couldn't laugh, private times when she was haunted by her own demons and tormented by an eating disorder that left her five-foot-ten frame rail thin.

Fahey and Capano started their secret affair late in 1993. Anne was working as Governor Tom Carper's appointments secretary. Capano, who was then a private lawyer who worked on many government bond issues, was a frequent visitor to Dover, the state capital, about 45 miles south of Wilmington. With their individual political involvements over the years, they needed no introduction.

Anne Marie told only a few close friends about how she was flattered and intrigued by the suave, articulate, high-powered lawyer 16 years her senior. He treated her, she said, like no other man ever had. They would meet secretly for lunch or dinner, sometimes in her small apartment a few blocks from the Wilmington business district, but more often in swank Philadelphia restaurants like the Saloon, Panorama or La Famiglia, where they were unlikely to be recognized.

In the aftermath of her disappearance, friends and relatives described Capano as a predator who played on her weaknesses and took advantage of her kindness. But it was more complicated and complex.

"It was difficult," said Kim Horstmann, a close friend of Fahey's who knew about the affair almost from the beginning.

"She loved him and he really loved her," Horstmann said in a lengthy interview with investigators shortly after Fahey disappeared. But the relationship was fraught with problems, not the least of which was Fahey's guilt over the thought that Capano might leave his wife and four daughters for her.

"She did not want the responsibility of having him leave his wife for her," Horstmann said. "But then she didn't know if she could ever meet a man that would take care of her the way Tom took care of her. . . . She was very confused."

On the one hand, she said, Fahey wanted to get away from Capano. On the other, she would ask, "Will anybody ever love me the way he loves me, or will anybody treat me the way he treats me?"

E-mail from Capano to Fahey, April 29, 1996, 2:08 p.m.:

> Hi,
>
> The guys from Smith Barney just left. . . . Anyway, here's the trivia question: Who owns Coach Leather? . . . I enjoyed our phone call this morning. Thanks for the time. Please call if you can. Oh, almost forgot. If you answer the trivia question correctly, you win a prize. Hope your day is okay.

From Fahey to Capano, same day, 2:26 p.m.:

> Well look here Mr. Smartie Pants. The owner of Coach Leather is SARA LEE!!! How do you like them apples? Thanks for making me laugh and getting my mind off my financial problems. Call you later.
>
> Annie
> P.S. Nobody does it like Sara Lee!!!

Kathleen Fahey-Hosey last spoke with her sister on the Wednesday before she disappeared. They had gone shopping together at the Talbots in Wilmington. Kathleen chided Anne Marie for trying on an expensive suit that she could not afford.

Anne Marie was supposed to join her brother Robert and his wife that Saturday night for dinner. She was to bring her boyfriend, Michael Scanlan, a young banker. She had confided to her sister and several friends that Scanlan was "the one," that they had been talking about getting engaged.

Kathleen was excited about that prospect. The family loved Scanlan and thought he was a stabilizing influence on Annie. Before they parted, Kathleen also expressed concern about Anne Marie's weight.

"She looked so thin when she tried on the suit," Kathleen said in an interview last year. "I hadn't noticed. She'd wear jeans and a baggy sweatshirt when she came over to the house. But at Talbots, when she came out of the dressing room, I could see how thin she was."

Anne Marie's anorexia often flared up when she was under stress. Kathleen had no way of knowing the source of the tension. Anne Marie said she was fine and appeared annoyed at Kathleen's comments. She said she would call and told her not to worry.

Around this same time, Capano told Kim Horstmann that he was frustrated over his inability to win back Fahey's love.

"He said that he was very frustrated . . . because he was . . . completely in love with her," Horstmann told a grand jury. "He said he could have anybody he wanted and he made the comment again about 'Look where she comes from and I can offer her the entire world. I could buy her anything she wanted. I have more money than I can spend in a lifetime. Am I crazy going after her? Am I crazy to be in love with this girl?'"

Horstmann said she suggested that Capano give Fahey space, that he back off. She and others in whom Fahey had confided also told investigators that at that time, in the spring of 1996, Fahey thought she had reached an understanding with Capano.

There had been a period, shortly after they stopped their sexual relationship at the end of 1995, when Capano had been abusive, calling repeatedly on the phone, sitting in his jeep outside her Wilmington apartment as if he were stalking her. Fahey told her friends—who later told the FBI—that Capano began reclaiming all the gifts he had given her: the clothes, the CDs, the television.

"No other man is going to see you in the dress that I bought you," he ranted. But that time had passed.

There were hints of the turbulence in the e-mail messages, but also indications that things had gotten better, calmer. Fahey believed, it appears, that Capano was content to be her friend. Investigators and her family say that was a fatal mistake.

"In order to understand why my sister was easily manipulated by a guy like Tom Capano, you need to understand the frailties of her nature,"

Robert Fahey told *The Inquirer* shortly before Capano was arrested last year. It is not pleasant, he said, to have his sister's private life—her hopes, her fears, her shortcomings—held up to public scrutiny, examined and analyzed, questioned and gossiped about.

"There are many things which we would have preferred not made public that have come out," he said. "You get numb to it. . . . It is what it is. . . . But this guy made a career of preying on vulnerable women. So I guess that stuff has to be there."

E-mail from Capano to Fahey, May 21, 1996, 10:54 a.m.:

> Good Morning Annie,
>
> Glad you enjoyed the fax and that you ate well at Debbie's. . . . I'm worried about you. Don't tell me not to because you know I do. Did you call [your therapist]? Probably not. . . . Please be sure to give her the $500 tomorrow since you're out of credit. . . . Could we have dinner tonight? It would be good for me and, at the risk of sounding pompous, I think you might get something out of it too. . . .

From Fahey to Capano, same day, 12:33 p.m.:

> Hey Capano,
>
> . . .Please do not worry about me. . . . I'm scared to death that I am killing myself, and that's a positive thing because I am forced to do something to make myself better. It's kind of a bittersweet device if you know what I mean. . . . I almost sent myself to St. Francis yesterday morning because of how weak I felt. Believe me Tommy when I tell you all of this is good for me, because for the first time, I am afraid that I am killing myself. . . . I'm ready to tackle this problem that I have—whereas before I did not see it that way. I know all you want to do is help, and believe me it's greatly appreciated, but I also need some time alone to work out a lot of stuff. I hope you can understand all this mumbo.
>
> Anne Marie

It was a balancing act for Fahey, like walking on a tightrope. She was trying to keep Capano at a distance without upsetting him. She was in agony over the thought that her siblings might learn of the relationship. And she was terrified that her boyfriend, Michael Scanlan, might find out.

"I don't want him to run," she wrote in her diary. "I don't know what he will think of me."

The one thing she could control at that time was her eating. And so she did. She stopped.

She lost weight at an alarming rate. Kathleen was not the only person to notice. On June 12, while at work in the governor's office in Dover, Anne Marie Fahey fainted. And when she came to, she called the one person she knew she could count on for help. She called Tom Capano, asking him to come and drive her home to Wilmington.

Why Capano and not Scanlan, her boyfriend, the man she hoped to marry? Kim Horstmann was asked that question during her testimony before the grand jury. She had spoken to Anne Marie both before and after the fainting incident and thought she knew the answer.

"She was afraid to death of Michael ever finding out that she had this problem," Horstmann said.

"She didn't want him to think that she was sick. She was aware that she was taking too many laxatives at night and she wasn't eating, but she did not want Michael to know because it would make her look weak in his eyes. She was afraid it might make him think less of her if she had this problem.

"Tom, she felt, was, I guess, more like a father figure to her because they had this friendship and so she could confide in him because he knew about the eating disorder."

A father figure. That's not the role, investigators believe, Capano had envisioned for himself.

"If he couldn't have her, no one would," state prosecutor Ferris Wharton said in what is a simplistic but, investigators contend, accurate description of the motive for Fahey's murder. But it hardly begins to tell the twisted saga of love and betrayal, obsession and control that lies at the heart of the case.

E-mail from Capano to Fahey, June 3, 1996, 12:19 p.m.:

> Hey you,
>
> You'll get this after I'm gone but I didn't want the day to go by without saying hi. I know you're having a rough day and hope it doesn't make you crazy. . . . How's about dinner Thursday night? Lobster at Dilworthtown? . . . AND TAKE YOUR VITAMINS.

From Capano to Fahey, Friday, June 7, 1996, 10:35 a.m.:

> Good Morning Annie,
>
> Thanks again for last night. I had a great time and hope you enjoyed yourself. I'm still stuffed. . . . Please call when you can.

From Fahey to Capano, same day, 12:49 p.m.:

> Hey,
>
> I am also still stuffed up to my neck. Hey, it was a great stuffing! . . . I'll call before I leave.
>
> Annie

Investigators say that even as he was writing notes of endearment and support to Fahey in May and June 1996, Capano was carrying on an affair with another woman and apparently trying to start an affair with someone else.

The other "other woman" is Deborah MacIntyre, who has since admitted that she and Capano had been having an affair for about 15 years at the time Fahey disappeared. MacIntyre, who left her job as an administrator at a private school in Wilmington earlier this year, is now cooperating with authorities.

She testified that she met Capano in the late 1970s when he and her then-husband were members of the same Wilmington law firm. She said Capano first told her how he felt about her at a New Year's Eve party in 1981. According to MacIntyre, they started sleeping together a short time after that and the affair continued into the fall of last year.

"I fell in love with him," MacIntyre said while testifying at a pretrial hearing in August. "He was charming. . . . He cared for me. . . . He listened to me. And I needed that."

MacIntyre says she was unaware of Capano's relationship with Fahey. She has admitted, however, that on May 13, 1996, she bought a handgun for Capano. At his request, she purchased the weapon in her name, then turned it over to him, she said.

The gun has never been found.

During this same period, Capano reestablished contact with the woman he had allegedly harassed back in 1980, the woman who said she had fled Wilmington to get away from him. The woman, whose identity has been withheld by authorities, told the FBI that she saw Capano again in 1987, after she had divorced, and he acted "as if nothing had happened." In fact, he asked her out. She agreed. They went to an Atlantic City casino to celebrate her birthday. He bought her a watch and had it engraved to commemorate the event. Then, she said, he asked if she was seeing any other men. When she replied that she was, he called her a "slut and a whore."

That was the last she heard from Capano until January 1996, when, she said, he called her "out of the blue," suggesting that they go out and proposing that she come to work as his legal secretary. This was shortly after Capano had separated from his wife and moved into a home on his own. At that time, investigators say, Capano was continuing his relationship with MacIntyre and trying to rekindle his affair with Fahey.

The woman said that in April Capano took her to dinner at La Veranda, another posh Philadelphia Italian restaurant, and that a month later he lent her $3,000 to pay off some debts, all the while encouraging her to become his legal secretary. She said she interviewed for the job at his law firm and was hired. She was supposed to start work on May 29. But after a series of phone calls in which Capano complained about the personal greeting on her home telephone answering machine—Capano told her she sounded "childish" and could not come to work for him unless she changed it—the woman thought better of the job offer.

Anne Marie Fahey may have decided that she, too, was better off without Capano. On April 7, she wrote in her diary that she had finally reached "closure" over Capano, describing him as a "manipulative, jealous, insecure maniac."

In May, Fahey told her hairdresser that she had been trying for several weeks to end her relationship with Capano, who, she said, "was crazy and . . . scared me." On one recent occasion, she said, they had gotten into a heated argument while sitting in his car outside her apartment.

"Fahey told Capano that she wanted to end their affair," according to an FBI affidavit outlining an interview with the hairdresser. "Capano started screaming and yelling at her and called Fahey a slut and bitch [and] grabbed her by the neck. Fahey jumped out of the car and ran into her apartment."

Fahey also told her psychologist, who later told the FBI, that "Capano had stalked Fahey and threatened to expose their relationship to others in order to force Fahey to continue" to see him. The psychologist said she had encouraged Fahey to report Capano's actions to the attorney general's office, but that she had not.

The psychologist also told the FBI that she thought "the only reason Fahey would have accompanied Capano to Philadelphia for dinner on June 27 would be to break off the relationship."

E-mail from Fahey to Capano, June 26, 1996, 4:24 p.m.:

> Io siento mucho [I am very sorry]. I would like to apologize for being such a downer today. I realize that your day has not been so great either, and I was not much help. I feel like some days I can handle my anorexia and other days I feel overwhelmed by the whole thing. Today has obviously been an overwhelming day. My appointment [with her psychologist] was hard and in depth . . . and quite

frankly it drained all my energy. . . . Right now I am going to focus on trying to get better. Sorry for being such a doggy downer today.

Take care,
Annie

From Capano to Fahey, same day, 6:19 p.m.:

Re: Io siento mucho

I didn't get a chance to react to this until after 6:00 and I assume you're gone and won't see this 'til tomorrow. . . . I appreciate the apology, but you don't need to worry about it. I just hope you know that all I want to do is help in any way I can. I promise to make you laugh tonight at Panorama, to order calamari and to surprise you with something that will make you smile. Please call when you get a chance.

Twenty-four hours later, Thomas J. Capano and Anne Marie Fahey sat across from each other at a table in the fancy Italian restaurant.

The waitress remembered them well.

They didn't look happy.

TRUMP VS. WYNN:
A REAL-LIFE SPY TALE

MARCH 12, 2000

They were the tools of the trade in a gritty, down-and-dirty corporate power struggle between companies controlled by casino industry giants Stephen A. Wynn and Donald Trump. Weapons in a war of words, lawsuits and executive one-upmanship that the two egocentric millionaires have been waging for more than 15 years. Inventory that even some lawyers involved in the case found unsettling.

Consider the implications:

Two briefcases, one with a hidden audio tape recorder, the other with a hidden video camera with audio capability.

A clock radio with a hidden transmitter.

A "modified jock strap" with hidden tape recorder and microphones secreted in a belt.

Microcassette tapes the size of postage stamps that could record for up to two hours.

All of that equipment, say lawyers in a controversial civil suit settled here last month, was used by a private investigator who became a "double agent," working first for Trump Hotel & Casino Resorts and then for Wynn's Mirage Resorts.

"I have never seen such unethical corporate espionage as I've seen in this case," said Gregory Smith, a Los Angeles lawyer whose client, former Mirage employee Laura Choi, was one of the defendants sued by Mirage. To date, Choi, a former marketing representative, is the only defendant not to have reached a settlement. "They [Mirage] operated as if they were a government agency coordinating a sting operation."

The case, which Mirage and Trump settled February 23, is replete with allegations of fraud, money-laundering, conspiracy, perjury and the theft of trade secrets. But the most outrageous of all the charges is the claim that Wynn's Mirage Resorts had secretly flipped a private investigator hired by Trump's company, turned him into a "double agent" and sent him back to meet and secretly record conversations with Trump officials who became defendants in the suit Mirage filed here back in April.

"Unethical" and "unbelievable," said attorneys for Trump before a confidentiality agreement at settlement barred them from further comment. "Chicanery" and a "Faustian deal" were two other descriptions that appeared in motions and pleadings along with references to corporate investigative operations dubbed "Operation Snake Eyes" and "Operation Seoul Train."

Mirage lawyers countered by arguing that the investigator, Louis "Curt" Rodriguez Jr., a former Los Angeles police officer who later worked for both the IRS and the U.S. Customs Service, was a "whistle-blower" who switched sides because he was asked to dig up dirt on Wynn and Mirage in an unethical manner.

Now overshadowed by last week's blockbuster announcement that Mirage has agreed to accept a $4.4 billion buyout offer from industry giant MGM Grand, the charges and countercharges offer a glimpse at the seamy side of a multi-billion-dollar industry.

Who is bigger? Who is better? Who has more staying power? Those are the bottom-line questions that define the legendary industry feud between Wynn, 58, and Trump, 53, say those who have followed the saga. The antipathy, says casino analyst Marvin Roffman, stems from the fact that both men are so "similar." The two University of Pennsylvania graduates are self-made and in many ways larger than life.

Trump toys with running for president and owns the Miss Universe and Miss USA pageants. Wynn builds billion-dollar adult fantasy lands on the Las Vegas Strip and owns some of the finest art in the world.

"They hate each other's guts," said Roffman. "It's like poison."

They have been sniping at each other for years.

This particular battle began in 1995 in Atlantic City where Wynn's plans for a grandiose, billion-dollar casino in the marina area were opposed by Trump and some other Boardwalk gambling operators. After two years of acrimony that included charges and countercharges of political manipulation, Wynn's Mirage company filed an antitrust suit in federal court in New York alleging that Trump and Hilton Hotels used sham lawsuits and illegal political influence in an attempt to keep Mirage out of Atlantic City.

As part of its defense, Trump Resorts hired a Manhattan investigative firm, William Kish International. Kish, in turn, contracted with Rodriguez, a partner in Pacific Empire Group, a Los Angeles-based investigative firm. Both parties in the suit concede those facts. What remains in dispute is what Rodriguez did and for whom he did it in the 18 months leading up to a second civil suit filed in federal court here by Mirage against Trump Resorts and several of its top officials. In that suit, Mirage charged that Trump Resorts and some of its top officials engaged in a conspiracy with current and former Mirage employees to steal trade secrets, primarily lists of Korean high-rollers.

"I wish I could talk about this but I can't," William Kish, a retired FBI agent, said in a brief telephone interview last week. "I really, really wish I could say something."

Because of a confidentiality agreement, Kish, like all other defendants in the case, is barred from discussing the litigation. Rodriguez, who is also covered by that prohibition, said through his attorney that he would have no comment. But both PIs had plenty to say on the record in sworn affidavits that are part of the settled lawsuit. Each tells a different story.

Rodriguez said that he was hired in February 1998 to dig up dirt on Mirage and Wynn, to purloin information about Korean high-rollers who frequented Wynn's casinos, and to spread rumors about Mirage's alleged involvement in money-laundering in Korea and its suspected mob ties in Atlantic City. Along the way, he said, he even gathered information about the gambling habits of Steve Wynn's elderly mother.

Rodriguez said the plan was dubbed "Operation Snake Eyes." He said that Kish repeatedly referred to Wynn as "the villain" and encouraged Rodriguez to share any information he developed with federal authorities, including the FBI, the Customs Service, and Korean and Japanese law enforcement agencies. Rodriguez said Kish told him that the Trump organization had a "three-pronged" attack plan that it hoped would result in the indictment of Mirage executives and would jeopardize Mirage's chances of winning a New Jersey casino license. But after after working for Kish and the Trump company for about six months and receiving about $88,000 in compensation, Rodriguez said he had a change of heart.

Rodriguez said he decided to approach the Mirage company "after becoming uncomfortable that the information that I had gathered . . . was being used . . . in an immoral and unethical manner to cause financial harm" to the Mirage company and to Wynn. Kish, in affidavits that are also part of the court record, said that was not the way it happened.

Attorneys for both Kish and Trump Resorts, pointing to a $10,000-a-month consulting deal Rodriguez had with Mirage and a golden parachute provision that guaranteed Mirage would not execute any financial judgment it might win in a lawsuit against him, say the private investigator had other motives for telling his tale.

Rodriguez's only mission, Kish said in two sworn affidavits, was to gather information that could be used by the Trump company to defend against the antitrust suit Mirage had filed in New York. Kish said that the phrase "Operation Snake Eyes" was the name of a continuing "intensive investigation by the FBI" into the Mirage company, not, as Rodriguez claimed, an operation launched by Trump. The FBI declines to comment about any investigation it may be conducting.

Kish also said that Rodriguez spent a good part of his time either looking over his shoulder or worrying about money. According to Kish, Rodriguez complained that his life was in danger, that Mirage agents were harassing him, that he was not being paid enough, and that Mirage investigators were making much more. At one point, he suggested that he and Kish "join up with the other side." Kish said that when he "strongly criticized" Rodriguez, "he told me not to get so upset, that he was only kidding."

By October 1998, however, Rodriguez was secretly meeting with Mirage officials. By November, they were talking about an arrangement that ultimately resulted, Trump lawyers now charge, with Rodriguez's turning over to Mirage officials all the confidential information he had gathered while working for Trump. Finally, Trump's attorneys contend, Rodriguez agreed to become a "double agent" and work "Operation Seoul Train," the name given to his counterintelligence foray.

Between January and April 1999, court records indicate, Rodriguez taped 20 conversations with Trump officials or other individuals who eventually would be named defendants in the civil suit filed here by Mirage. Those secretly taped included Kish, Trump's head of security, Joseph Guzzardo, and Paul Liu, a Mirage employee who worked the Korean high-roller market.

On April 20, 1999, Mirage filed suit in U.S. District Court here alleging that the Trump company had engaged in a conspiracy to harm Mirage and purloin trade secrets. At that time, Steve Wynn called the case an example of "the most outrageous misconduct, the most flagrant violations of law and decent behavior in the history of the resort hotel industry." Trump Resorts, Kish, Guzzardo, Liu, Choi and Rodriguez were named as defendants. When Trump's attorneys learned of Rodriguez's actions as a double-agent, they responded in kind.

"Rodriguez dishonored his fiduciary duty in a fashion that would have made Judas Iscariot proud," wrote Donald Campbell, Trump's Las Vegas lawyer, in a blistering motion filed in August that included the argument that Mirage was perpetrating a "sham" on the court by listing Rodriguez as a defendant.

The charges and countercharges continued for months. All of it was expected to become part of a sweeping evidentiary hearing set to begin here on February 22. But after a one-day delay, lawyers announced that a settlement had been reached here and in the antitrust suit in New York.

No one would comment, but both sides acknowledged that the cases had been dismissed "with prejudice," meaning they could not be refiled, and that none of the defendants would pay any damages to Mirage. A week later, MGM made its first offer to buy Mirage Resorts for $17 a share. Last week, after private negotiations, the deal was finalized. The sale price was $21 a share, a deal worth about $4.4 billion. Wynn, as the largest Mirage stockholder, will receive about $300 million after taxes, if the deal is completed, as expected, by year's end. Left unresolved is the fate of the billion-dollar marina casino-hotel Mirage had hoped to build in the marina section of Atlantic City.

While a controversial $330 million inner-city tunnel, partly funded by the state, to the marina site is under construction, not a spade of dirt has been turned on the grandiose Palais Le Jardin that Wynn had trumpeted in 1995 when he announced his return to Atlantic City. That casino project, which sparked the antitrust suit in New York and the civil suit here and which eventually led Trump to hire Kish and Kish to hire Rodriguez, may never be built, casino analysts were saying last week.

GETTING TO GUILTY:
THE MURDER OF CAROL NEULANDER

DECEMBER 15, 2002

It was never a question of whether the rabbi had been involved in the murder of his wife. During the first few weeks of the investigation eight years ago, detectives were certain that that's where the case was headed. They knew it in their guts. Despite the trappings that surrounded the crime—the upper-middle-class, suburban setting, the religious backdrop, the status and community standing of the principals—they knew that at its core the murder of Carol Neulander was a domestic matter.

Play out the basics of this case in a blue-collar neighborhood in Camden or Marcus Hook or South Philadelphia, and the first suspect who comes to mind is the husband. More often than not, such a case is solved in a month. So, from the investigators' perspective, there was a strong sense from the start that Rabbi Fred J. Neulander was somebody worth looking at for the horrific murder of his wife, Carol. The question for the investigators was always: Would they be able to prove it?

Carol Neulander, 52, was found bludgeoned to death and lying in her own blood on the living room floor of her home on Highgate Lane in Cherry Hill on the night of November 1, 1994.

Four years later, the rabbi was charged with conspiracy to commit murder. The charge reflected the fact that, at that point, the case was largely circumstantial.

Two years later, with the surprise confession of the hit man—a character who could have walked out of a grade-B film noir—the charges against the rabbi were upgraded to capital murder.

And two years after that, three weeks after the eighth anniversary of Carol Neulander's death, a jury finally reached a decision, finally confirmed in a court of law what the investigators sensed and felt and knew intuitively almost from the night of the murder.

The rabbi was guilty.

The investigation that got the jury to that point began on the night Fred J. Neulander dialed 911 and reported his wife bloody and beaten. It is a story of police work, sometimes fascinating, often mundane. It is about gathering bits and pieces of evidence, about interviewing and reinterviewing witnesses. It is about taking all those bits and pieces, all those details and statements, and using them to create a picture that could be offered to a jury of 12 men and women so that they could determine, beyond a reasonable doubt, how and why Carol Neulander was murdered.

The jury saw the finished product. The production is another matter.

"He thought this was the perfect murder, but it started to unravel before it was committed," said a satisfied Marty Devlin as he sat in the Penrose Diner in South Philadelphia, eating a breakfast of eggs-over-easy with bacon the day after a Monmouth County jury had rejected the death penalty, thus handing Fred Neulander a life sentence.

A former Philadelphia homicide detective, Devlin is the investigator with the Camden County Prosecutor's Office who worked the case for nearly eight years. Street-smart and feisty with intense green eyes that display both the joy and seriousness he brings to the job, the five-foot-nine homicide cop set the tone for the investigation. Dogged. Relentless. Determined.

Early on he learned that the rabbi recognized him as an adversary. Devlin was told that Fred Neulander used to refer to him by a nickname that combined Devlin's Irish heritage and what the rabbi considered his abrasive style. "He called me the 'mick prick,'" Devlin said, the rhyming words dancing off his tongue. "I liked that." Others describe Devlin in more endearing terms. He is, some say, a leprechaun with an attitude.

"Through Marty Devlin we learned how the criminal justice system works," said Barbara Lidz, Carol Neulander's sister-in-law and the point person for the family with law enforcement throughout the investigation. "And we learned about those who try to heal with justice. . . . There is no way I can explain how much this family loves and respects him."

"You look up the word detective in the dictionary," added Ed Lidz, one of Carol Neulander's two brothers, "and you see a picture of Marty Devlin."

Martin Devlin, 57, grew up in the Mayfair and Port Richmond sections of Philadelphia. He graduated from Father Judge High School and worked for 28 years with the Philadelphia Police Department, most of it as a homicide detective, before joining the Camden County Prosecutor's Office in December 1994, about six weeks after Carol Neulander was killed.

Devlin, who is quick and effusive with his praise of others in the office, got the case about a week after he took the job. He and James P. Lynch, the first assistant Camden County prosecutor who tried the case twice, brought the same approach to the investigation. Both are career law enforcement men. And both have that calm strength that comes from not wanting to be anything other than what they are.

"I've been at this for 36 years," Devlin said as he sat in the diner that Saturday morning, dressed in a "Fightin' Irish" Notre Dame football jersey. "My only regret is I can't do it for 36 more." Then he starts talking about the case.

"The chances of Rebecca receiving those two phones calls at just the times she received them were," Devlin says, pausing slightly for effect, "none and none." Yet it happened that way. Sometimes, Marty Devlin says, there is a higher authority at work.

Looking back now on all the pieces that went into the puzzle—the evidence, the interviews, the pretrial motions that set the stage for the courtroom drama, the first trial that ended with a hung jury, the retrial that resulted in the conviction—he comes back to those phone calls between Carol Neulander and her daughter, Rebecca Neulander-Rockoff. They are one of four key elements that underpinned the case from the early days and give perspective to what Devlin, Lynch and a dozen other investigators, prosecutors and staff workers accomplished during the marathon investigation that began on the watch of one county prosecutor, peaked during the term of another, and concluded after a third had been sworn into office.

"Nobody ever said, 'Get the rabbi,'" Devlin said of his three bosses, county prosecutors Edward Borden, Lee Solomon and Vincent Sarubbi. "The only thing I was ever told was, 'Find out what happened. Do what you got to do.'"

The easiest way to understand what happened and why Rabbi Fred J. Neulander, the 61-year-old founder and former leader of Cherry Hill's Congregation M'kor Shalom, will spend the rest of his life in prison is to look at four crucial pieces to the puzzle: the phone calls, the fight, the mistress and the Torah.

THE PHONE CALLS

It was like a message from the grave. It was as if Carol Neulander herself was telling those she had left behind where to look.

"There's a man here with a package for Daddy," Carol Neulander told her daughter during a phone conversation on a Tuesday night a week before she was killed. "Daddy said to expect him."

Daddy said to expect him.

Rebecca, then 24 and a student in a master's program at Temple University, told detectives about the phone call after she was rushed to her home in Cherry Hill on the night her mother was killed. She was sitting in an EMT van outside the house, which was awash in flashing lights and cordoned off with yellow crime-scene tape. Inside, detectives took pictures and gathered evidence. They were disappointed. There wasn't much.

"It was an organized crime scene," Lt. Arthur Folks, the lead homicide investigator that night, later testified. "As opposed to a disorganized crime scene."

By that, Folks meant that nothing seemed out of place. Other than Carol Neulander lying dead and bloodied on the floor, nothing had been disturbed. Pieces of valuable crystal were on shelves and tables nearby. None of the drawers in a secretary where large sums of cash were stored had been disturbed. None of the jewelry Carol Neulander was wearing—a watch, a diamond ring, a gold necklace—had been taken.

"Whoever went there that night went there to kill Carol Neulander," Folks said.

"You can't re-create the crime scene," Devlin noted. "You only get one chance. You have to do things right. The guys working that night did everything right. They set the table for me," he added, having joined the case seven weeks later.

Rebecca was eager to tell investigators about the first phone call—and about another conversation she had had that very night with her mother. As she sat in the EMT van next to her father, she blurted out the story.

A man had come to the house a week before claiming to have something for her father. Rebecca and Carol were talking on the phone at the time, Carol sitting in her car in the driveway of the home. She told Rebecca a man was approaching, then knocking on the car window. He said he had something for the rabbi.

Carol Neulander let the man into her home and ended the conversation with Rebecca. He asked to use the bathroom. Then he gave her an envelope and left. Carol called her daughter back that night and told her what had happened. She said the whole thing was a little strange and that there was something bizarre about the delivery. The envelope the man left that night was empty.

But there was more. The man had come back. He had come that very night, just hours ago, Rebecca said as she sat in the van. She added that she was supposed to come home that night, but wasn't feeling well. So her mother called her at her Philadelphia apartment and they were talking—they talked on the phone constantly, sometimes for a few minutes, sometimes for an hour or more. They were talking and there was a knock on the door, her mother said. So while she was still on the phone, she went and looked through the window.

"Oh, it's the bathroom guy," Carol told her daughter. Rebecca said she then heard muffled conversation, but she remembered her mother saying, "Come on in. Have a seat. He'll be home soon."

The bathroom guy.

"You look at this as an investigator," Devlin said, "and you're saying to yourself, 'All right. This is dynamite. This is a lead.' So they ask the rabbi as he's sitting next to Rebecca, 'What about this delivery? Who was this guy?' And he says, 'I don't know anything about that.'"

Later that night, the rabbi would change his story, offering a version that fit with what his daughter had said. Someone had come to the house a week before, he now remembered Carol telling him. But he had no idea what it was about.

And the envelope? He said he thought Carol had thrown it away.

Devlin says he tries not to take a case personally, tries not to get too close to the family of the victim. You do that and you lose your perspective. What's more, you can get eaten alive.

"This job takes all your time and your energy and your spirit," he says. "You can't weep over the death. It takes too much out of you."

Marty Devlin has seen a lot of death. He estimates he's investigated nearly a thousand homicides over his career. But the Neulander case was special.

"I'll never forget that family." And for a moment the streetwise and hardened homicide detective has to pause and compose himself. This time he did get close. Carol Neulander's brothers and sister and their spouses, he said, "were the salt of the earth."

"They were innocent to the dangers of the world," Devlin adds. "I think I was the first detective they ever met." He would go to New York to visit them and they would talk.

"They grilled me, as they should have. I couldn't tell them anything that would compromise what we were doing, but I did try to keep them informed about where things stood."

Over time Devlin began to suggest the direction in which the investigation might be heading, that their brother-in-law, the rabbi, was somebody investigators were taking a hard look at.

Any time you deal with families, he says, it's difficult. They have ideas and perceptions about how the system works, but you have to let them know that "I'm the one that does this and I know how to do this."

In time, the family totally supported Devlin, offering him insights and information that fleshed out the profile of the rabbi that investigators were building.

The children were another matter.

Devlin says that Rebecca never wavered. Her story was the same from the first time she was interviewed.

"I think she knew the danger she put her father in, but she never changed that story. It had to hurt her a lot. But she was telling the truth."

Her brother Matthew came along more slowly. A student at Rutgers University in Camden, he would stop by the prosecutor's office and talk with Devlin from time to time.

"He was a bright kid and he loved his mom so much," Devlin says. But Devlin also knew he was agonizing over what he knew and what it meant.

"All these kids, they lost their mother and now they were in danger of losing their dad. That's a horrible position to be in." Matthew would talk and Devlin would listen.

"At first, the point I was trying to make was that nobody was trying to railroad his dad," Devlin says. "So I let him talk. I just let him know, wherever the truth was, that's where we were going."

THE FIGHT

It had occurred two nights before the murder. Carol and Fred Neulander arrived home that night from a trip to New York, where Carol's relatives lived. When they got home, they were already in a heated argument.

Matthew, the only one of the three children living at home at the time, had never seen anything like it. At one point, Carol Neulander looked at her son and said, "Tell your father good-bye." Matthew thought his father was going on a trip.

"No," his mother said, "he's leaving the house."

Later, she went down to the basement and returned with a suitcase that she handed to her husband. Fred Neulander said hardly anything. Matthew would testify later that he had no idea what caused the fight, but said he had never seen his parents so angry with each other. For the next two days, he tried to get his father to talk about it, but the rabbi avoided any meaningful discussion.

By that point, investigators say, the murder plan was already in place. In fact, they now believe, Carol Neulander was lucky to be alive. She was supposed to have been killed a week earlier, during the first visit from the "bathroom guy." But it would be several years before that piece of the puzzle fell into place.

Devlin read the reports of the statements of Rebecca and Matthew and then he listened to the 911 tape, the call Fred Neulander made when he came home from the synagogue that night and found his wife lying on the floor in a pool of blood.

Neulander did nothing you would expect. He didn't rush to his wife's side. He didn't try to help her. He didn't try to comfort her. She was dying—or dead—on the floor, and the rabbi said he couldn't touch her. This was the woman he had been married to for nearly 29 years. He said he couldn't look at her.

"I knew not what to do," he would later tell a jury.

I knew not what to do.

The tape of the emergency call caught the same oddness. To Devlin, the rabbi sounded scared and anguished, but in a forced way, as if he were talking the way he thought someone in his position would talk. Marty Devlin picked up on that as soon as he heard the tape. Lt. Folks and Cherry Hill detectives John Long and Rich Rublewski (who are both now retired) had the same reaction.

"At first blush, it sounded contrived to me," Devlin said of the voice and the words of the man he heard on the phone.

"He never touched her," Devlin said, echoing parts of the devastating testimony of Matthew Neulander at the second trial. Matthew brought tears to the jury's eyes when he described the scene at his home that night.

Now a doctor working in a hospital emergency room in North Carolina, he was working part time as an emergency medical technician for the Cherry Hill ambulance squad on the night his mother was killed. His squad got the call to respond to the address on Highgate Lane that he knew was his home. "Someone was bleeding," was the initial report.

When Matthew Neulander got there, friends grabbed him and forcibly stopped him from rushing into the home. His father stood in the driveway watching.

"I would have given my right arm to spend five minutes with her," Matthew told the jury during the retrial. Yet, he said, his father made no effort. He was standing there, he remembered, in a neatly pressed suit, hardly wrinkled. Impeccably dressed. And totally indifferent.

The statements of Rebecca and Matthew were keys to the investigation. Their stories painted a picture of crucial events in the life and death of Carol Neulander.

"They had no reason to lie," Marty Devlin said. "They were totally believable."

THE MISTRESS

Elaine Soncini, on the other hand, had several reasons to lie. And she did. The former Philadelphia radio personality at first denied she had been the rabbi's secret paramour. But within a month of the murder, after being questioned by police and overhearing—or perhaps being allowed to overhear—two investigators say, "The bitch is lying," she told police all that she knew. It had little to do with the murder, but everything to do with the "other life" of Rabbi Fred J. Neulander.

When the movie is cast, as it surely will be, the actress chosen to play Elaine Soncini will have to decide which way to play the character. After two appearances on the witness stand—she was a star prosecution witness at both trials—there's still a question about Soncini's motivation.

The backstory is clear. She was a South Philadelphia girl who made good. She started as a secretary and ended up a bona fide radio personality. She married Ken Garland, the dean of AM radio, a star in his own right. They were a media couple, on the air together each morning for five years, sharing their thoughts with thousands of listeners.

But in December 1992, Garland was dying, ravaged by leukemia and related problems. He was rushed to the hospital one night, and a friend arranged to have a rabbi come to see him: Fred J. Neulander. Two days later, the rabbi conducted the funeral service for Garland, delivering a stirring eulogy. Less than two weeks after that, he was in bed with Elaine.

Their affair would grow more and more torrid. Toward the end he was visiting her five afternoons a week, two nights a week, and early each Saturday and Sunday morning. There apparently were other women in the rabbi's life, but none had the spot that Elaine Soncini had. She was the woman, prosecutors say, for whose love the rabbi was willing to kill. So do you play her as vulnerable and naive or hard and calculating? Was she obsessed with him? Or was he obsessed with her?

Soncini's story filled in gaps and helped Lynch, Devlin and the others develop a potential motive for the killing. While not essential, if you're going to try to sell a murder conspiracy charge to a jury and if the defendant is a highly regarded religious leader, it is best to have some explanation for why he did what you claim he did.

"*Cherchez la femme*," look for the woman, Devlin observed. "Homicide detectives say that all the time. In this case there were many. And they all seemed vulnerable at the time that he met them. That was the common thread. . . . This guy must have been smooth as silk. I mean, physically he's not that imposing."

In terms of the actual crime, Soncini didn't bring that much to the table. She did, however, tell investigators that she had given the rabbi an ultimatum. In the fall of 1994, after returning from a cruise to Alaska, she told the rabbi that, come the first of the year, she was starting life over. She would no longer be his mistress. The rabbi asked her not to give up on them. They would be together, he promised. Somehow. They would be together, he vowed, by her birthday. Elaine Soncini was born on December 17. Carol Neulander was killed on November 1.

THE TORAH

Devlin never lost his focus during the probe. There were times when he was frustrated, but he says he always kept in mind what prosecutor Lee

Solomon told him after taking office in 1996: Find out what happened, find out why Carol Neulander was killed.

Patience is always the key in working a homicide, Devlin believes. "It's like a birth. It's going to come knowing its time." That's how it was with Pep Levin and figuring out where he fit in the puzzle.

Devlin needed to know what a rabbi was doing playing racquetball each week with an ex-con who, law enforcement authorities in Pennsylvania and New Jersey have long maintained, had strong underworld connections. So he went to see Pep.

Myron "Pep" Levin did business out of an office tucked in the back of Flower World, a large floral warehouse on Route 38 in Pennsauken. Marty Devlin showed up there one day unannounced.

"He's a serious man," Devlin says, "and I wanted to look him in the eyes and let him know I was a serious man, too. I really didn't say that much to him that day. I just told him I was going to find out what had happened to Carol Neulander and that I was going to expect everyone's cooperation."

"If I knew anything, kid, I'd tell you," Levin, then 70, replied.

It was the start of a game of cat and mouse that would play out over several months. Levin gave up bits and pieces of information, telling investigators that during one racquetball game the rabbi had angrily thrown his racquet on the floor and told Levin he wished he would "come home one night and find his wife dead on the floor."

"What else did he say?" Devlin asked.

"That's all," Levin replied.

"There had to be more," Devlin says. "That kind of conversation doesn't end like that."

A short time later, the detective heard about the Torah. Originally, the story was that Levin had donated a Torah to M'kor Shalom in memory of his wife, Reta.

Ever the cynic, Devlin remembered reading and hearing about a spate of robberies in the 1980s in which valuable Torahs had been stolen and were being sold on the black market. He wondered if the Torah that Levin had donated to M'kor Shalom was hot and whether he could use that to pressure the reluctant witness. In the midst of his research, Devlin learned that Levin had not actually donated a Torah, but rather had given Rabbi Neulander between $16,000 and $20,000 to purchase a sacred scroll in Reta Levin's memory. Devlin contacted a rabbi in Philadelphia who was an expert in authenticating Torahs and arranged for him to visit M'kor Shalom and examine the Torah. The scribe brought another expert along. What Devlin learned that day, he kept in his pocket. It was a card to be played at a later date.

Several months later, in September 1997, grand jury subpoenas went out. Levin was one of about a dozen witnesses called to testify before the panel investigating the murder. By that point, Devlin and Lynch had Solomon's approval to prepare a murder conspiracy case. It would be built around the testimony of Rebecca and Matthew Neulander, Elaine Soncini and several others, including Levin and Levin's former driver.

The driver, Anthony Federici, said Levin had complained to him about a conversation he had had with the rabbi during a racquetball game in the fall of 1994. He said Levin told him the rabbi had said he wanted to come home one night and find his wife dead. He also said Levin told him the rabbi had asked, "Do you know anybody who could do that?" It was the second half of the conversation that Devlin knew had to exist.

Before Levin appeared before the grand jury, he was made aware of Federici's statement. Investigators hoped Levin would confirm the second part of the conversation before the grand jury. If true, testimony that the rabbi had solicited the murder of his wife would be crucial to the circumstantial case being built.

"We just want you to tell the truth," Devlin told Levin during a meeting prior to his grand jury appearance. Then they talked about friendship and loyalty.

"Next to love, loyalty is probably the most important thing a man can have," Devlin told Levin. "You have to make up your mind what side you're on."

With that, Devlin said, Levin began to talk about what a good friend Rabbi Neulander had been, about how he had purchased a Torah that came from Krakow, Poland, a "Holocaust Torah."

"You know what the Holocaust is, kid?" Devlin says Levin asked him.

"Yes, sir, I do," Devlin replied.

Levin said the rabbi had "scoured the world" for the sacred scroll, and he talked with pride about how he, Levin, had carried and proudly displayed the Torah at his grandson's recent bar mitzvah.

"That's the kind of man Fred Neulander is," Levin told Devlin.

Devlin paused, and then told Levin, "What I'm about to tell you doesn't give me any great pleasure. I had a couple of scribes look at that Torah. You know what they told me?"

"What did they tell you, kid?" Levin asked.

The experts whom Devlin had brought to M'kor Shalom several months earlier had determined that the Torah was not what Rabbi Neulander had claimed. Devlin sums up their assessment of the Torah this way: "It wasn't kosher." There were numerous mistakes and errors in the script. Pages were faded and poorly maintained. They doubted it was from Krakow. Devlin asked one of the two experts what he thought the scroll was worth.

"Let me be kind," the scribe said to Devlin. "Maybe $3,000, $4,000."

Marty Devlin told Pep Levin what the experts had said. He let the words hang in the air. But his message was clear and direct. That's the kind of man Fred Neulander is.

Levin, when he appeared before the grand jury, confirmed what Federici had told Devlin. Not only had the rabbi said he wanted to find his wife dead, but he also asked Levin if he knew anybody who could do it. The murder conspiracy case was complete.

It would take one more year before the indictment was handed up, but on September 10, 1998, Fred J. Neulander was arrested on murder conspiracy charges. Marty Devlin was the investigator who clapped the cuffs on him.

"He was in his car when we stopped him," Devlin recalled. "He's built funny. He's got a thick body and really short arms. I couldn't cuff him behind his back. His arms wouldn't reach. So I cuffed him in front and we put him in the back of the car." And that's when Devlin and Rabbi Neulander had their first significant conversation.

"What's this all about?" the rabbi asked in a stammering voice that sounded frightened and concerned, yet also contrived. Marty Devlin recognized it immediately. It was the same voice he had heard on the 911 tape.

"What's this about?" Devlin said as he turned and looked at the rabbi. "This is about Carol Neulander. And you're under arrest for murder."

In Hollywood, the story could end there. But in the spring of 2000, shortly before Rabbi Neulander was to go on trial on the murder conspiracy charge, Len Jenoff confessed to having killed Carol Neulander, claiming the rabbi promised him $30,000.

Jenoff, a struggling private eye and recovering alcoholic who had built a fantasy world for himself around boasts of having connections to the CIA, Oliver North and President Ronald Reagan, said he was "the bathroom guy." His story, another tale of manipulation and betrayal, added a whole new dimension to the case. Now the circumstantial evidence that Devlin, Lynch and the others had developed would be the framework for the testimony of Jenoff and his accomplice, Paul Michael Daniels. Both admitted beating Carol Neulander to death. Both testified for the prosecution.

The first trial, in Camden last year, ended in a mistrial. Jenoff's credibility was apparently too big a hurdle for the entire jury to get over. The panel in that trial, according to those familiar with the deliberations, voted nine to three in favor of conviction on all three charges the rabbi faced: capital murder, felony murder and the original conspiracy charge.

The retrial, moved to Freehold because of the extensive publicity the case had received, unfolded this fall in the Monmouth County Courthouse. Lynch used most of the same witnesses and evidence, although he emphasized much more strongly the corroboration the prosecution had for Jenoff's story. The phone calls to Rebecca, the fight Matthew had witnessed, the ultimatum Soncini had delivered and the conversations with Pep Levin—the four crucial pieces in solving the puzzle before Jenoff made it seem easy to the casual observer—were all writ large the second time around.

Jury deliberations began on a Friday morning. They would last nearly four days. But during the first day, the panel of seven men and five women who would decide Rabbi Neulander's fate asked for the first of several read-backs of trial testimony. What they wanted to hear, they said, was the testimony of Rebecca Neulander-Rockoff. They wanted to hear about the phone calls.

When Marty Devlin heard that, he smiled. He knew the jury understood the case. The phone calls were crucial, and they got it. And if they understood the case, Marty Devlin knew they would find the rabbi guilty.

FINAL VERDICT?

JUNE 1, 2003

It was supposed to be a second honeymoon, a trip to a national park in Utah for hiking and communing with nature, a chance to be alone. James and Patricia Bottarini, a Medford couple who seemed to have it all, left New Jersey on May 7, 1997. Two days later, they were walking Observation Point Trail, a five-mile trek that offered spectacular views of sandstone cliffs, mesas and canyons along the eastern edge of the sprawling 229-square-mile Zion National Park.

Around noon that day, Patricia Bottarini fell—or was pushed—to her death. A witness hiking in the park said he looked up and saw a woman "cartwheeling like a cheerleader with her arms and legs out" as she came over the side of a cliff several thousand feet above him.

Six years later, with hundreds of documents bulging from legal briefs filed in three states, the demise of Patricia Bottarini, an athletic, 36-year-old wife and mother, remains clouded in mystery. Members of her family, law enforcement investigators and federal prosecutors believe her husband killed her.

"Nobody knows exactly what happened," said Patricia Buccello, the National Park ranger who was the lead investigator on the case, "but I think we had good proof that she didn't go over on her own. . . . Mr. Bottarini assisted her."

James Bottarini, from the witness stand and through legal documents, has denied that allegation. A criminal trial in U.S. District Court in Utah last year ended with his acquittal, yet in a bizarre twist, several jurors later told reporters they had deadlocked ten to two in favor of convicting.

State prosecutors in St. George County, Utah could still bring a murder charge, but their evidence, like that presented by federal prosecutors, is entirely circumstantial. There are no witnesses to the alleged crime. No one, other than James Bottarini, was there when Patricia, who family members said had a fear of heights, fell to her death.

Bottarini, 44, is negotiating a settlement in two civil cases that have effectively tied up his wife's assets. These include her interest in a family-owned real estate partnership in California valued at more than a million dollars and a $250,000 life insurance policy that was purchased in September 1996. A month later, on October 29, 1996—seven months before she died—Patricia Bottarini signed a one-page will leaving all of her assets to her husband.

The civil litigation includes an action filed in Superior Court in Burlington County by a lawyer assigned by the court to protect the interests of the Bottarinis' two sons, Jon, now nine, and Jacqui, now six, in the dispute over who will receive the proceeds from her life insurance policy. In another suit, filed in California, an attorney for the real estate partnership in which Patricia Bottarini and her two older sisters were shareholders argued that James Bottarini was not entitled to claim any of the partnership's assets.

"The preponderance of the evidence against James clearly indicates that he killed Patricia and that the killing was felonious and intentional," the suit read in part.

Because of the pending litigation, all the parties involved, including James Bottarini, have declined to comment publicly. Still, the court record in New Jersey, Utah and California provides an intriguing look at a twisted and tragic case that may never be solved, a case that leaves two compelling and sharply contrasting questions hanging in the air.

Has James Bottarini, described by some as a manipulative, controlling spouse who was living off his wife's wealth, gotten away with murder? Or has a loving and caring father and husband had his life and reputation ruined because his wife accidentally slipped and fell over a cliff?

"It just happened so quickly that she was already off the trail on the face of the cliff area going down almost like she had caught herself and was trying to scramble up. . . . She was saying, 'Jim, do something.' . . . I didn't even get halfway there and she like moved a finger and her foot slipped. . . .There was no way for her to stop."

"Did you push her?"

"No, I didn't push her."

Jim Bottarini is "a good guy and he's gotten a bum rap," said August Von Matt. "I can't believe some of the things people were saying about him."

Von Matt, 68, of Mount Laurel, got to know Bottarini through his wife, Alice, who was the family's baby-sitter for nearly three years. Alice Von Matt, after checking with James Bottarini, declined to be interviewed for this article. But in court last year in Utah, where she testified as a defense witness, she had nothing but positive things to say about her former employer.

"Jim just glowed when he was around Patty," Alice told the federal jury. "You could see the love."

She went on to describe James Bottarini as a "quiet, reserved man" and "a very gentle person." Those same jurors, however, heard others describe Bottarini in less glowing terms.

Bottarini was tried last year on charges of interstate domestic violence, wire fraud and giving a false statement to authorities. The allegations were contained in a six-count indictment handed up by a federal grand jury in Utah in April 2001.

While not specifically charging Bottarini with murder, the indictment alleged that he "willfully, deliberately, maliciously and with premeditation caused the death of his wife, Patricia . . . while they were hiking together on the Observation Point Trail."

The murder, the indictment alleged, was part of a scheme to defraud both the insurance company that had issued the policy on his wife and the California real estate partnership in which his wife had an interest.

In opening arguments, a federal prosecutor described James Bottarini as a "systematic gambler who bet he could get away with murder." The prosecution contended that Bottarini was in an unhappy marriage, had been living off his wife's wealth, and had lost a substantial amount of money in his commodities trading business. Friends and family members of Patricia Bottarini described him as controlling and cold, a man who told his wife what to wear and how much makeup she could use. At least two witnesses at the trial described separate incidents in which they saw him wipe off his wife's lipstick, telling her, "You know what the rules are." They said the marriage was in trouble, that the couple slept in separate bedrooms, and that Patricia Bottarini was terribly unhappy.

And there was this from Patricia Buccello, the park ranger, who told the jury about the spot where Patricia Bottarini left the trail and fell to her death, a five-foot-wide pathway where children sometimes hike and where high school cross-country teams sometimes train. In 30 years, Buccello testified, there has never been an accident reported on that trail. Not so much as a sprained ankle. She said that when she and other rangers were first alerted to the fall, they looked at one another in disbelief.

"Nobody falls off Observation Point Trail," she said.

"I didn't need any material things," Patricia Bottarini once remarked. "Our idea about money was just that you make more than you spend or you spend less than you make. That is our attitude."

The Bottarinis were, in many ways, children of privilege. Both from upper-middle-class families, they lived comfortably if not lavishly. Patricia came from Carlsbad, California, a seaside town just north of San Diego. Her British-born father, Arthur Howard-Jones, made a fortune in Southern California real estate. After he died, his real estate holdings—which include two motels on the beach in Carlsbad—were left in a trust to his wife and daughters. Patricia, who received $250,000 when her father's estate was settled in 1994, would receive periodic payments from the partnership. The payments, according to court records, could be as much as $100,000.

"Patty" was the youngest of the three Howard-Jones daughters. Tall, athletic and outgoing, she was named the most valuable player on the Carlsbad High School basketball team and was a member of the varsity girls' tennis team. She was also the homecoming queen. She attended the University of Arizona on a basketball scholarship, but after injuring a knee, she returned to California, graduating from the University of San Diego. Friends called her "Sunshine." They said she "lit up the room" when she walked in.

James Bottarini had grown up in Ottawa, Illinois, outside Chicago. He was one of four sons. After graduating from the University of Mississippi in 1983, he joined the Navy and eventually was assigned to a base in San Diego. Then a Navy lieutenant, he met Patricia Howard-Jones in Mazatlán, Mexico. Bottarini was on an assignment, part of a Navy goodwill program.

"Building school buildings and helping kids with disabilities and all that," he said.

Patty was in Mexico traveling with friends. They met on the beach one day and later that night bumped into each other at a local disco. They danced and joked and flirted with one another. He said he remembered the date, February 14, 1986—Valentine's Day. Back in California, they dated for about a year and a half, married while traveling through South America, and then set up house in the Carlsbad area. Patty had a job with a company owned by her cousin that trained professional trainers and fitness instructors. After his Navy discharge in December 1987, Bottarini was "self-employed," describing himself as a real estate and investment consultant.

They traveled frequently, sometimes for a month at a time. They visited Europe on three different occasions, hiking in Switzerland, visiting his relatives in Italy and hers in England. James also frequented the casinos in Las Vegas, employing a "system" at the craps and blackjack tables.

"I like to believe I took the gambling out of gambling," he said when asked during the trial about his frequent trips—53 in four years—to Las Vegas while living in California. A juror later said he felt that Bottarini exhibited more passion when he testified about and defended his gambling "system" than he did in responding or reacting to any of the details about his wife's death.

The Bottarinis moved to New Jersey in 1994, shortly after their first son was born. They lived briefly in a townhouse in Marlton before buying a ranch-style home on a heavily wooded lot in Medford. Their second son was born in July 1996. While some friends and family members from California said they were led to believe the Bottarinis had moved East because of a job James had lined up, he remained self-employed. He would later testify that his wife "just had enough of Southern California," implying that she wanted to get away from her family.

In Medford in 1996, James Bottarini started his own commodities trading company. Edge Investment Corporation, listed as having the same address as the Bottarinis' home, 118 West Centennial Drive. James and Patricia were the chief shareholders and investors in the fund. Others who "pooled" their resources for James to invest included his parents and a friend.

According to court testimony, Bottarini struggled in the commodities trading business, losing $73,000. He testified that he stopped trading shortly before his wife died.

"I mean, you're a pretty high-stakes gambler, true? . . . Put a thousand bucks on the craps table is a gamble, even if it is a systematic bet, isn't it?" he was asked during the trial.

"In your eyes, I guess," Bottarini replied.

"How about in your eyes?"

"It is a decision that you make based upon what you expect is the probable outcome. Just as simple as whether you're going to buy stock in a company. You don't know the outcome. It is a risk. Everything is a risk."

Shortly after Patricia Bottarini's death, TOBO, the family real estate partnership, filed suit to block James from exercising any control or claiming any assets. That Bottarini was at least contemplating that move is detailed in a series of e-mails that are now part of both the California and Burlington County actions. In one, dated May 23, 2000, James Bottarini wrote a lawyer for the partnership, complaining about his failure to gain access to the business' records.

"Effective immediately," he wrote, "I intend to participate in the control, management and direction of the business of the partnership." With that, he asked that a set of keys to the firm's office be left for him when he was next in California. The lawyer for TOBO replied that nothing would be provided until the criminal case was resolved.

In another document, an attorney for Patricia Bottarini's sisters claimed that James had received one disbursement of $136,074.62 from the partnership before things were put on hold. The lawyer alleged that Bottarini had "depleted" and "wasted" those assets of the estate. The $250,000 life insurance policy has also been on ice. The money, paid by the United States Automobile Association, has been held in an escrow account collecting seven and a half percent interest since July 1, 1997, when James Bottarini first tried to collect it.

In a letter to the court in February 1999, David H. Dugan 3rd, the lawyer serving as guardian for the interests of the Bottarinis' two sons, detailed the "suspicious" death of Patricia Bottarini. Among other things,

Dugan wrote that "Patricia's death involved her falling from a 500-foot cliff. However, the trail above the cliff is not treacherous. It is five foot wide and paved. Between the trail and the cliff is a 40- to 50-foot slope. It is difficult to imagine an accidental fall."

Dugan also noted that "At the time of Patricia's death the marriage between her and James was faltering. They had stopped sleeping in the same bedroom. Patricia was not happy. For years Patricia had kept a private journal of the activities of her life and personal reflections. Following her death, James turned the journal over to her family, but many of the pages had been torn out. James claimed that he burned them.

"For the last few years or so, James had no employment. His basic occupation was investing Patricia's money, which she received from her father's trust and from her family real estate partnership. James was also a heavy gambler, making regular trips alone to the Mirage Casino in Las Vegas."

"Did you sleep in separate beds at some points in your marriage?" he was asked.

"Absolutely. . . . After she had given birth . . . she was into breast feeding so the baby would be there and it just—I considered it impossible for me to get a good night sleep and uncomfortable for her and the baby. . . ."

James Willmott, who with his wife lived next door to the Bottarinis on West Centennial Drive, said he couldn't believe it when he read in the paper, on Mother's Day 1997, about Patty Bottarini's death in Utah. Like other friends and neighbors, he said his shock and sorrow quickly changed to anger and suspicion. Willmott, who testified for the prosecution—as did his wife and several other neighbors—described James Bottarini as "cold and distant."

"Patty was more outgoing," Willmott said. "She had a lot more friends than he did."

Willmott said he noticed a difference in the Bottarinis after they returned from a three-month trip to California to visit Patty's family early in 1997.

"After they came back from the Christmas trip to California, something had changed," Jim Willmott noted. "You could feel the tension."

"She didn't seem happy," added Paula Carlson, another Medford neighbor and close friend of Patricia Bottarini's. Carlson was opening a tea shop at the time. She said Patty spent hours helping her get the place ready.

"It seemed like something was bothering her," she said. "I know she didn't want to go on that trip [to Utah]. Her youngest boy, Jacqui, had an ear infection and she didn't want to leave him. But she said, 'Jim wants to go' and so she went. I think she did a lot of things because he wanted to."

Willmott said that from the moment he read about Patricia Bottarini's death in a local newspaper, he had a bad feeling.

"There are just too many questions," he added.

After her death, he said, James Bottarini told different people different versions of what had happened. Other witnesses also testified about discrepancies in Bottarini's story.

"He told my wife she stumbled and fell down a dangerous, rocky cliff," Willmott said. "He reached back for her, but couldn't get her.

"He told someone else she slipped while swatting at a bee. Another time he said she was looking over the edge. In different stories he was in front of her or behind her."

"I didn't want to talk about it so . . . quite possibly there are many times when I just offhandedly, I would say I didn't see her," Bottarini testified.

"So depending on how you felt on a given day, you just told them whatever you felt like saying when people inquired, is that true?"

"Bingo. I think you hit it on the head right there."

"No reason to be accurate about something as incidental as your wife's death?" Bottarini was asked.

"Unless you were talking to an authority . . . I mean, I'm talking to people, like, none of their business, some of them."

Patricia Bottarini was afraid of heights. Several friends and family members testified about that at the trial.

"It wasn't so much being high as it was a fear of falling," her mother told the jury.

On the morning of May 9, Patricia and James Bottarini had hiked about three miles up Observation Point Trail before deciding they were too tired to continue to the top, about two more miles. Instead, James told the jury, they paused to rest, drink some water and have some snacks, then began to walk back down. He was about 30 feet ahead of his wife when, he said, he heard a scream, turned and saw her slipping over the side.

By the time he reached the spot, he said, she was gone, tumbling over the edge of a cliff and falling into Echo Canyon. Her body was found about 500 feet below by a hiker, part of a group who came upon Bottarini as he raced down the mountain for help.

Another hiker in the park that day testified that he and his wife had heard voices, scuffling, and what they thought were children engaged in "horseplay." He said he looked up and saw some stones coming over the side. Then, Donald Cox said, he saw a woman, her arms and legs stretched out, "cartwheeling like a cheerleader" as she fell off the edge of the cliff.

Investigators found a bloodstain on the cliff face about 11 feet below the spot where Patricia Bottarini allegedly slipped and fell to her death.

Experts during the trial attempted to interpret what it meant. A witness for the prosecution said the blood splatter indicated the victim had gone over the side in the air as if she had been pushed or jumped. The splatter was not consistent with someone who was clinging to the rocks, desperately trying to hold on, someone who slid over the side. The splatter also indicated, the prosecution expert said, that Patty Bottarini was already bleeding when she went over the side.

An expert for the defense, however, told the jury that the blood splatter marks were "inconclusive" and that trying to draw an inference from them was meaningless. A detective testified that the crime scene had been disturbed and that weather could have distorted the bloodstain by the time it was discovered. Jurors also heard witnesses who described James Bottarini's mental state in the hours after his wife's body had been found. He was described as distant and reserved.

The hiker who found Patricia's body said he waited there with James for two hours while other members of his party went for help. He noted that Bottarini said very little, that he occasionally mentioned his children, and that he threw rocks at vultures that had begun circling overhead.

Patricia Buccello, one of the first park rangers to reach the body, said she mistakenly approached the hiker, assuming from his demeanor and apparent anguish that he was the husband of the victim. Investigators also said that James Bottarini gave conflicting statements about how his wife fell and later about the life insurance policy he subsequently tried to collect.

"Do you blame yourself for her death?"

"There are times when I blame myself for her death, yes. . . . Because I went up there and I'm alive and she is not. . . . Because she had a wonderful life and I couldn't, for the life of me, understand why it had to end."

"Did you want your wife dead for any reason?"

"No. There is no possible way that I would have killed my wife. . . . I'm sick and tired of people asking me that."

The jury deliberated for about 16 hours over two days before announcing its verdict.

Not guilty.

As he left the courthouse, Bottarini thanked his parents and family for supporting him and added, "I plan to continue to raise my children in memory of my wife." His lawyer, Ron Yengich, said the prosecution's case was "permeated with doubt."

"The government overreached," Yengich said in a telephone interview last month. "They would not listen to anybody but her family. And her family refuses to consider the fact that she could have fallen and that this could have been an accident."

Eighteen months after trying the case and more than six years after Patricia Bottarini's death, Yengich said he remains convinced his client is innocent. He added that he is troubled that Patricia Bottarini's family "has a continuing agenda and won't let it go" and by the attention a sensation-fueled media continues to give to the tragedy.

Paul Warner, the U.S. Attorney for Utah, said it was his decision to prosecute; he denied that influence from Patty Bottarini's family or anyone else led to the indictment.

"This was the result of a dogged investigation," said Warner, who decided to try the case himself. "There was one piece of evidence after another. The cumulative effect led to the charges." Warner said he was convinced the charges were valid after he visited Observation Point Trail.

"You have to see the trail," he insisted. "It's an improved path. There's a berm that juts up and then a runout. . . . I looked at it and I said to myself, 'She didn't fall off this trail.'"

To hammer home that point, Warner requested during the trial that the jurors be permitted to view the scene. As a result, the court moved from Salt Lake City to Zion National Park—about a five-hour car ride—in the middle of the trial and the jurors, defense and prosecution attorneys, and James Bottarini hiked to the spot where Patty died.

"We thought that was essential," Warner said. "We felt that if the jury had a chance to see the trail where she fell to her death, they would understand . . . how unlikely the scenario the defendant was painting was. Unfortunately, we were not able to convince all 12 jurors."

In the days following the verdict, several jurors spoke to reporters about the case. One said there was no way the government had proved its case, that there was too much reasonable doubt. But others claimed the jury had originally voted ten to two in favor of conviction and that a "misunderstanding" about the judge's instructions led to the acquittal.

"The way we interpreted the instructions, if we couldn't reach a unanimous decision, we were supposed to acquit," said Cameron Howell, one of those jurors.

Howell said the initial vote was eight to four in favor of conviction. A second vote, he said, was ten to two in favor of conviction.

"At that point, the two holdouts told us, no matter what, they would not vote to convict," he recalled. "It was a stalemate. They just didn't think the prosecution had proven its case. It was all circumstantial." Howell stated that had he realized the jury could have hung, he would have held out.

"There are probably five or six of us who don't believe he should be walking the streets," he said of James Bottarini. "Some of the others were just happy to go home."

Howell noted that while the prosecution continually focused on the money issues—the insurance policy, the real estate holdings, Bottarini's gambling and business losses—the jurors thought that was "secondary."

"They both came from rich families," he said. "Money didn't seem to be the underlying issue."

Howell said that despite his eventual vote to acquit, he was convinced Bottarini was guilty. But he acknowledged that "What I think now doesn't matter. The acquittal stands. . . . But I don't trust the guy. I wouldn't want to be his neighbor."

State prosecutors could file a murder charge in the case. There is no statute of limitations. Federal authorities could not bring a murder charge because they did not have jurisdiction. The actual scene of the death was a portion of state land within the national park.

"Was your wife happy, Mr. Bottarini?"

"She was very happy," he replied.

Jon and Jacqui Bottarini have been living with their father since their mother's death. Neither, according to a letter filed by a lawyer for Patricia Bottarini's two sisters, is currently enrolled in school. Both, according to several people familiar with the situation, are being home-schooled by their father, who has moved back to Ottawa, Illinois, where his parents still live. According to the lawyer's letter, however, Bottarini spent most of last year on the road with his sons, traveling in a recreational vehicle in Florida, California and Illinois and staying for a good part of that time in RV parks.

In a brief telephone conversation last month, Bottarini said he would be happy to talk about the case once the civil litigation was settled, but could not comment before then. Friends of Patricia Bottarini on the West Coast also declined to comment about the case because of the pending litigation.

"The family is concerned about the boys and thinks it would be best right now not to say anything," said Joanne Remillard, who was described as one of Patricia Bottarini's oldest and best friends. Patricia's sister, Carolyn Howard-Jones, also said she felt "this was not the right time to say anything."

Both women testified for the prosecution at the trial. Remillard recounted how her friend had told her she did not want to make the trip to Utah. From the witness stand, Carolyn Howard-Jones was asked about her sister's troubled marriage and read from Patty's journal. One of the items was a list Patricia Bottarini had made shortly before she died. It was headed "These things make me sad." They included "Jim pushing me in Edinburgh," "Separate Thanksgivings" and "Sleeping in separate beds (except for sex nights). Then I touch him on the back of the neck. He doesn't like it. He leaves afterwards."

Under cross-examination, however, Carolyn Howard-Jones admitted she had no firsthand knowledge of the relationship between her sister and James Bottarini. Ron Yengich, Bottarini's lawyer, who had told the jury in his opening argument that "their love transcended any problems they had," then asked Carolyn Howard-Jones to read from a letter Patricia had written to her husband shortly before her death.

"Jim, I cherish the way you bring to life a spark in me," she wrote.

Last month, with negotiations in the civil litigation continuing, the Utah state medical examiner finally issued a death certificate in the Patricia Bottarini case. Her family had been anxiously awaiting the certificate, even though it would have no legal impact. The document, filed on April 11, said Patricia Bottarini died from "blunt force injuries to the head, torso and extremities." The death certificate listed the cause of death as homicide.

MURDER IN THE SUBURBS

DECEMBER 7, 2003

She was stabbed six times in the back, and her throat was slit nearly to her spinal cord. A diamond engagement ring, a gift from her fiancé, was taken off her finger; two bracelets were missing from her wrist. Then, as Janice Bell bled to death on the kitchen floor in her well-kept home in an upscale section of Voorhees, New Jersey, family members say, her killer or killers went into the refrigerator/freezer to remove some audiotapes hidden in a Folger's coffee can she had stored there, took some home videos and a children's quilt from the family room, and rifled a secret compartment in her upstairs bedroom where she kept some coins and letters. Nothing else was taken, members of her family say. The audiotapes, she had told family members, were phone messages—angry calls left by her ex-husband, against whom she had filed at least five complaints with the police. The last was on December 2, 1995.

"If anything happens to me, you'll know who did it," her sister said Bell told the officer who took that complaint. Five days later, Janice Bell was dead.

It is now eight years since the brutal slaying. No one has ever been charged.

Pasquale DeTommaso, Janice Bell's former husband, was identified in an affidavit by a federal investigator as a "suspect" about a year after the slaying. DeTommaso, who now operates a pizzeria in Maryland, has denied any involvement. Although declining to be interviewed—"I'm not interested, thank you," he said before hanging up the phone at his pizzeria—he had previously said that the Bell family has a "vendetta" against him. The family, he said in court papers, "blames me for Janice's murder."

Solomon Fisher, who represented DeTommaso in a tax evasion case brought by the IRS in 2000, said he could not comment on any other allegations. But he pointed out that DeTommaso has never been charged and was awarded custody of his two young sons by a judge who determined that he was "a good father."

Frustrated, Bell's family—her mother and father, her older brother and sister—contends that law enforcement has allowed the case to go cold.

"The court system failed Janice," Joan Dombrowski, the oldest of the three Bell siblings, wrote in a letter to the New Jersey attorney general in October. "The police failed Janice. . . . The Prosecutor's Office has failed her as well."

Janice Bell was murdered about a year after Carol Neulander was found beaten to death in her Cherry Hill home and about six months before Anne Marie Fahey disappeared in Wilmington. Those two cases, murder investigations built around dogged police work and underscored by intense media coverage, are the benchmarks the Bell family uses in discussing the investigation. Both ended with murder convictions based in large part on circumstantial evidence.

The Bells spend hours ticking off the circumstantial evidence—the bitter divorce, the stalking and harassment, the murder-robbery in which only personal items were taken—that they believe points to the man responsible for Janice's death. But investigators, sympathetic to the family's anguish, say it is one thing to suspect what happened and another to prove it. The bottom line in the Bell investigation, they add, is that the evidence gathered to date is not strong enough to make a case.

"Sometimes you have a feeling in your gut," said Jeff Nardello, the former Voorhees police detective who worked the investigation. "But unless you can prove it. . . . "

So investigators move slowly—too slowly, the Bells say—trying to reexamine and revisit what they have, looking for anything that might have meaning.

"Together with the Voorhees Police Department, we have spent countless hours investigating this horrible crime," Camden County Prosecutor Vincent P. Sarubbi said in a statement. "In spite of our efforts, it is our considered judgment that the state of the evidence at this time does not support the filing of criminal charges."

"It has been eight long, heart-wrenching, difficult years since my . . . sister . . . was brutally murdered," Dombrowski wrote in her letter asking Attorney General Peter C. Harvey to intervene in the case. Single-spaced and covering five pages, the typewritten note outlines the history of the investigation and the frustration the family is feeling. Handwritten notes, complaints filed with the local police, and legal briefs that are part of a bitter divorce proceeding provide more details. Like a voice from the grave, they echo around the investigation.

"Ms. Bell states that she is in fear of Mr. DeTommaso [who] has harassed her in the past and has made several threats to her life," reads a portion of a police report based on a complaint filed by Bell at 11 a.m. on Saturday, December 2, 1995. By that point, the energetic, 33-year-old mother was a familiar figure at the Voorhees Township Police Department.

"She was worried," said Nardello, who was aware at the time of the complaints she was filing against her ex-husband. "She was a nice woman, and I think she was doing what she thought was right. She was apprehensive, but that didn't stop her."

The story Bell told police was the same one that had been outlined in her divorce filings: Her ex-husband was jealous and possessive; he had been following her and making harassing telephone calls.

"He said that this was just the beginning and he continued yelling, saying they would find me in the woods," Bell wrote in March 1994 in one of the first complaints she filed with the local police. "This is not the first time he has threatened me."

At that point, the couple, who married in May 1988, had been separated for about a month. And on the day their divorce was finalized, she told her lawyer and family members, DeTommaso came up behind her in the hallway of the Camden County Courthouse and told her: "Watch your back."

"Everybody knew," Joan Dombrowski said. "Nobody did anything. They thought Janice was just a hysterical housewife until they found her dead."

It was a fairy-tale romance built around friends, family and strong ethnic roots.

Within two years of their marriage, the couple had two sons, Vincent and Nicholas. DeTommaso, a La Salle College graduate who came to this country from Italy as a teenager, was in the pizza business, running shops in New Jersey, Florida and Pennsylvania. Janice worked in her family's business—a training school for those preparing to take civil service exams—but after suffering a back injury, she spent her time at home, taking care of the children. Her family and friends say the marriage was rocky from the start.

"They went on a month-long honeymoon to Italy," Joan Dombrowski said. "When she got back, she said to me: 'I made a mistake.'"

Pasquale DeTommaso, the smiling, fun-loving suitor who had been one of her brother's best friends in college, was not what he seemed, her sister said Bell told her. Bell and DeTommaso stayed together for about six years. Court records in their divorce case and in a subsequent child custody dispute that the Bell family instituted after Janice Bell was killed paint a picture of constant friction.

She described him as irrationally jealous, a "vindictive and very threatening individual" who would secretly tape her phone calls and who would rant and rave when she went out with friends. He described her as a spoiled spendthrift who loved to go shopping with her mother and who was unduly influenced by her own family.

"She thinks I want to kill her," Pasquale said of his wife in one document filed in the divorce proceedings. In another, during the custody fight, he said the Bell family had a vendetta against him because they blamed him for Janice Bell's killing.

"He wanted to keep her barefoot and pregnant," said Rene Messina, a longtime friend of Bell's. The irony, she added sadly, is that all Bell ever cared about was having a family.

"All she wanted was to get married and have children," Messina recalled. "Janice was one of the sweetest girls you'd ever wanted to meet. She was fun to be around . . . and she would give you the shirt off her back."

Pasquale DeTommaso, who lives in Maryland with his mother and two teenage sons, has consistently denied that he had anything to do with the death of his wife. He was questioned by police on the night of the murder, explaining that he was at his pizzeria in Hatfield, Montgomery County, on the morning of the slaying. After that, the Bells say, he stopped talking to police. In an interview in an Italian newspaper shortly after the murder, he described his wife as his "princess" and said he grieved constantly.

About a year after the killing, Gerald Loke, an investigator with the IRS, told a federal judge that DeTommaso was a suspect in the murder. Loke, who had several conversations with Camden County investigators, built an income tax evasion case against DeTommaso. The agent spent several months combing through records and interviewing friends and employees of the pizza shop owner.

"I wish we could have done more," Loke said.

DeTommaso eventually pleaded guilty to a tax evasion charge—the government alleged he had evaded more than $135,000 in taxes—and served about a year in prison.

The Janice Bell murder investigation took a bizarre twist last year during the murder trial of Rabbi Fred J. Neulander. A jailhouse snitch, testifying for the defense, alleged that Len Jenoff, the hit man who confessed that he had murdered Carol Neulander, had admitted in prison that he also was involved in the Bell murder. The testimony of the snitch, convicted pedophile David Beardsley, was discredited by the prosecution. Jenoff has denied the allegation. The Bells openly wonder whether authorities don't want to pursue the Jenoff angle in their case because it might undermine the rabbi's conviction. While declining to comment about specifics, Vincent Sarubbi and others in his office say they are pursuing every lead.

"We very much look forward to the day when . . . we can go forward with a prosecution," Sarubbi said. "We can only imagine the heartache suffered by the families of homicide victims and . . . would like nothing more than to be able to bring Janice Bell's killer or killers to justice."

Janice Bell spoke to her brother, Michael Bell Jr., on the phone about 9:30 on the morning she was killed. At 10:45 a.m., when her sister called, the answering machine picked up, and Joan Dombrowski jokingly speculated that her younger sister was out Christmas shopping. She left a "Ho, Ho, Ho" message. Authorities believe that Janice Bell was lying dead on the floor as that message was recorded. Her mother and father, Joan and Michael Bell Sr., had left for their annual vacation in Puerto Rico a day earlier. Ordinarily, Janice's mother would have been with her.

"I was at my daughter's house every day after her divorce," Joan Bell said. "Every day. . . . Now, a day does not go by that I don't think of her. I go to her grave. I talk to her. It hurts. It hurts like it just happened."

"Nothing will bring Janice back," Joan Bell said. Then she paused, and very quietly said: "A mother shouldn't have to bury her child."

TERRORISM ON TRIAL

SEPTEMBER 28, 2008

It was paintball and jihad, Dunkin' Donuts and Osama bin Laden—terrorism come to suburbia. And if the plot had been carried out, prosecutors say, the bodies of U.S. Army personnel would have been strewn across the fields of the Fort Dix military base. Jury selection begins tomorrow for the trial of five foreign-born Muslims from the Philadelphia area, charged with planning a jihad-inspired attack on the South Jersey military complex.

The government's case is built primarily around secretly recorded conversations made by two cooperating witnesses who befriended the defendants. Those conversations, prosecutors say, detail "plans to attack Fort Dix and kill American soldiers" and include "discussions of the supposed justifications for such attacks rooted in radical jihadist ideology." But defense attorneys contend their clients talked a bigger game than they intended to play, portraying them as easily manipulated individuals led into a plot by paid FBI informants who created a conspiracy out of hollow words and empty threats.

"Any conspiracy that plots death and destruction has to be taken seriously," said Bruce Hoffman, a terrorism expert who teaches at Georgetown University and who is following the trial of the so-called Fort Dix Five. But Hoffman said that there are no stereotypical "homegrown" terrorists and that each case has to be evaluated on its own. Challenging the credibility of informants and arguing entrapment have been common defense strategies used in other terrorist trials, he said. Sometimes effectively, he added.

Those are the issues jurors will have to wrestle with during the trial, which is expected to last several weeks. The first of an estimated 1500 potential jurors will report to U.S. District Court in Camden tomorrow morning and begin filling out questionnaires designed to determine how much they know about the case and whether that knowledge or any other inherent beliefs or biases should preclude them from the jury. Twelve jurors and six alternates will be chosen to determine the fate of the defendants, all in their mid- to late 20s, who face potential life sentences. Opening arguments, before Judge Robert Kugler, are expected next month.

The Fort Dix trial is one of three major prosecutions of suspected terrorists under way, or soon to begin, across the country. In Houston, the retrial of the leaders of the Holy Land Foundation, a Texas-based Muslim charitable organization charged with funneling $12 million to Palestinian terrorists, began this month. The first trial ended with a hung jury last year. And in Miami, prosecutors are gearing up for a third try at convicting members of the so-called Liberty City Seven, who were charged with plotting to blow up the Sears Building in Chicago and several federal offices in Florida. Two earlier trials ended with hung juries. In the first, one of the defendants was found not guilty.

Six suspects were originally charged in the Fort Dix case. One, Agron Abdullahu, 25, a baker in a ShopRite store near Williamstown, pleaded guilty to a conspiracy charge, admitting he had given weapons to three of the other defendants who were illegal immigrants. He was sentenced to 20 months in prison. The five other defendants, charged with the more serious offense of plotting to kill soldiers, are brothers Dritan Duka, 29, Shain Duka, 27, and Eljvir Duka, 24; Mohamad Shnewer, 23; and Serdar Tatar, 24.

The Dukas and Shnewer are from Cherry Hill. Tatar is a former Cherry Hill resident who was living in Philadelphia when he and the others were arrested. Shnewer, who was born in Jordan, is a U.S. citizen. Tatar, born in Turkey, is a legal resident immigrant. The Duka brothers, ethnic Albanians from what is now Macedonia, have been living in the country illegally since arriving as young children by way of Mexico in the late 1980s. The Dukas were in the roofing business. Shnewer drove a taxi and worked in his family's food market in Pennsauken. Tatar was a clerk/manager of a 7-Eleven store. His father owned a pizzeria just outside the gates of Fort Dix. Among other things, Tatar is accused of supplying a map of the base he got from his father's pizza shop. The conspirators allegedly planned to launch their attack from a pizza delivery truck.

The arrests of the plotters in May 2007 capped a 16-month investigation that started after a worker at a Circuit City store in Mount Laurel contacted authorities about a "troubling" tape he was asked to copy onto a DVD for some customers. The tape, which will be played at trial, shows the defendants at a shooting range in the Poconos firing guns, calling for jihad (a holy war or struggle) and shouting "*Allahu Akbar*" (God is great). It will be one of several videos shown to the jurors. Others were made by FBI surveillance teams. There will also be dozens of tapes recorded by two cooperating witnesses who befriended the defendants at the behest of the FBI.

Those informants, authorities allege, took part in "training sessions" that included paintball games in wooded areas and farms around South

Jersey. They also recorded conversations and were shown Islamic militant videotapes that promoted the ideals of al-Qaeda and bin Laden, investigators contend. Several of those conversations took place at a Dunkin' Donuts near a Palmyra mosque where some of the defendants attended Friday prayer services. After prayers, they would meet at the shop where they discussed politics, religion and, among other things, how to repair cars.

The defense is expected to argue that their clients were young men blowing off steam and occasionally making ill-advised comments to government informants who were wearing body wires. The prosecution and defense arguments in the case are similar to those made in other terrorism trials where wiretaps, electronic audio and video surveillance, and informants have been employed.

According to a study by the Center on Law and Security at New York University Law School, 62 terrorist suspects were convicted between September 11, 2001 and September 11, 2007. In most of those cases, as in the Fort Dix probe, there was no link between the defendants and any foreign terrorist organization. In the Fort Dix case, however, prosecutors are expected to use taped conversations to support their argument that the defendants were aware of and often celebrated the radical Muslim philosophy that is at the heart of the terrorist movement. They include potentially damaging quotes already cited in court papers in which:

> Tatar tells one of the cooperating witnesses, "It doesn't matter to me whether I get locked up, arrested or taken away, it doesn't matter. Or I die, doesn't matter. I'm doing it in the name of Allah."
>
> Shnewer says, "My intent is to hit a heavy concentration of soldiers."
>
> Eljvir Duka explains, "When someone attacks your religion, your way of life, then you go to jihad."

Whether attacking the credibility and motivation of the cooperating witnesses will be enough to offset incriminating conversations by the defendants is one of the biggest challenges for the defense in the case, legal observers say. One of the cooperators has a criminal record for bank fraud and was facing deportation to his native Egypt when he began working for the FBI. Both cooperators were paid. The exact amounts are expected to be made public during the trial, but defense attorneys have already estimated cash in excess of $50,000 changed hands. The defense will argue that was another incentive for the witnesses to steer the alleged conspirators into a plot they never intended to carry out.

A similar argument appeared to resonate with some jurors in the Liberty City Seven case, which has ended twice with hung juries. Some defendants, in fact, testified they were trying to scam a cooperating witness out of $50,000 by claiming they needed it to finance planned attacks when, in fact, all they were doing was trying to get his money.

Bruce Hoffman, the terrorism expert from Georgetown, said that could be an effective defense strategy. He noted, however, that the alleged Liberty City Seven plot "sounded more amateurish than the Fort Dix plot," in which defendants are accused of, among other things, scouting out the perimeters of Fort Dix and other area military complexes and arranging to purchase weapons from an undercover agent introduced into the investigation by one of the cooperating witnesses. Two of the Duka brothers were arrested after allegedly purchasing AK-47 and M-16 assault rifles from someone they thought was an illegal gun supplier.

MAHMOUD OMAR AND THE FORT DIX FIVE

OCTOBER 5, 2008

Five years ago, he was a bankrupt felon with a conviction for passing bad checks. He was facing deportation. And he was living in a subsidized, low-income apartment complex in Paulsboro, New Jersey, scratching for cash by trying to sell used cars from the complex's parking lot. Today he is the central figure in the Fort Dix terrorism trial, an FBI informant who may have received more than $3,000 a month to wear a body wire and record conversations.

Mahmoud A. Omar, whose immigration problems appear to have gone the way of his financial difficulties, spent more than a year working undercover in the case. While some details about his role have surfaced in pretrial documents, Omar's actions and motivation will be the focus of what could be the most important testimony in the high-profile trial. Was he the FBI's eyes and ears inside a conspiracy to gun down Army personnel on the sprawling Burlington County military complex? Or was he an agent provocateur who took the hollow words and empty threats of five hot-headed young Muslims and turned them into a terrorist plot?

"He is a consummate con man," said Rocco Cipparone, the lawyer for Mohamad Shnewer, the defendant who spent the most time with Omar. "He wasn't in this for patriotic or altruistic motives," added Cipparone, who has spent hours going over transcripts and FBI memos detailing Omar's activities. "He was very adept at manipulating conversations."

Prosecutors have declined to comment about the 39-year-old Egyptian Muslim or a second cooperating witness in the case. Jury selection began last week. Opening statements are expected this month.

The defendants, in addition to Shnewer, 23, are brothers Dritan Duka, 29, Shain Duka, 27, and Eljvir Duka, 24, and Serdar Tatar, 24. The five foreign-born Muslims, all raised in the Philadelphia area, were arrested in May 2007 and charged with planning to gun down Fort Dix military personnel in a jihad-inspired attack. Shnewer and the Dukas are from Cherry Hill. Tatar was a former Cherry Hill resident living in Philadelphia.

Cherry Hill, that quintessential American suburb, was the primary setting for much of the action in the probe, arguably one of the most sensational "homegrown" terrorism investigations in the country. Omar routinely met with his FBI handlers at public locations in the township: the parking lot of the library, in front of the Cherry Hill Skating Center, at the Steak & Ale restaurant on Frontage Road and outside the public works garage. At those meetings, he would turn over tapes of conversations, get his instructions, have his car fitted with audio and video recording devices, and receive cash payments, usually $1500. Defense attorneys, who will receive a tally of the cash paid to Omar and the second cooperating witness before they testify, estimate it will exceed $50,000.

The lawyers are expected to argue that money motivated Omar, that he brought the ethics and style of a sleazy used car salesman to the undercover operation, doing and saying whatever was necessary to close the deal. All five defendants interacted with him, and most were picked up on tape. Those conversations and Omar's testimony are at the heart of the case. How Omar comes across on the stand may determine the fate of the defendants, who face possible life sentences.

"The more he talks, the more problems he's going to have," said Juannae Gunter, an office manager at Paulsboro Gardens, the 150-unit complex where Omar lived until about two years ago. "He tries to talk slick, but you know there's something else going down," she said.

The FBI has said Omar began working undercover in its investigation early in 2006, shortly after a videotape of the defendants waving weapons and shouting for jihad turned up at a Circuit City store in Mount Laurel. He had just settled into an apartment in Cherry Hill with his wife and baby, and had apparently put the money problems detailed in a 2002 bankruptcy filing behind him.

Before the move, Omar spent several years at Paulsboro Gardens. According to his Chapter VII bankruptcy papers, his monthly rent was $79. Omar lived in Apartment 37A, a two-story corner unit near the rear of the complex. Gunter described him as "just an OK tenant." She said she had a run-in with him because he was trying to sell cars he bought at auto auctions from one of the complex's parking lots.

"He had three or four cars out there," she recalled. "They had dealer's tags from Pennsylvania."

In his bankruptcy filing, Omar said he was a self-employed auto mechanic with assets of $835 and debts of $37,877.21. At the Hampshire Houses, a middle-class apartment development off Cooper Landing Road in Cherry Hill, his financial status seemed markedly improved. Whether Omar was already working for the FBI when the investigation began could not be determined, but his cash-flow problems were behind him. He was driving a new Honda Accord and living in a two-bedroom apartment that rented for about $1200 a month.

Omar's entry into the alleged Fort Dix conspiracy came through Shnewer, the youngest defendant and, Shnewer's lawyer argues, one of the most gullible. Shnewer was working at his father's Plaza Food Market in Pennsauken. Omar was a regular, and struck up a friendship with Shnewer and his family. The two men would socialize, play pool, and talk about cars, politics, and their ethnic and Muslim heritage.

Shnewer is a U.S. citizen born in Jordan. He is a high school graduate and has attended community college. Omar, according to his testimony in the check-passing case, entered the country illegally through Mexico in the 1980s. He got a green card after marrying an American. He boasted on many of the tapes of his life experiences and claimed to have served in the Egyptian military. On one tape, Shnewer discussed attacking Fort Dix.

"I assure you that you can hit an American base very easily," he said. But he appeared to defer to his older friend. "I am at your services, as you have more experience than me in military bases and in life," he told Omar.

An earlier conversation, cited in an FBI memo, demonstrated how Omar used his ethnicity to solidify his bond with Shnewer. In March 2006, Omar asked Shnewer's mother to cook a lamb for what the memo describes as an aqiqa, a traditional welcoming party for a newborn. This was soon after Omar's daughter was born. Shnewer suggested a mosque where Omar could have the party, and, according to the document, Omar agreed to pay Shnewer's mother $350 for preparing the lamb feast.

Tapes and FBI memos also refer to conversations about jihad and attacks on Fort Dix, surveillance trips to the base and other targets, and philosophical discussions about Muslim extremism. Other evidence includes a map of Fort Dix given to Omar by Tatar, whose family owned a nearby pizza shop, and an attempt by two of the Dukas to purchase seven assault rifles from an undercover agent posing as a friend of Omar's who was an illegal gun dealer. There are also conversations noted in FBI investigative memos but not recorded because Omar said he wasn't wearing a wire or because the recording device malfunctioned or the tape ran out.

Defense attorneys point to those alleged lapses—and to the fact that Omar had the ability to turn his recorder off—as opportunities for Omar to fabricate information or steer the conversation in a certain direction before he turned on his tape.

Omar was "an extremely good used car salesman," Rocco Cipparone, Shnewer's lawyer, said last week. He was adept not only at closing the deal but, "in many respects, creating it."

FATHER AND SONS

NOVEMBER 23, 2008

It's the American dream turned nightmare. Ferik Duka said last week that he had brought his family to the United States nearly 25 years ago for a better life. Once, he thought he had found it. Now, he and his wife, Zurata, sit in a federal courtroom in Camden each day watching and listening as their three oldest children, sons Dritan, 29, Shain, 27, and Eljvir, 25, stand trial on allegations that they plotted a jihad-inspired attack on Fort Dix. The charges, Ferik Duka said, are ridiculous; his sons are not guilty.

"I'm confident in the American justice system," he said. "My sons are innocent."

So he sits in the fourth-floor courtroom, dressed in a sports coat over either a shirt and tie or a turtleneck, his thick arms folded in front of him, watching the system work. His wife, wearing a head scarf, is always by his side. Occasionally other family members—a son and daughter born in the United States, a daughter-in-law and grandchildren—attend the sessions.

When the defendants enter the courtroom, the relatives smile and nod. When court ends promptly at 4:30 p.m. each day, they wait for the jury to exit, then exchange nods, smiles and waves again as the Duka brothers and their co-defendants, Mohamad Shnewer and Serdar Tatar, are led away by U.S. marshals. All five have been held without bail since their arrests in May 2007. All five are foreign-born Muslims who were raised in the Cherry Hill area. Eljvir Duka is married to one of Shnewer's sisters. All face life in prison if convicted.

Ferik Duka, 61, shook his head at that prospect and then talked about better times.

Standing on the steps of the federal courthouse on Market Street one morning during a break in the trial, the burly roofing contractor lit a cigarette and told the story of his coming to America. In many ways, it is the story of millions of other immigrants who have come looking for something better.

"I came . . . because we heard a lot of good things," he said. "Freedom of speech, democracy, opportunity. And it was true. I chose America because of those things." His sons were five, three and a half and 18 months old. "I bring them here to build a better life," he said.

It was 1984. He had left Yugoslavia, where, he said, there was little work and less opportunity, especially for ethnic Albanians like himself. He and his wife fled to Italy and were trying to decide where to go next. They chose America, entering illegally through Mexico. They stopped in Texas, then Brooklyn, before settling in Cherry Hill, the quintessential American suburb. To this day their immigration status remains murky. The government has labeled them illegal immigrants. But Ferik Duka said he had a lawyer and had been trying for years to straighten out his status.

"I came in illegally, but since 1985 I have been applying [for legal status]," he said. "I work. I pay taxes."

Duka operates a roofing and construction business out of his home on Mimosa Drive. His three oldest sons worked with him. They are religious, he said, but not fanatical.

"For Muslims, it is not easy to live in the United States," he said. "But still, it is better than in Muslim countries. We are not extremists, not terrorists. We are," he said with no little pride, "Albanians."

"We do not have a history of terrorism. We fight man to man."

And, he added, all Albanians are grateful to the United States for coming to their aid in the war with Serbia and for ending the ethnic cleansing that cost tens of thousands of Muslim lives.

It was against that backdrop that Duka offered his assessment of the case against his sons. The charges, he said, are built around the lies of two FBI informants, Mahmoud Omar and Besnik Bakalli. Ferik Duka met both men, befriended them, invited them to his home for dinner. He shook his head and smiled.

Broad-shouldered and tan, with a thick shock of snow-white hair and a neatly trimmed white beard, Duka was blunt in his assessment, his eyes flashing anger and hinting at a short temper. But he puffed on his cigarette and spoke in a calm, even tone. Omar pretended to be a friend, Duka said. He got close to Shnewer and, through him, the Duka brothers. And for most of that time, he was wired for sound.

"He's a liar and a hypocrite," Ferik Duka said of the government's star witness.

Mahmoud Omar, a convicted felon with a history of passing bad checks, spent 13 days on the stand, his testimony finally ending Thursday. Among other things, the jury learned that the FBI had paid the 39-year-old Egyptian national nearly $240,000 for his work in the investigation, and that he hoped to avoid deportation as a result of his cooperation.

"I feed him like my sons," Duka recalled. "I try to encourage him to just continue working and stay away from trouble." Then he shook his head again, remembering Omar's comment from the stand that he had never wanted to hurt anyone.

"He never hurt anybody? He hurts everybody. He's a bad guy. He just wants to save himself."

Omar's secretly taped conversations—more than 200—are central to the government's case. Most were discussions with Shnewer. The talk is alternately disturbing, frightening and outlandish. Shnewer spoke incessantly and with admiration of jihad, Osama bin Laden and the "brothers who changed the world" by carrying out the 9/11 attacks. The jury has seen and heard it all.

Omar "found a soft spot talking to Shnewer," Ferik Duka said. Shnewer is "a child. He doesn't mean what he says." That, in fact, has been one of the defense's themes in the now month-old trial. Shnewer, the defense has argued, talked a game he never intended to play. Eljvir Duka may have said it even better in a conversation Omar secretly recorded.

"A barking dog never bites," he said.

Ferik Duka said his sons never had any intention of attacking a military base. And, again echoing a defense argument, he said Shain and Dritan had bought seven assault rifles from Omar not because they planned to launch an assault on Fort Dix but because they liked to target-shoot.

The trial is expected to last about four more weeks. Ferik Duka will be there each day. Besnik Bakalli, the other government informant, will probably take the stand after the Thanksgiving break. Like the Dukas, he is an ethnic Albanian. And like the Dukas, his immigration status is questionable. Among other things, the government has said Bakalli, who lived in Northeast Philadelphia, agreed to cooperate in exchange for assistance in his fight against possible deportation. Ferik Duka offered another ironic smile.

"I invite him to my house," he said of Bakalli. "We are hospitable people, accepting, trusting." Bakalli, like Omar, has made a deal to help himself, regardless of who is hurt, Duka said.

"It's hard," he said. "I talk to my sons. They say, 'Dad, don't worry. God knows and we know that we are innocent. Whatever they do is up to them.'"

Even if they should beat the most serious charge of conspiring to kill U.S. military personnel, the Duka brothers appear certain to be convicted of weapons offenses. At the very least, that would likely result in their deportation.

"They came here as children," Ferik Duka said. "I'm the one who brings them here. When you are five years old, three years old, you can't tell you father, 'No.' I don't think they deserve to be deported. I bring them here."

Despite the allegations that have turned their lives upside-down, Duka said he and his sons wanted to stay in the United States.

"I love this place," he said.

And then he headed back through the revolving doors of the federal courthouse, through the metal detector and up the elevator to the courtroom where an anonymously selected jury will decide whether his sons live the rest of their American dream as inmates in a federal prison.

Drug kingpin and former professional boxer Kaboni Savage

GANGSTAS AND DRUG LORDS

A few days after a bug—an electronic listening device—was discovered in Philadelphia Mayor John Street's office in 2003, I got a call from Maria Panaritis, who is also a reporter at *The Inquirer*. She had gotten a tip that the bug, planted by the FBI, was somehow connected to an ongoing drug investigation. She asked if I wanted to work that end of the story with her.

It was the beginning of an 18-month trip into the drug underworld that changed my outlook on organized crime in the city. Until that point, I had written a few stories about drug gangs and dealers—the first three pieces in this section are examples of that—but I had focused most of my attention on traditional organized crime, the wiseguys from Downtown. By 2003 that crime family was a shell of its former self and, in most respects, a minor player in a much more volatile and violent underworld.

In the midst of reporting the drug story that tied into the City Hall bug, a low-level wiseguy from South Philly, John "Johnny Gongs" Casasanto, was killed. He was found slain in his own rowhouse on a Saturday morning. I got a call at home to go out and cover the shooting. When I got to the neighborhood, half a dozen reporters from newspapers, television and radio were already there. Everyone did a major story about the mob hit. This is not to belittle the late Mr. Casasanto, but Maria couldn't understand the extent of the coverage. We had already spent months looking into drug dealers and murders that were tied directly or indirectly to the story we were chasing.

In most cases, none of the violence had been reported in the media. And if it had been, it was usually two or three paragraphs buried deep inside the paper. But we were coming to realize that these were events tied to major players in a criminal underworld that was literally ripping the city apart. Why was it, Maria wanted to know, that Johnny Gongs got all this attention while the drug lords and their victims were ignored? There was no good answer to the question.

The Mafia, of course, has become part of American pop culture. Everyone has a frame of reference built on *The Godfather* books and movies or *The Sopranos* television series. So when there's a mob hit in real life, it resonates with readers and viewers. The drug underworld, not so much.

But it shouldn't be that way. The drug lords who appear in these stories, particularly individuals like Kaboni Savage, Felix Summers and the McKendricks, father and son, have had as great a negative impact on the city as any recent Mafia boss. Factor in the level of violence, the wanton murders and the astronomical amounts of money involved in their businesses and they make mob bosses like Ralph Natale, Joey Merlino and John Stanfa look like minor leaguers.

That's the point I think Maria was making when she asked the question. And the drug stories that I've pursued and written about since then are an attempt to provide a better answer. It turned out, by the way, that the tip was accurate. But like everything else in journalism, there were other circumstances that needed to be explained.

The FBI was working a narcotics investigation that focused on one of the bigger drug gangs in the city. A wiretapped conversation between one of the drug dealers and a prominent and politically connected imam at one of the city's bigger mosques included a reference to political payoffs unrelated to the drug case. That conversation launched a separate, political corruption investigation that led to the bugging of the mayor's office. Mayor Street was never charged with any crime. The bug, according to some, was discovered before that part of the probe got anywhere. Several of his top associates, including the city treasurer and a major fundraiser, ended up indicted. To many it was just an example of business as usual.

The drug investigation also led to a series of indictments and provided details about murders, witness intimidation and hundreds of thousands of dollars generated from the sale of kilogram shipments of cocaine and heroin. Unfortunately, that also seems to be an example of business as usual.

THE NEW FACE OF ORGANIZED CRIME

JUNE 20, 1988

Even in high heels, she is under five feet. She wears a plain, blue denim dress that looks more like a housecoat. She has soft, round features, deep brown eyes and a constant look of bewilderment as she sits at a courtroom defense table in the federal building. Her name is Eucaris Ceballos. She is known as "Dona Tulia." And she is an example of one of the new faces of organized crime in America today.

Ceballos, who went on trial earlier this month along with 10 co-defendants, is the first woman charged under the so-called federal kingpin statute. If convicted, she could face life in prison without parole. She is charged with supervising a ring of Colombian drug dealers who prosecutors say sold and distributed more than a million dollars worth of cocaine a week in the North Jersey-New York City area.

"She's a four-foot, ten-inch female Al Capone," said one law enforcement source familiar with the case.

Based in Hollywood, Florida, where she had a house and owned a beauty parlor, Ceballos, 54, headed an operation that put between 80 and 100 kilograms of cocaine on the streets each week, according to federal prosecutors. Members of her organization, according to the charges, used apartment houses in Queens and several North Jersey communities as distribution centers. They traveled in nondescript cars so as not to attract attention. They hid behind several legitimate business fronts. They conducted their dealings over cellular phones and with automatic beepers.

The ring, which the government contends operated between April and November 1987, netted profits of $100,000 a week, according to Assistant U.S. Attorney Donna Yurow Sonageri, who is prosecuting the case. That would amount to profits of about $2.8 million during the period covered by the indictment.

"They sold cocaine 24 hours a day, seven days a week, week after week, month after month," Sonageri told the jury in her opening statement on June 8.

Law enforcement sources at the federal and state levels say that hundreds of similar organizations operate today, bringing thousands of kilograms of cocaine and other illicit drugs into the country and taking out tens of millions of dollars in profits. Those sources say that the trial of Ceballos and her co-defendants, which is expected to last most of the summer, offers an inside look at one of those organizations and how state and federal investigators attached to the Organized Crime Drug Enforcement Task Force cracked it open.

It started with the garbage in front of an apartment house on Chestnut Street in Ridgefield Park, a small North Jersey community a few miles west of the George Washington Bridge. This was in the spring of 1987, and police were getting complaints from neighbors about the constant flow of people into and out of the apartment at 73 Chestnut Street, where a man named Francisco Betancourt lived.

"The police noticed that, at all hours of the day and night, there were a lot of people coming in and out of that apartment," Sonageri told the jury.

They would drive past the apartment, she said. Even if there was a parking space right in front, they would park six or seven houses away. They would go to a pay phone on the corner and make a call. Then they would go into the apartment. A few minutes later, they would emerge and "they would be carrying a plastic bag, something like you get in ShopRite, the plastic ones with the little handles."

So, at 4 a.m. one day, after the garbage had been put out for trash pickup, a state police detective began sifting through the house's trash. He came up with snips of duct tape and wrapping paper that narcotics agents say are commonly used in the cocaine trade. The tape and paper were sent to a New Jersey State Police laboratory for testing and showed traces of cocaine. With that information, state police and federal authorities got permission for a wiretap on the pay phone. And with that, investigators say, the Ceballos organization began to unravel.

"It started out with the little things," said Colonel Clinton Pagano, superintendent of the New Jersey State Police. "A detective goes to the curbside 4 a.m. in the morning. . . . And it just kept expanding and expanding to the point where we have such a broad investigation of a Colombian cartel."

In the course of the investigation, state and federal investigators had eight additional wiretaps, including taps on phones in apartments in North Jersey and Queens and on two cellular phones and a mobile beeper used by alleged couriers in the organization.

From the garbage in Ridgefield Park, the investigation stretched across the Hudson River to Queens, down to Hollywood and, ultimately, to

Colombia. State and federal authorities think that Ceballos' ultimate source was the notorious Medellín cartel, which supplies an estimated 85 percent of all the cocaine smuggled into the United States. While the state police had dubbed the investigation "Operation Kingpin," detectives were surprised and somewhat taken aback when their surveillance and wiretaps eventually led them to Dona Tulia.

"It was certainly out of the ordinary," Pagano said. "Disarming in a way. And it's much more incredible when it comes to presenting this case to a jury. They're looking for some kind of major tough guy. . . . And instead, there's this motherly type in a housedress."

"There have been other women involved [in drug networks]," added Victor Pedalino, an agent from the Newark office of the federal Drug Enforcement Administration, which directed the investigation, "but she is one of the few to have such a high position and give orders in all facets of the operation."

Pedalino said that, when federal and state agents began arresting suspects in the case in November, several investigators who had never seen Ceballos could not believe that the woman brought through the door in handcuffs was Dona Tulia, the drug boss they had been tracking for months.

"But then, what does a dope dealer look like?" Pedalino asked.

Among those arrested was Francisco Betancourt, who had since moved to an apartment in Queens. Investigators confiscated $40,000 in cash and nine kilograms of cocaine at that apartment, the only drugs seized in the case. Several other suspected couriers and Hector Sanchez, Ceballos' 21-year-old son, also were arrested. Sanchez was living at his mother's Hollywood home at the time. He has been accused of transporting the profits from his mother's drug operation from New York to Florida. Prosecutors say Sanchez drove the money back to Florida in a gold Porsche that he had bought from a grocery owner in Queens. It was paid for, they say, with a little more than a kilogram of cocaine.

DEA agents seized a 42-foot boat and 15 cars, including the Porsche, a BMW, a Ferrari and a Lincoln Continental, when they arrested Sanchez in Florida. All have been linked to Ceballos, according to DEA investigators. The government is also trying to seize Ceballos' home and the home of another defendant in Queens.

The cocaine sold by the Ceballos organization, according to investigators, was marketed under the "Reina" name. In Spanish, reina means queen. But Ceballos, according to her court-appointed attorney, is hardly the queen of an international drug network. John S. Furlong, a Trenton lawyer, paints a decidedly different picture of Dona Tulia. She is a Colombian immigrant who came to the United States 12 years ago on a tourist visa and stayed to find a new life. She worked for years as a seamstress in a sweatshop in Queens and was abandoned with four young children by a husband who returned to Colombia. Eventually, she saved enough money—$15,000—to buy a small beauty parlor in Hollywood.

Her son, Hector Sanchez, bought an auto body shop there with the proceeds he received from a negligence case after an accident that broke both his legs. The home in Florida is worth about $100,000, not that much for a residence in South Florida and certainly "not the kind of *Miami Vice* drug mansion you see on television." Three of her children, two of them married and with children of their own, live there with her.

Furlong said that both the Porsche and Ferrari were cars that Sanchez had bought as wrecks and repaired. He said he knew nothing about the other cars and the boat that federal investigators say are owned by Ceballos or her son. Furlong pointed out that authorities found no drugs in the Jersey City apartment where Ceballos was arrested in November and none in the Hollywood home where her son was picked up.

"There are drugs in this case, and there are culpable people who have been swept up by the government," Furlong remarked, stopping short of pointing a finger at any co-defendant. But, he said, Ceballos, who has been held in the Metropolitan Correctional Center in Manhattan since her arrest, is not the boss, supervisor or drug "kingpin" that the government has made her out to be. Furlong says he is not even sure that Ceballos grasps the significance of the charges against her. Furlong speaks with Ceballos through an interpreter. She does not speak English. The trial is being translated into Spanish for the defendants, who listen through earphones.

"She's in over her head intellectually," Furlong noted.

"Like many South American women, she is a God-fearing woman. She prays frequently and her conversation is laced with phrases like 'I trust in God.'

"You look at her, and you look at some of the other defendants in this case and it's awfully difficult to believe that this woman [ordered] these guys around."

TAT MAN HO:
TRIADS GIVE THE MAFIA A RUN FOR ITS MONEY

JUNE 4, 1991

The drug deal began more than a year ago in the casinos of Macao, the Portuguese-controlled island off the coast of China, where a man named Tat Man Ho was part of an international drug-dealing and loan-sharking operation. It ended last June in the bowels of 30th Street Station, where an Amtrak investigator confronted Ho and a companion in the sleeping compartment of a train bound for New York City and found more than 17 pounds of high-quality heroin.

The heroin was "China White," 81 percent pure, with a wholesale value of about $25 million. Diluted and cut into street-level doses, a federal judge later said, the stash amounted to "enough heroin to get everyone in the United States high 1.8 times."

The bust was one of the largest single heroin seizures in Philadelphia history. Yet after a lengthy investigation, two trials and two convictions, authorities acknowledge that the case still raises many more questions than it answers. In that light, Tat Man Ho and the Amtrak heroin bust may be the preface to a story that is just beginning, a saga of organized crime in the 1990s.

Ho, say agents of the Drug Enforcement Administration, is an active member of the 14K Triad, one of the oldest and most powerful Chinese criminal organizations in the world. Over the last 10 years, the triads, secret societies that trace their origins to 17th-century China, have emerged as a major force in the American underworld. They are, some authorities believe, more powerful, more secretive and potentially more dominant than La Cosa Nostra, the legendary mob of modern America.

Testimony before the Senate Judiciary Committee last August included a description of the triads as "a new super Mafia," an organization that might have more than 9,000 members in the United States before the end of the century. Membership in La Cosa Nostra in this country, the committee was told, peaked in the mid-1960s with an estimated 4,500 initiated members.

Ho, a short, stocky man with thick black hair and horn-rim glasses, is what law enforcement thinks is the American mobster of the future. Asked during a sentencing hearing in February if he wanted to make any comment to the court, Ho, through an interpreter, politely replied: "You are an honorable judge. I have nothing to say."

Honor and silence. Those are two of the cornerstones of the triads, societies that were formed—like the Mafia in Sicily—to fight oppression and that grew into highly structured criminal associations that have become shadow governments wherever they operate.

The 14K Triad, according to DEA Special Agent John McCarty, who testified at Ho's trial, is one of the biggest. It has 24,000 members worldwide and is considered, he said, the second largest of the six major triads now based in Hong Kong.

Overall triad membership has been estimated at from 80,000 to as many as 100,000, according to several government reports. The organizations operate throughout Southeast Asia and in many European countries, and have shown up in ever-increasing numbers in major Canadian cities, particularly Toronto, and on the East and West Coasts of the United States. Authorities predict an even larger influx of triad members when Hong Kong reverts to China's control in 1997.

A HIGHLY ORGANIZED FOE

McCarty likened the triads to the Mafia, but are more highly organized.

"They involve themselves in heroin dealing, counterfeit currency, counterfeit checks, stolen credit cards, prostitution and illegal gambling," he said. And, according to other law enforcement officials, in almost any other racket that will generate a profit. Federal and local law enforcement agencies in New York and San Francisco have developed the most detailed information about the triads, but even that is somewhat sketchy.

Officials say those cities serve as two of the main distribution points for Southeast Asian heroin in the United States. From New York, shipments of heroin would be cut and diluted, then shipped to East Coast cities such as Philadelphia and Boston for street sales. In the Philadelphia area, the FBI, DEA, and local and state police departments have been building files, expertise and cases, but they say they have only begun to scratch the surface. The Pennsylvania Crime Commission said in its 1990 report, released in April, that "investigators are only beginning to unravel the web of Asian organized crime."

A TOUGH TASK

The crime commission, like other federal and local authorities, pointed out that cultural and language differences, coupled with the Asian-American community's general distrust of authority, make the task of confronting the triads a difficult one. It is not unlike law enforcement attempts in the early part of this century to crack the emerging, highly secretive, ethnocentric Sicilian and Calabrian crime organizations that became the American Mafia.

More troubling, say authorities, is the worldwide scope of triad organizations and their heavy involvement in drug trafficking, particularly heroin. Bootleg liquor was the contraband upon which the Mafia built its early empire in the United States. It then expanded into other rackets. Heroin could play the same role for the triads as they begin to move to America.

Investigators say Tat Man Ho, 37, typifies the American-based triad member. He came to this country from Hong Kong in 1984, settling in the San Francisco area, where he operated a messenger service. Despite what appeared to be a modest existence, he traveled to Hong Kong and Macao frequently. At the time of his arrest he was the target of drug trafficking investigations in San Francisco, Japan and Hong Kong.

AN EARLIER PROBE

The DEA developed a portrait of Ho during an unsuccessful undercover investigation in San Francisco in 1986. During a six-month period, Ho met on several occasions with a DEA agent posing as a would-be drug dealer. During those meetings, Ho said he could smuggle any amount of heroin into the United States and that "his people" had a direct connection with a heroin manufacturing laboratory in Chiang Mai, Thailand, an area within the opium-rich Golden Triangle that encompasses parts of Burma, Thailand and Laos.

Ho also told the undercover DEA agent that he "made frequent trips to Bangkok, Thailand, to bring . . . girls into Macao for the massage parlors" and that he was part of a loan-sharking operation in and around the casinos there. It was at those casinos that Hin Ping Lo, Ho's traveling companion on the day of the arrest at the 30th Street Station, gambled and lost. And lost. And lost.

Lo, a $4,000-a-month electrical engineer from Hong Kong, said his string of bad luck led him to a loan shark named Ah Keuhng, a shadowy figure who traveled back and forth between China and Macao and who, Lo said, clearly had triad connections.

"I borrow sometimes," Lo said of his dealings with Keuhng in the casinos. "I win some, I pay them back some and pay some interest. And when I lose, I borrow again."

Lo, 40, testified at his trial in October that his debt to Ah Keuhng reached $50,000. He was under constant pressure to pay. Eventually, he said, Keuhng told him that he would forgive the debt if Lo went to the United States and did him a favor. Lo said he was told to go to San Francisco, contact Keuhng's associate, "and do whatever he tells me to do." And that, Lo said, is how he met Tat Man Ho and ended up traveling by train with him from Houston to New York at the time they were arrested.

Steve Goldstein had been working as a captain in Amtrak's drug interdiction unit for about a year when he got the call from a fellow agent in New York whose duties include scanning computerized reservation lists for potential drug traffickers. Amtrak has developed a set of "indicators" that investigators look for in an attempt to ferret out narcotics couriers. These include points of departure and destination, types of reservations, accommodations and travel routes.

"A guy in New York was doing the computer check and he called down to me and said, 'I've got a funny reservation that I want you to take a look at,'" Goldstein recalled.

The reservation, which had been changed a few times, was for two men, Ho and Lo, traveling out of Houston, through Chicago and Philadelphia, to New York. They were traveling in a sleeping compartment and had not checked any luggage.

When the train pulled into 30th Street Station for a scheduled 20-minute stopover, Goldstein was there to greet it. He asked and received Lo's permission to search their sleeping compartment. Lo, he said, spoke haltingly in English and "appeared very nervous." Ho, he said, was sitting on a couch, eating a sandwich when he entered the compartment. Goldstein, with two agents stationed in the corridor, searched the room and examined their luggage. He also looked in the bathroom that is a part of the compartment. He found nothing.

"Then, just as I was leaving, I noticed a shelf above the bathroom. I go up on the couch and, stuffed way in the back, out of sight, was this bag."

Inside the bag was a knapsack. Inside the knapsack, wrapped in brown paper, were nearly a dozen bricks of a white substance.

"I thought it was cocaine," Goldstein recalled.

Amtrak authorities took Ho and Lo into custody. Goldstein took the bricks to his office above the bustling train terminal and ran a field test on a sample of the substance.

"I did the test for cocaine and it came up light blue instead of dark blue. I said to myself, 'This is either [poor quality] cocaine or it's dope [heroin].'"

Goldstein called the feds.

L.C. Wright Jr., the Assistant U.S. Attorney who prosecuted both Ho and Lo, called it a "fascinating case." He described Ho, sentenced to 15 years and eight months, as "an international criminal." Lo, who was convicted of a lesser charge and testified against Ho, was sentenced to three years. Like the DEA and Amtrak agents who handled the investigation, Wright said the 30th Street Station bust was just a skirmish in the war on drugs.

"There's a lot more getting through," said Wright, who has prosecuted dozens of drug cases for the government. "It's a tremendously lucrative vocation . . . if you can get away with it."

Last year, according to federal authorities, nearly 360 kilograms—about 792 pounds—of heroin were seized. Most of it came from the processing laboratories of Southeast Asia. During the same time, authorities estimate, more than 300 tons were produced in those labs. While it is impossible to determine how much of that made its way into the United States, an FBI official told the Senate Judiciary Committee last year that "the increasing prevalence of Southeast Asian heroin may be a harbinger of a new drug epidemic." Officials estimate that there are between 500,000 and a million heroin addicts in the United States today, and that those addicts spend $8 billion annually to support their habit.

The stash of 17 pounds confiscated at 30th Street Station was an infinitesimal piece of the market. And the money lost by the drug traffickers was just a small part of the financial base of an expanding organized crime operation.

"As the triads grow, so will the heroin trade," Senator Joseph R. Biden Jr., the Judiciary Committee chairman, said during last summer's hearings. "As the heroin trade grows, so will the triads. The two will feed each other."

PIZZA, PASTA AND COCAINE

APRIL 20, 1997

Pizza and pasta. Cocaine and calamari. They all were on the menu for those in the know at Stefano's Pizzeria & Ristorante, according to federal authorities, who last week called the small restaurant in Mount Laurel, New Jersey, the "clearinghouse" and nerve center of a multi-million-dollar drug distribution ring ultimately linked to the Sicilian Mafia.

Cocaine, authorities said, was literally sold over the counter at Stefano's. It was as readily and easily available there as a pizza with pepperoni. Orders for a $20, one-gram bag of the addictive white powder, they added, could be called in the same way regular customers might ask for a cheesesteak, panzarotti or antipasto to go.

"The amazing thing was that it was so open and notorious," said Assistant U.S. Attorney Robert Mintz, the prosecutor in the case. "If you knew the right person to ask for, you could order over the phone."

Mintz said two young Stefano's waitresses and a pizza maker, who were among the 14 defendants arrested in the drug case, had plugged into a customer network of friends and associates—mostly young, middle-class suburbanites in their teens and 20s. The word, the prosecutor said, quickly spread that Stefano's was the place to go if you were looking to score.

"They were one step above the street-level user," Mintz said.

At the other end of the investigation, authorities tracked larger cocaine and heroin sales involving three other defendants with possible organized crime links back to Sicily.

Mount Laurel and Medford, the neighboring Burlington County community in which the investigation began, are thousands of miles from Palermo, the spawning ground of the Sicilian mob, but authorities said last week that their investigation had shown that it was a distance easily traveled.

Two of those arrested Thursday—including Giacomo Gallina, owner of Stefano's—have family ties to members of the Sicilian Mafia prosecuted in the infamous Pizza Connection case in New York in the 1980s. Another, according to authorities, once worked for a company controlled by jailed, Sicilian-born Philadelphia mob boss John Stanfa.

"There are a lot of interesting connections in this case," Mintz said last week. "Not all of them have come out yet."

In fact, most of what has been made public comes from a 10-page criminal complaint filed by FBI agent Michael P. Holeman, one of the chief investigators in the case. The probe, federal authorities said last week, was a joint, 14-month investigation by the FBI, the Internal Revenue Service, and the Mount Laurel and Medford Township Police Departments. It included talks secretly taped by undercover agents and their operatives, who made drug purchases, and phone conversation picked up by a wiretap at Stefano's.

From their listening posts, investigators heard and recorded it all: from the routine, over-the-counter, one-gram coke sales to the larger and more circumspect sales of up to a kilogram (2.2 pounds) of cocaine or heroin to wholesale or retail drug dealers. All of it played out against the hustle and bustle of a busy pizza shop and restaurant in a small shopping center off Church Road in Mount Laurel, a restaurant and a shopping plaza not unlike hundreds scattered all over suburbia.

"An everyday institution—the local pizza parlor," noted Faith S. Hochberg, the U.S. Attorney for New Jersey, in announcing the arrests.

While Gallina, 32, used his employees to sell small quantities of cocaine routinely, authorities said he personally handled the larger cocaine and heroin sales. Most were to drug dealers, according to the criminal complaint, but several unknowingly were made to undercover FBI agents and their operatives. As a result, the feds got most of it on tape.

Some of the conversations were in code, with such words as cheese and pizza sauce used in place of heroin or cocaine. To federal agents who have worked or read about earlier investigations into Sicilian-linked drug networks—including the Pizza Connection case and a South Jersey offshoot of that probe known in federal circles as Pizza Connection II—it was all too familiar.

In a July 26 conversation shortly after the wiretaps went up at Stefano's, an undercover FBI agent called Gallina to ask about a prearranged drug deal.

"I have your pizza ready," the short, stocky, dark-haired restaurateur said.

Later that day, the agent showed up at the restaurant and picked up 160 grams—about a third of a pound—of heroin, according to court papers. But in another conversation, recorded September 6, Paul Testa, 38, the pizza maker at Stefano's, and Christopher Grosso, 25, did not even bother with a code, investigators said. Both have been charged in the case, in part because of that conversation.

"I really hate talking on here," Grosso said.

"It's OK," Testa told him reassuringly.

"How many have you got?" Grosso asked.

"We got, ah, as many as you want, really. . . . OK? They're $20 a bag, OK? And there's a gram in each bag, OK? And it's good stuff, because everybody has been buying it."

Later that month, Julie Arcaini, 20, a Stefano's waitress also arrested and charged last week, inadvertently pointed the feds to a secret stash of cocaine at the restaurant. On September 16, federal authorities said, Arcaini called Testa from home to say she would not be able to make it to work that night. Federal authorities said she then explained that drug customers would be coming in and that Testa should take care of them.

"Listen," she said, "I can't leave my house, because I'm baby-sitting my brother. People are probably going to be coming up to the store."

"OK," Testa answered.

"OK?" Arcaini replied. "You don't know where it is, though."

"No," Testa said.

"You know where the cans of cheddar cheese and stuff like that is, in the back? . . . Look in one of those boxes. It's kind of like shoved in between two cans."

Later in the conversation, Testa asked whether he should put the money from the sales into the cash register.

"No," Arcaini replied. "Don't put it in the register. Just keep it and, ah, give it to Jack [Giacomo Gallina] later. OK?"

But of all the sales and conversations recorded during the investigation, none was as startling as one picked up by an FBI undercover agent who wore a body wire to a prearranged heroin sale at the Sage Diner in Mount Laurel on January 16, two months before the investigation would shut down.

Giacomo Gallina and Giovanni Saponara, 36, the owner of a Philadelphia food distribution company and a suspected drug dealer, met that day with the undercover agent. Saponara, federal authorities said, brought his 14-year-old son along. In the diner, the boy provided the agent with a sample of the heroin, authorities said. Gallina, meanwhile, was accompanied by his 16-year-old nephew.

Saponara, a thin man with long, black hair pulled into a ponytail, told the undercover agent that he wanted his son to learn how to conduct drug business, a federal authority said incredulously last week. That day, the undercover agent purchased 162 grams of 95 percent pure heroin.

Gallina, Saponara, who owns Don Giovanni Foods on Belgrade Street in Philadelphia, and Vito Evola, 31, who operates Sal's Pizza on Market Street in Palmyra, were identified by investigators last week as principal targets of the investigation. Each faces a sentence of 10 years to life in prison on drug conspiracy charges. And all three, investigators said, have links to mobsters with ties to Sicilian crime families.

Gallina, according to investigators, is the nephew of Gaetano Badalamenti, a Sicilian heroin kingpin convicted in the Pizza Connection case. Plus, Gallina's father, Stefano—after whom the restaurant was named—was killed in Sicily in 1981, making him one of more than 300 alleged mobsters murdered during a bloody war that pitted country-based Mafia clans against crime families operating in Sicily's major cities.

Evola, like Gallina, migrated to the United States about 10 years ago from Carini, a small village west of Palermo, authorities said. And, they added, he had relatives tied to the Pizza Connection investigation. Saponara, according to Mintz, opened Don Giovanni Foods a few years ago. Prior to that, the prosecutor said, he worked for Continential Imported Food Distributors Inc., a company controlled by Stanfa.

Evola and most of the other defendants were released on $100,000 bail last week. Gallina and Saponara were ordered held without bail pending another hearing Wednesday in federal court in Camden. At that time, with federal authorities pressing to keep both men in jail, more information about the case may be made public.

"All I can say," Mintz said, "is that the investigation is ongoing."

MONEY, POWER AND REVENGE

DECEMBER 4, 2005

It was a combination of hip-hop arrogance and street-corner fatalism, a rare look at the mindset of a man federal authorities say once dominated Philadelphia's drug underworld. For several hours Wednesday and Thursday, a federal court jury heard reputed drug kingpin Kaboni Savage, 29, talk about his life and times. Boasting about never having held a job, bragging about his wealth, and promising to kill anyone who might be cooperating against him, Savage unknowingly provided prosecutors with an expletive-laden final chapter in a month-long trial that could land him in jail for the rest of his life. The jury of six men and six women is expected to begin deliberations this week. The conversations, picked up by an FBI listening device hidden with court approval in Savage's prison cell, were played just before the prosecution rested its case.

"They're gonna pay," Savage said during one discussion about "rats," adding that he didn't really care who had to be eliminated. When another inmate suggested that Savage knew who "got to go," he replied, "and if I was wrong, so be it. . . . That's how this . . . supposed to be, man."

Insisting that he had no regrets about the way he had lived his life, Savage boasted on another tape that he was arrested more than a month before his co-defendants in April 2004 because the government feared he might start eliminating witnesses.

"They know if they left me out there . . . they wouldn't had no case," he said in a conversation recorded on November 11, 2004 in the Federal Detention Center at 7th and Arch Streets.

For the last month, prosecutors Mark Ehlers and Gregory Lisa have used the testimony of witnesses, including some of those Savage had allegedly targeted, and conversations from other wiretaps to paint a picture of Savage as a ruthless narcotics trafficker whose lifestyle was built on a combination of cocaine and murder. The prison tapes allowed the prosecutors to dramatically underscore that point in the defendant's own words.

Here was the reputed kingpin proudly describing all the improvements he had put into his North Philadelphia home—"wooden floors, wall-to-wall mirrors . . . the carpet, you put your foot in there and your footprints stay in there for a day"—while lamenting the fact that he could lose it all because of "these . . . rats." And there, in another conversation, was Savage bragging about his lifestyle while belittling the prison guards who, he claimed, worked six months to earn what he sometimes spent in a week.

"They wanna be us, they just ain't got the heart," he said on November 13. "But trust me, [they] ain't never gonna know how it feel to go to a car dealer, say 'Give me that!' That feeling where you go buy what you want. That's a hell of a feeling. . . . Spend a dime on some [women] . . . twelve thousand . . . just to trick.

"You just [spent] six months of their salary having fun. See what I'm saying? You drove the finest cars, you [made love] to the finest broads. . . . And you shopped at the finest . . . clothing stores."

Savage, in the same conversation, said he had no regrets for anything he had done. Instead, he said, he was proud of what he had accomplished.

"I mean, my mom never worked," he said. "My sister ain't have to work, she's got her education. Put my wife through school, got her education. My other sister got a house. I mean, fruits of my labor!"

Savage, who is charged with heading a narcotics network that brought hundreds of kilograms of cocaine into Philadelphia between 1999 and 2003 and that routinely used intimidation and murder to advance its ends, could be sentenced to life in prison if convicted. Four co-defendants face related charges. More than a dozen others indicted with Savage in May 2004 pleaded guilty. Several have testified for the prosecution.

A onetime professional boxer, Savage has long had a reputation for violence. Before his arrest in the current drug case, he beat a murder rap in Common Pleas Court when a key witness was killed just days before he was to testify. In more than a dozen other conversations, prosecutors were able to provide an image of Savage that jibed with the charges he is facing. On only one tape played for the jury did Savage appear to have any second thoughts about how he had lived his life, claiming that things might have been different had his father not died when he was a child.

"I know I didn't sell drugs because I wanted to," he said on December 8, 2004. "My pop was living, I never looking at drugs."

But when another inmate asked why he couldn't have "went and got a job," Savage laughed.

"Come on, man," he said. "Where . . . am I gonna work at? What, am I gonna work and go to school? Yeah."

That same sarcasm was evident in yet another conversation in which he again belittled his jail guards.

"I like to live, man. . . . They're gonna die miserable. They're waiting for that . . . pension, for the Social Security.

"What you wanna get, $2,000 a month? I ain't living that way. I like to live. . . . Those [guards] aren't never gonna get experience going down there and just buying what you wanna buy. . . . I mean, they don't know that feeling. They gotta wait for their next check.

"I ain't waiting."

CHICKEN WINGS AND MURDER

MARCH 8, 2005

The night started with some "weed" and chicken wings and ended with the murder of a witness. That, Sherrie Hewett told a jury yesterday, was how things played out on March 29, 1999, when her former boyfriend, Felix Summers, allegedly gunned down Charlotte Presley in the doorway of a South Philadelphia apartment to keep Presley from testifying against him.

"She could have put him away for the rest of his life," Hewett said when asked the motive for the killing. Hewett, 27, appeared on the witness stand more than three years after agreeing to cooperate with authorities, who have gone to extraordinary lengths to keep her alive.

She and her children were twice relocated—once to North Carolina—by the District Attorney's Office. She was also placed in protective custody in a Philadelphia prison because of threats against her. Through it all, she said, Summers continued to reach out to her, calling her on a cell phone that he managed to have smuggled into prison or contacting her through friends and associates, including a prison guard. The message was always the same: Change your story or die.

Hewett's testimony, coming on the second day of the murder trial in Common Pleas Court, not only provided details about the killing of Charlotte Presley, but also offered a glimpse into the underworld of Summers, a man who once had a spot on the FBI's Ten Most Wanted list and who has been a suspect in four murders and seven other shootings in South Philadelphia. Summers, 24, could be sentenced to death if convicted of first-degree murder in the case. He also faces charges of conspiracy, burglary, possession of a firearm, and retaliation against a witness. The suspected drug dealer—who has been acquitted in two other homicide trials in which witnesses were killed, disappeared, or changed their testimony—could be freed if he is found not guilty.

The trial, before Judge John J. Poserina Jr., attracted a near-capacity crowd to the 10th-floor courtroom yesterday. On one side of the room sat Summers' mother, aunt, and about two dozen other friends and relatives, including two suspects in murder cases tied to the Summers investigations. On the other side of the room were relatives of slaying victims John Niles, a 19-year-old gunned down on January 12, 1999, and Veronica Rios, 15, killed in a drive-by shooting on August 16, 2001. Charlotte Presley, a witness to the Niles shooting, was dead before Felix Summers was tried in that case. He was found not guilty. Summers and two codefendants were acquitted last year of the Rios slaying.

Sherrie Hewett, dressed in Muslim garb including a head covering and veil, said she began cooperating in the Presley investigation after the Rios murder and the killing of another friend, Diana Meirino, five weeks later. Hewett told the jury that she and Meirino were with Summers on the night Presley was killed. She said she was with him at a motel near Philadelphia International Airport when he suggested they "go for a ride."

According to Hewett, they picked up Meirino at her home in South Philadelphia about 2 a.m., drove to North Philadelphia where they bought and smoked some marijuana, and then returned to South Philadelphia where they bought chicken wings. About 4 a.m., Summers allegedly persuaded Meirino to knock on the door to Presley's apartment. Hewett said she stayed in the van they had been riding in. Minutes later, she heard three shots and then saw Summers and Meirino running back to the van. Hewett stated that as she and Meirino sat in the back of the van crying, Summers again drove to North Philadelphia where he threatened to kill them.

"He asked us why were we crying over that bitch," she said. "She could have put him away for the rest of his life."

KING HOMICIDE

JANUARY 8, 2006

He called himself "King Homicide," and, according to federal authorities, he oversaw an underworld reign of terror that included murder, kidnappings, brutal beatings, torture and rape. This week, William "Homi" Sosa and seven top associates will go on trial in U.S. District Court in a racketeering case aimed at the fledgling Philadelphia chapter of the Almighty Latin King Nation. Sosa, 27, was described as the "Inca," or leader, of the local Latino mob family in a 26-count indictment handed up last year. Audio and videotapes made during a two-year investigation and the testimony of several former "kings" and "queens" who clashed with Sosa are expected to highlight the trial.

At least a half-dozen were on the dangerous end of "terminate on sight" orders allegedly issued by the Latin King leader as he maneuvered to take control of a Vineland-based branch of the national organization, authorities say. One woman was kidnapped in New Jersey, taken to Philadelphia, beaten and then raped, according to the indictment. Another, who was suspected of being an informant, was targeted for an assault that included burning off her Latin King tattoos.

The case also includes a homicide and heroin dealing in North Philadelphia, kidnapping and murder conspiracies in Vineland and Trenton, and a beating in a Philadelphia rowhouse in which the victim was to have had his hands chopped off with a machete.

These accounts come from court documents and FBI reports that paint a disturbing picture of Sosa, a slightly built, five-foot-six, 140-pound Ocean County College dropout who authorities say took over the top spot in the "Lion Tribe," the Philadelphia branch of the Latin Kings, about three years ago. Sosa's mother, on the other hand, says her son is being railroaded by a jilted girlfriend and her current lover, two disgruntled Latin King members who "caused all this trouble."

"What they are saying, that's not my son," said Rosita Cotto as she sat in a diner not far from her Lakewood, New Jersey home one night last month. "He wouldn't hurt anyone."

The witnesses who are scheduled to testify—including five co-defendants who have pleaded guilty and have agreed to cooperate—tell a different story. While heading up the Philadelphia organization, Sosa set at least six murder plots in motion, ordered a series of kidnappings and beatings, and continually battled with a Latin Kings group based in the Vineland-Millville area that resisted his attempt to take over, they contend.

"If they don't want to be with us, they're against us," one witness quoted Sosa as saying. "Crush them."

Several witnesses also provided the FBI with details about armed forays to the Vineland area by members of the Lion Tribe. At least one led to a standoff with police and a SWAT team at the Vineland Gardens Apartments and ended with more than a dozen arrests.

Prosecutors David E. Troyer and Barry Gross are expected to spend several weeks presenting the government's case, which offers a rare look inside an organized crime group that has garnered headlines and an underworld reputation in both Chicago and New York, but that has received little attention in the Philadelphia area. Jury selection begins Tuesday.

The Latin Kings are "a national organization, based in Chicago, [that] holds itself out . . . as a benevolent or social organization," according to an FBI affidavit that is part of the case. But in reality, the affidavit contends, they are "a criminal organization involved in drug trafficking and violent crimes, including murder, kidnapping and robbery."

A five-pointed crown is one of the key symbols of the organization. The group's colors are black and gold. Members take aliases or nicknames preceded by the word king or queen. The Philadelphia chapter included "King Terror," "King Tiger," "King Pleasure," "Queen Heart" and "Queen Legend."

Sosa's reign as leader of the group ended several months before his arrest last February, according to court documents. At the time, he was on the run, ducking both an indictment and an internal power struggle in which he had been targeted for death. Arrested in Brick Township, New Jersey, Sosa told authorities that he had quit the Latin Kings. He claimed that he had been an adviser to, but never the leader of, the organization and said he was aware that "the Latin Kings had a hit on him."

Sosa's court-appointed lawyer, William DeStefano, said last week that there was no physical evidence linking his client to any of the charges, and that the government's case was based on the tainted testimony of unreliable witnesses.

"What you're left with is the testimony of immunized or plea-bargained knuckleheads," he said. "And the question is, do they have a motive for saying what they're saying?"

One of the witnesses is Joseph "King Smiley" Wallenberg, a Chicago-based Latin King who was indicted with Sosa and who was charged with being part of the group that plotted to kill him. In fact, only one of the nine murder conspiracies listed in the case led to a killing—a shooting outside the Zip Code Bar in North Philadelphia, in which the victim was shot multiple times in the back of the head. In addition, the plot to chop off a victim's hands was never carried out, nor was the plan to burn off the tattoos of another member.

"These were a bunch of guys who had an overblown opinion of who they were," said another defense lawyer familiar with the case.

The drug charges outlined in the indictment underscore that point. There are six minor ($40 to $120) street-corner heroin transactions listed. All took place near Hope and Cambria Streets in North Philadelphia where, authorities allege, the Latin Kings controlled all drug dealing. But according to one informant, the group shut down the operation because addicts were stealing drugs and because Sosa was demanding 10 percent of all the earnings.

"Between the drugs that were being stolen . . . and the required 10 percent . . . the drug corner was not profitable," the informant told the FBI.

The indictment, the allegations, and the testimony of informants, some of whom spent time in her home, have Rosita Cotto, 45, shaking her head in disbelief.

"They made my son look like a monster, a monster with no heart," she said. "And that's not the way he was raised. . . . He's not a violent person."

Cotto, an administrative assistant at Ocean County College and the mother of four other children, scoffed at the description of her oldest son as the homicidal leader of a crime family. In fact, she said, he had signed up for criminal justice courses while briefly attending college several years ago.

"He wanted to be a cop," Rosita Cotto added.

WITNESS INTIMIDATION

MARCH 19, 2006

Shock, dismay and disbelief were the typical reactions last week after six witnesses recanted their testimony in the trial for the murder of Faheem Thomas-Childs, the 10-year-old North Philadelphia boy killed in February 2004 outside his elementary school by cross fire from feuding drug gangs. Typical, that is, for those not familiar with the criminal justice system in Philadelphia. For those who work in the trenches, the fact that the witnesses "went south" was business as usual, with Assistant District Attorney Mark Gilson calling it "fairly typical and commonplace."

"This case is not the exception. It's the rule," said Gilson, who prosecuted the case.

The recantations underscore what state Superior Court Judge Seamus McCaffery, a former homicide detective, described as an epidemic in major homicide cases—an epidemic based in fear of retribution.

"I've never seen anything like this," said McCaffery, who has built a career on a no-nonsense approach to law and order.

The Philadelphia District Attorney's Office does not keep statistics on witness intimidation, spokeswoman Cathie Abookire noted. As a result, it is virtually impossible to determine the impact such intimidation may have had when witnesses failed to appear or changed their stories. But anecdotal evidence, particularly in cases involving drug gangs and homicides (both factors in the Faheem case), seems to illustrate a thin line between becoming a witness and becoming a victim.

Consider just three other cases in Philadelphia courts last week:

On Thursday, less than an hour after Common Pleas Court Judge Jane Cutler Greenspan found reputed drug gang members Kareem Johnson and Kennell Spady guilty of first-degree murder in Faheem's death, there was a scheduling hearing in another room of Common Pleas Court for the retrial of Felix Summers. A reputed South Philadelphia drug dealer, Summers has been tried twice in the last year in the 1999 killing of Charlotte Presley. Both trials ended with hung juries.

Presley was killed, police say, because she was a witness against Summers in another murder case. Before that trial, police allege, Summers walked up to Presley's door and shot her: the ultimate form of witness intimidation. Presley was one of two women—the other was Diana Meirino—who authorities believe were killed because they offered information about Summers. Once on the FBI's Ten Most Wanted list, Summers has yet to be convicted of a major crime.

Also Thursday, just hours after the verdict in the Faheem case, a federal prosecutor filed a 56-page sentencing memo outlining the criminal curriculum vitae of convicted drug kingpin Kaboni Savage. The memo includes references to dozens of secretly recorded conversations in which Savage threatened to kill witnesses and their families. Savage beat a murder case in Common Pleas Court two years ago when the key witness, boxer Tybius Flowers, was gunned down just days before the trial was to start.

Savage is suspected as well of ordering the arson that killed relatives of Eugene Coleman, a witness against him in his federal drug case. Coleman's mother, her niece and four children ages 15 months to 15 years all died. Prison tapes secretly recorded by the FBI detail Savage's ranting about killing Coleman's family and joking after learning that Coleman, a federal prisoner, had been permitted to attend his mother's funeral.

"They should've took him and got him some barbecue sauce," Savage said.

In yet another Philadelphia courtroom last week, Brian Rogers quietly explained to a federal jury why he killed a woman named Tracey Saunders. Rogers, who began testifying Wednesday, is an admitted member of the Boyle Street Boys, a Chester gang whose leaders are on trial for trafficking in cocaine and violence. After he agreed to cooperate, Rogers told investigators that he had pumped several shots into Saunders' head as she sat in a car outside her home October 8, 2001.

"She's got to die," Rogers quoted Vincent Williams, a leader of the Boyle Street Boys, as saying after learning that Saunders, his cousin, was cooperating.

Although federal authorities, because of their resources, are credited with supplying better security for witnesses, the Coleman fire and the Saunders slaying are two stark examples of how "street justice" can trump even the Department of Justice.

The Philadelphia District Attorney's Office, with money supplied in part by the state, has a protection and relocation program. Time and again, District Attorney Lynne Abraham has promised to provide the resources to protect any witness who requires it. But neither Abraham, nor any of her assistants, nor any homicide detective working a murder case can force a witness to take advantage of that offer. There is often more at play.

"Witnesses . . . don't exactly tell you everything at first," Assistant District Attorney William Fisher said at a hearing in a 2004 murder case in which witness intimidation was an issue. "They don't tell you everything for a number of reasons. One of the reasons is that they're afraid for their lives."

Has the problem gotten worse? Or is there simply more media attention and public awareness because of cases such as Faheem's? Charles "Joey" Grant, a highly regarded former chief prosecutor in the district attorney's Homicide Unit, said witness intimidation was not new. By and large, he argued, the District Attorney's Office does a good job dealing with it. But unlike many federal cases in which cooperating witnesses are criminals, the police and district attorney often deal with witnesses who are innocent residents.

"These are good people who want to stay . . . with their friends and their families," Grant pointed out. They are also acutely aware that they could become victims themselves, he added.

"They get a message, and they know that the message could have been a bullet as opposed to a conversation," Grant said. That's the risk witnesses take "just because we ask them to tell the truth."

The tedious process of taking a case from the streets to a courtroom is fraught with all kinds of risks, Grant and McCaffery acknowledged. And often, McCaffery said, police must overcome a neighborhood culture of lawlessness based partly on distrust of authority and partly on fear of retaliation. It is a street code that tells many residents that it is smarter—and certainly safer—not to "snitch," even if someone gets away with murder.

"The mind-set in some communities is that it's cool to be a criminal," McCaffery said. "It's almost imbedded in the community: Don't snitch."

Indeed, street campaigns touting that slogan have surfaced in several cities, including Philadelphia, Baltimore and Boston. T-shirts emblazoned with that message were sold. In a video distributed in Baltimore, a rap group glorified the "no cooperation" mind-set. In one high-profile Boston case, the supposedly secret grand jury testimony of a cooperating witness in a drug case was circulated in the witness' neighborhood.

All were less than subtle forms of intimidation. So, too, was this: In a pending murder case in Philadelphia, police found in a suspect's jail cell a picture of a witness who was to testify against him. The photo had been circled with a bull's-eye; underneath it was a caption.

"Dead man walking," it read.

BENJAMIN TON:
THE DIZZYING RISE AND FALL OF A DRUG LORD

FEBRUARY 11, 2007

When he came to the attention of federal drug agents three years ago, Benjamin Ton, then 30, was an unemployed copy-machine repairman inexplicably living the American dream. A Vietnamese emigre, he and his wife, Lena Le, had just moved from a modest rowhouse in Folcroft, Pennsylvania to the upscale Cobblestone Farms section of Sicklerville, New Jersey. Parked in the driveway of their new home were a Corvette, a BMW and a Lexus.

"It was obvious there was a lot of money coming from somewhere," said Christopher A. Jakim, the Drug Enforcement Administration agent who supervised the squad working the case.

Eight months later, Ton was arrested on charges of heading a $50 million drug operation that in just two years had brought nearly 10 tons of high-quality marijuana and more than 300,000 ecstasy pills to the Philadelphia area from Canada, a quietly growing source for those illegal drugs in the United States. At the time of his arrest, Ton was a major player in the Philadelphia region's thriving drug market, an industry with at least a billion dollars in illegal street sales annually, authorities say. The rise and fall of Benjamin Ton, who has pleaded guilty and is awaiting sentencing, offers a glimpse into that highly lucrative drug underworld and a look at a new breed of American gangster.

Operating in close-knit ethnic groups and using language and culture as shields, these Asian, Latino and African American mobsters pose a more difficult challenge to law enforcement than the overexposed and largely disorganized American Mafia. Wiretapped conversations during the Ton investigation, for example, were recorded in four languages.

"In two years, this guy was making more money than Nicky Scarfo ever dreamed of," said Assistant U.S. Attorney David Fritchey, who helped bring down Philadelphia Mafia bosses Scarfo, Ralph Natale and Joseph "Skinny Joey" Merlino and is prosecuting the Ton case. Ton's story also is a look at the top of a drug empire. Authorities seized about $500,000 when he and 25 associates were arrested.

SEDUCED BY MONEY

Benjamin Ton's organization sprang from a chance encounter, say Christopher Jakim and other DEA agents who have debriefed Ton since he began cooperating. In 2002, Ton said, a Vietnamese friend from Canada told him that he was having trouble moving 100 pounds of marijuana he had shipped to Philadelphia. Would Ton be interested in finding buyers? Ton agreed, and a drug operation was born. With connections to the Vietnamese communities in Philadelphia and Toronto, Ton was the right person in the right place at the right time.

"He was an ambitious, aggressive young guy who saw an opportunity and seized it," Jakim said. "We don't think he was involved in drugs before that."

"He's remorseful for what he has done," said Ton's lawyer, Elliott M. Cohen, who said his client could not be interviewed. "He started out living an honest life and got seduced by the money." Ton faces a life sentence, but his cooperation could result in less jail time.

Ton took his first deliveries on consignment. Eventually, he had a network of Canadian suppliers who competed for his business through a broker he hired in Toronto. Weekly, he received shipments of 100 to 300 pounds of marijuana, hidden in trucks transporting legitimate goods across the border. One major shipment, for example, came in a tractor-trailer loaded with futons heading for Kmarts in North Carolina, according to the DEA. The ecstasy, usually in shipments of 40,000 pills, was typically hidden in the door panels of cars, sometimes driven by Ton or his associates. Cash was brought up; ecstasy pills were brought back.

Fritchey estimates that Ton sent $25 million to $50 million to Canada over two years. Ton paid between $1700 and $2700 a pound for marijuana and $2.25 to $3.00 per pill for ecstasy. His wholesale network would then sell the drugs for about double those amounts. According to the indictment, that network included about two dozen Asian American associates in Camden, in Eddystone near Chester, and in Massachusetts, Georgia and North Carolina.

The most potent and expensive marijuana was cultivated by the "Vietnamese Mafia" in "grow houses"—indoor hydroponic operations that have proliferated in Canada in the last decade, according to a Royal Canadian Mounted Police report. Labeled "AAA" or "purple haze," this premium marijuana had a level of THC (the psychoactive ingredient) that was sometimes 25 to 30 percent, investigators said, instead of the usual three to five percent. The even more potent ecstasy pills were stamped "puppy" or "strawberry," and sold for $25 to $30 apiece at "rave parties" popular with teenagers and young adults.

PHONY RECEIPTS

By late 2003, Ton and his wife were buying fine clothes and jewelry and enjoying vacations abroad and visits to Atlantic City casinos. In his debriefing sessions, Ton said he had always kept about $100,000 in cash in a home safe and hundreds of thousands more in bank accounts and safe-deposit boxes. He traveled to Canada and Vietnam for business and pleasure, meeting in both countries with a Vietnamese movie star and singer with whom he had begun an affair, authorities said. Ton would eventually spend $300,000 to build his girlfriend a home in Vietnam, a bit more than he and Lena Le had paid for their South Jersey house. But just as a chance encounter brought Ton into the drug trade, another sparked his downfall.

In March 2004, DEA agents in New York City, working a different case, overheard a target on a wiretap discuss a shipment of marijuana and ecstasy to Philadelphia. Within days, DEA agents here had won court authorization to set up their own wiretaps, which quickly pointed to Ton.

"He was the guy in charge," Christopher Jakim realized.

In all, Jakim and agents Philip Bernal, Carl Rideout and William Schohn would record more than a thousand conversations in English, Vietnamese, Chinese and Spanish as they worked the case. They still shake their heads at the business acumen and ingenuity of the young, charismatic former Canon copier repairman.

At one point, Ton was able to write off a debt of $200,000 after police in the United States stopped one of his couriers en route to Canada and seized the cash he was carrying. As is standard procedure, police gave the courier a receipt. Ton showed that receipt to his Canadian supplier, who accepted Ton's explanation and wrote off the loss. Later Ton and one of his top associates, Sergio Caldera, faked a similar incident to save $600,000 earmarked for another Canadian supplier.

"They went on the Internet and copied the logo of a police department. Then they dummied up another seizure receipt," Jakim recalled. "One of the interesting things was the phony cash-seizure receipt wasn't for $600,000 but for something like $580,000." This made the seizure seem even more realistic, the agent said, because many drug dealers assume police pocket some of the cash they seize.

"Ton and Caldera split the $600,000," added Jakim, whose investigators found a copy of the phony receipt during searches after Ton, Caldera and 24 other members of the organization were arrested.

HIDDEN CASH, HIDDEN PILLS

Early on November 6, 2004, a Saturday, Jakim was scrunched down in the back seat of his car, conducting what he hoped would be the last night of surveillance on Ton's home. Parked a half-block away, the agent focused on the garage, where, he knew, Ton and Caldera were running $525,000 in bills collected that week through a machine that counted and bundled them.

Shortly after sunrise, Caldera pulled a silver Acura out of the garage. Based on wiretaps, Jakim knew that the cash was hidden behind the car's door panels and fenders and was destined for Canada to cover a previous drug buy and to "front" a shipment of ecstasy coming back down. Caldera drove to his girlfriend's apartment in Northeast Philadelphia. She then set off alone on the journey north. Diana Rivera, who owned the Acura, had made several trips for the drug ring, usually for a two percent fee. This trip was worth about $10,500 to her.

All day, the DEA listened as Caldera and Rivera, who have pleaded guilty to drug charges and are cooperating with authorities, talked on their cell phones. Investigators learned when she crossed the border, dropped the car off in Toronto, and picked it up later for her journey south. As Rivera crossed the Rainbrow Bridge at Niagara Falls, DEA agents began tailing her. At the Fort Washington exit of the Pennsylvania Turnpike, they pulled her over and quickly found the stash of pills behind the car's door panels. At $30 each, the shipment of 55,000 tablets had a street value of $1.65 million.

"It was time to shut them down," Jakim concluded.

ICE AND THE *CAP SAN LORENZO*

APRIL 27, 2008

Late last year, almost by chance, federal investigators pulled off the second-biggest heroin bust in the city's history, grabbing more than 12 pounds of Colombian white and arresting five suspects. The aborted deal, which began in a South American seaport, came undone in a South Philadelphia parking lot.

Now pending in U.S. District Court, the case offers a glimpse into the gritty, loosely organized and highly lucrative world of international drug trafficking—a world through which an estimated 20 tons of heroin and more than 500 tons of cocaine pour into the country every year.

The seized heroin, with a street value of $3.5 million, had been hidden in the shorts and boots of three hapless crewmen off the *Cap San Lorenzo*, a cargo container ship that docked November 5 at the Packer Marine Terminal. That night, the seafarers were wandering around the Home Depot/Walmart parking lot on Columbus Boulevard, trying to contact a man they knew only as Richie at a cell phone number given to them in Venezuela a month earlier by a man named Tony. As drug deals go, it was not the French Connection.

Chaotic and disjointed, it fell apart when agents with Immigration and Customs Enforcement (ICE) swooped in and arrested the crewmen and two alleged couriers who drove down from New York to rendezvous with them. In this instance, law enforcement prevailed. What no one knows is how many times, and in how many different places, such deals go undetected.

"More often than not, heroin is coming in by body," said Jeremiah A. Daley, director of the federally funded Philadelphia-Camden High Intensity Drug Trafficking Area program. "Most of the time we're dealing with swallowers or body carriers."

The crewmen, from the tiny South Pacific island nation of Kiribati (formerly the Gilbert Islands), were mules, apparently hired at random to handle what is arguably the most dangerous end of a smuggling operation.

"They were pawns of a drug trafficker," said Daley, minor players in a game that ebbs and flows through the nation's ports and along its borders, despite terrorism-heightened surveillance. Last month, the crewmen, who are cooperating with authorities, pleaded guilty to drug-trafficking charges in U.S. District Court. The New York couriers and "Richie" are awaiting trial.

Investigators believe the drug deal was set in motion by Colombians who have established a heroin pipeline to New York. From there the product is diluted, packaged and funneled into networks extending into New England, New Jersey and eastern Pennsylvania, part of what authorities estimate is a nationwide $10 billion heroin underworld.

THE DEAL IS BORN

The deal began in Puerto Cabello, Venezuela, a Caribbean seaport about 70 miles west of Caracas. The city of 190,000, with a quaint district of narrow streets and Colonial-style architecture, has been a port of call for merchant ships plying the Atlantic for three centuries.

On October 5, the Liberian-registered *Cap San Lorenzo*, a cargo ship nearly the length of three football fields, docked there on the first leg of a voyage that would take it to six other South American ports before it headed for Philadelphia and New York. Its ever-changing cargo would include tens of thousands of metric tons of clothes, shoes, food and fruit—products loaded at one port and delivered to another. In Puerto Cabello, the *Cap San Lorenzo* also took on cargo that did not show on the ship's manifest.

Crewmen Bakaie Tatonga, 26, and Thomas Teweia, 37, have provided authorities with an account of how the operation was set in motion. Their story is detailed in court documents, affidavits and ICE reports obtained by *The Inquirer*. With the ship taking on cargo, Tatonga said, a man approached him and asked if he wanted to make some money. A few minutes later, at a motel, the man Tatonga knew only as Tony gave him a pair of boots and form-fitting athletic shorts in which drugs were hidden. If Tatonga delivered the boots and shorts to a source in the United States, Tony said, he would be paid $20,000. For a crewman making about $1200 a month, the offer amounted to more than a year's salary.

Tatonga agreed to the deal and took Teweia that day to a second meeting, where Tony gave the crewmen two more pairs of Spandex-like shorts with plastic packets sewn into them. He also gave Tatonga a cell phone number to call when the *Cap San Lorenzo* docked in Philadelphia. Ask for Richie, Tony said.

Tony decided the transfer would occur in Philadelphia, not New York, after Tatonga told him the crew would have more downtime there. Tatonga hid the boots and shorts among some cables in a passageway near the engine room during the month the *Cap San Lorenzo* sailed the Atlantic, making stops in Argentina, Uruguay and Brazil. On the voyage, crewman Taanioto Barao, 47, agreed to wear the third pair of drug-laden shorts off the ship.

"A HOME RUN"

On November 5, Immigration and Customs Enforcement agents set up what they described as a routine surveillance of the *Cap San Lorenzo*—the kind of job that, given resources and time, they conduct whenever a ship arrives from a South American source point.

"Usually, nothing happens," said Brian A. Michael, an ICE investigations unit supervisor. "This time we hit a home run," he said. (In fact, the 12-plus pounds was the second largest heroin seizure in Philadelphia history. In 1990, Amtrak authorities confiscated 17 pounds from a drug courier arrested on a train stopped at 30th Street Station.)

About a dozen agents from ICE and Customs and Border Protection took part in the surveillance of the *Cap San Lorenzo* that afternoon and night, with teams of agents following different groups of crewmen off the ship. The seamen did what most on shore leave do: They went to stores and restaurants. But Tatonga, Teweia and Barao didn't fit the pattern. The seamen, arriving by taxi at the Walmart, wandered around the parking lot. Tatonga, with a cell phone to his ear, was approached by a woman also talking on a cell phone. Agents watched as she signaled him to follow her into a red Mazda SUV with New York tags and a man at the wheel. Agents, now dispersed around the shopping plaza, watched as the two other crewmen joined Tatonga in the backseat.

SPRINGING THE TRAP

Angel Gonzalez, 45, and his wife, Angela Estrada, 44, had driven the red Mazda from New York City that afternoon. They'd had lunch at a McDonald's before making their way to the plaza on Columbus Boulevard, where Estrada did some shopping. Then they waited for the call from Richie in New York that connected them with the crewmen.

With the three seamen in the back seat, the deal was apparently about to go down. But then Estrada spotted an agent eyeing the Mazda. Her husband quickly ordered the three crewmen out, telling them he'd meet them later at the Home Depot. He then drove across Columbus Boulevard and went into a Dunkin' Donuts. The seamen headed for Rocco's Italian Sausage & Philly Cheesesteaks, located near the entrance to the Home Depot. With more than three million dollars in heroin hidden under their baggy jeans, they ordered sandwiches, sat down at a picnic table and began to eat.

That was when agents closed in. After just a few questions, the crewmen admitted they were carrying drugs. Simultaneously, ICE agents approached Gonzalez coming out of the Dunkin' Donuts. Asked why he was in Philadelphia, he said he had come down "to try a cheesesteak." But after a search turned up $12,400 in cash hidden behind the lining of his wife's purse, the couple was taken into custody. In less than an hour, all five were being questioned at ICE headquarters in the historic U.S. Custom House at 2nd and Chestnut Streets. The crewmen agreed to cooperate, and with investigators taping the conversation, Tatonga called Richie.

"How are you doing?" Richie asked, apparently aware of a problem. "What happened?" Tatonga said he was still waiting to make the transfer.

"They're scared," Richie said. "I don't know what they're doing." Tatonga offered to meet the couriers at midnight.

"Let me see. Let me see," Richie said. "Oh, my God, I don't know what can I do, man. Let me call you back."

Moments later, agents had Gonzalez listen to a tape of that conversation. He identified Richie as his brother-in-law, Ricardo Estrada, 40, a Colombian with suspected drug ties living in Queens. Gonzalez then agreed to call his brother-in-law using his wife's cell phone and to allow authorities to record the conversation.

Between 11:39 p.m. on November 5 and 12:49 a.m. on November 6, the men had four conversations. Each was recorded, but what was said remains sealed in court documents. Authorities now allege that Ricardo Estrada sent his sister and brother-in-law to Philadelphia to complete the heroin deal that a Colombian associate had set up in Venezuela. Ricardo Estrada already was known to ICE agents in New York. He had been questioned in October in an investigation into the electronic transfers of tens of thousands of dollars in suspected drug profits to Colombia.

On November 7, Estrada was arrested and brought to Philadelphia, where he was charged with conspiracy to distribute more than 12 pounds of heroin. He faces a possible life sentence. He, his sister and Gonzalez are being held without bail. No trial date has been set. The three crewmen are to be sentenced July 1. They face 10 years to life, but they hope their cooperation will result in less time.

YET ANOTHER ARREST

As ICE agents were sorting out the Estrada case on the night of November 5, officers with Customs and Border Protection continued the surveillance of the *Cap San Lorenzo*. At 9:36 p.m., they stopped Siila Mauteti, another crewman from Kiribati, as he walked off the gangway at the Packer Marine Terminal. Mauteti, 36, "appeared nervous," according to the CBP officers, who noticed "unusual bulges" under his pants. Patting him down, they discovered four packets of a white powder duct-taped to his thighs and ankles. It field-tested positive for heroin—nearly a pound.

Mauteti was arrested; court documents indicate he is working out a plea agreement. To date, no details are available about the source of his heroin or its destination. Agents say Mauteti had a slip of paper with two phone numbers, one with an area code in Houston, the other with an area code in New York.

Less than two hours after the arrests on Columbus Boulevard and again almost by chance, authorities had uncovered a second heroin smuggling operation on the docks in South Philadelphia.

KINGPINS IN SUBURBIA

JULY 7, 2008

They were living the American dream. A lavish home in the suburbs. Fine clothes and jewelry. Expensive cars. All financed, if federal investigators are correct, with narco dollars. The description was applied most recently to the lifestyle of Vicente and Chantal Esteves, a young couple arrested on charges of running an international cocaine distribution network from their home in Monmouth County, New Jersey. But it could apply to a number of convicted or suspected drug kingpins whose cases have surfaced in the last two years.

They live in comfortable, upper-middle-class communities where BMWs are commonplace, swimming pools dot many backyards, and the school system is top-notch. And they accumulate the kind of luxury items—authorities found nearly 100 Rolex watches and 100 pairs of Prada shoes in the Esteves residence—that separate the really wealthy from the merely well-to-do.

"It was an enterprise concealed in suburbia," said agent Douglas S. Collier, spokesman for the Drug Enforcement Administration's Newark office that worked the Esteves case. "They had so much money they didn't know what to do with it."

While several neighbors, who would only speak anonymously, said last week that they wondered about the Esteves' ostentatious lifestyle, narcotics investigators say it fits a pattern. Drug kingpins move to the suburbs for the same reasons as anyone else: for comfort and security. And, like other goal-oriented entrepreneurs, many flaunt their success.

"It's about the money and living the lavish lifestyle," said FBI agent John M. Cosenza, who supervises a drug task force out of Philadelphia. "We're seeing more and more moves out to the suburbs."

"They move to an affluent community because they want a nice home and better schools for their children," said Jeremiah A. Daley, executive director of the Philadelphia-Camden office of the federally funded High Intensity Drug Trafficking Area (HIDTA) program.

Another factor, he said, is safety. Living in the suburbs usually removes a kingpin—and his family—from the violent world of drug dealing and competitors who often use guns to settle disputes. "They move away from the field of fire, so to speak," Daley said.

Vicente Esteves, 35, and his wife, Chantal, 30, were living in a spacious new house on Taylors Mills Road in Manalapan when they were arrested. Gerald McAleer, who heads the DEA's New Jersey office, compared the 5,000-square-foot residence (with its dance floor and DJ booth, weight room, game room and home theater with stadium seating) to "something out of the movie *Scarface*."

Alton "Ace Capone" Coles, convicted this year of using his Southwest Philadelphia hip-hop record company as a front for a $25 million crack cocaine operation, was arrested shortly after moving into a $500,000 home he had built outside Mullica Hill in Gloucester County. In the garage was his $250,000 Bentley.

Ricardo McKendrick Jr., part of an alleged father-and-son team that has been described as a major source of cocaine to Philadelphia drug dealers, lives in an upper-middle-class development in Woodstown, Salem County. The night of his arrest, police found nearly a million dollars in cash in the trunk of his Mercedes, parked in the driveway. The home is on Rockwell Lane between Kingsberry and Queensberry Lanes, around the corner from the posh Town and Country Golf Club, where an annual membership is $1,750.

"It's a long way from 25th and Federal," said Daley, referring to the South Philadelphia neighborhood where McKendrick's father lives in a rowhouse and where, that same night, authorities found 274 kilograms of cocaine. The drugs, in brick form and ready for distribution, had a street value of about $28 million, police said. The McKendricks, arrested on April 1, are awaiting trial.

Benjamin Ton, who pleaded guilty last year to heading a $50 million marijuana and ecstasy distribution network tied to Canadian-based Vietnamese drug dealers, was living in a spacious home in the Cobblestone Farms section of Sicklerville, Camden County, when he was arrested three years ago. Outside were a Corvette, a BMW and a Lexus. Not bad for a 30-year-old who, two years earlier, lived in blue-collar Folcroft, Pennsylvania and worked as a copy-machine repairman.

"There has been a perception in the past that law enforcement wasn't looking out there," Daley said of the rationale of suspected drug dealers for moving to the suburbs, and even to some exurbs. But case after case developed by HIDTA investigations, he added, has led authorities to enclaves in Chester and Delaware Counties, in South Jersey and in New Castle County, Delaware.

Alton Coles, the Southwest Philadelphia kingpin, lived in a posh townhouse in Newark, Delaware before relocating to South Jersey. Convicted with five associates in March, he faces a potential life sentence. A codefendant, girlfriend Asya Richardson, lived with him in Gloucester

County at the time of their arrests. They moved there 10 days before the DEA swooped in.

Richardson, 28, faces a possible 10-year sentence on money-laundering charges. According to evidence introduced during the trial, she was a relatively minor player in the drug ring. On wiretapped conversations that were part of the investigation, Richardson was repeatedly heard discussing plans for the house that was being built, the draperies she wanted to install, and the shrubbery she hoped to plant.

Wiretaps also figure to be a part of the Esteves case, now before a grand jury. Peter Warshaw, first assistant Monmouth County prosecutor, declined to comment on the investigation. At a news conference about the arrests, authorities alleged that Vicente Esteves was leader of a smuggling operation that imported more than a ton of cocaine a month from Mexico and Colombia. They charged that the operation generated about a million dollars a week for the organization, cash that Esteves turned into his version of the good life.

His home, built on a corner lot in an upper-middle-class neighborhood, is assessed at about $1.7 million. Its market value may be millions more. When police raided the residence they seized over a million dollars' worth of jewelry, including the cache of Rolex watches, stored in one of the many walk-in closets. In another closet, authorities found Chantal Esteves' Prada shoes, many with photos taped to the boxes, presumably so that she could keep track of her footwear.

There were a dozen plasma TVs in the two-story home, a pool and cabana, and patio furniture that still had thousand-dollar price tags attached. The neatly groomed grounds were lined with arborvitae trees that provided a measure of privacy. The entrance to the property was barred by an eight-foot-high iron gate and a plaque that warned "Entire Site Protected by Video Surveillance."

"They were a young couple, and I said to my wife, 'How are they making it?'" said one of several neighbors who asked to remain anonymous. "People get greedy and don't know what to do with their money," he said as he stood in front of his ranch-style home down the block from the Esteves residence. "But it catches up with you. . . . You don't put a house like that on the corner so that everybody can look at you."

Across Taylors Mills Road at the Carchesio Farms nursery, a clerk who also didn't want to give her name said the arrests have been the talk of the town. The clerk said she always wondered about the couple.

"There was something funky," she said. "They planted trees at the wrong time of the year, and when they died, they just planted more. It was like they couldn't care less. They put in these expensive pavers all over the property, walkways that led nowhere. What was that about?"

And, finally, she added, there were the linens. After the arrest, customers said that Chantal Esteves had a running tab at a local, high-end linen shop where she spent about $6,000 a month on items she had delivered.

"How many freakin' sets of towels do you need?" the clerk wondered.

A FAMILY AFFAIR

JANUARY 26, 2009

They were known in law enforcement circles as "suppliers to the suppliers," father-and-son narcotics traffickers who sold cocaine in bulk to big-time drug dealers in Philadelphia and its suburbs. In the spring, Ricardo McKendrick, 56, and Ricardo Jr., 36, were arrested in one of the biggest drug raids in Philadelphia history. On April 2, authorities found 274 kilograms of cocaine—more than 600 pounds—stashed in the elder McKendrick's South Philadelphia rowhouse. They also uncovered more than a million dollars in cash, most of it in the trunk of a Mercedes-Benz parked in the garage of the younger McKendrick's house in Woodstown, New Jersey. Authorities touted the bust as a major blow to the city's multi-million-dollar narcotics trade.

"We are taking the city back" from drug dealers who bring "death and destruction to our streets," Mayor Michael Nutter said the next day at a news conference attended by Police Commissioner Charles H. Ramsey and then-U.S. Attorney Patrick L. Meehan.

Last month, with little fanfare and no media attention, the McKendricks entered guilty pleas in the case. Potentially more significant, it appears that at least one of them could be cooperating with law enforcement, a development that could lead to several other cases.

"They know everybody," said a detective who asked not to be identified because of his role in continuing investigations. "It would be a major break."

If either McKendrick has flipped, investigators will have access to inside information about the movers and shakers who populate Philadelphia's highly secretive and violent drug underworld.

"It could be monumental," noted Sean Patrick Griffin, a professor at Pennsylvania State University and a former Philadelphia police officer who has written two books on black organized crime in the city. "They know the landscape. They've known it for decades." Griffin's book, *Black Brothers Inc.*, places the elder McKendrick in the hierarchy of the Philadelphia Black Mafia in the 1970s. He was a "narcotics entrepreneur, a businessman-drug dealer," Griffin added.

Authorities have described the McKendricks as expediters, highly compensated brokers who bought from out-of-town suppliers in bulk and sold to local distributors who funneled drugs to neighborhood dealers and street-level traffickers.

"The sheer amount of drugs and money involved in this case is truly staggering," a federal prosecutor wrote in a pretrial document that described the McKendricks as part of a "large-scale drug distribution ring."

Father and son are scheduled to be sentenced by U.S. District Court Judge Gene E.K. Pratter in March. They have been held without bail since their arrests. The elder McKendrick has pleaded guilty to a drug conspiracy charge. He faces 10 years under terms of a plea agreement filed in federal court on December 10. Originally he was looking at a mandatory life sentence. McKendrick Jr.—known as Li'l Rick—entered a guilty plea on December 3, but documents relating to his plea agreement are filed under seal and unavailable for public examination.

Though it is not the only reason, records often are sealed in cases involving individuals who are cooperating with authorities. The move is intended to protect them from retribution and to keep investigations that come from information they provide secret.

Contacted last week, Assistant U.S. Attorney Leo Tsao, the prosecutor in the case, declined to comment on Ricardo Jr.'s status and would not respond to questions about why parts of his court record had been sealed. The younger McKendrick's lawyer, Brian McMonagle, stated that he could not talk about the case. Arnold Joseph, who represents the elder McKendrick, said his client was not cooperating. Joseph called the potential 10-year sentence a fair deal, but would not comment on whether the father had benefited from any arrangement worked out by his son.

Ricardo McKendrick Sr. has a string of narcotics arrests dating to the 1970s. Among other things, sources say, he was a suspect in the murder of a Black Mafia member who was decapitated. The younger McKendrick was jailed in 1995 on assault and weapons charges and served about a year in prison. He has no other arrests.

In a memo filed during a detention hearing in April, Tsao said the 274 kilograms of cocaine found in the elder McKendrick's rowhouse had a street value of roughly $28 million. It was "one of the biggest drug seizures in the history of the city," he noted.

"The sheer quantity of the drugs involved in this case confirms that the defendant is a major drug supplier," Tsao wrote in separate memos seeking to bar each defendant from obtaining bail. Authorities have been tight-lipped about the case ever since.

The McKendricks were arrested after being targeted by the FBI and the Philadelphia Police Department's Narcotics Bureau. Tipped by an informant that a major shipment of cocaine was due at the elder McKendrick's rowhouse at 2606 Federal Street in the city's Grays Ferry section, investigators set up surveillance. After observing Ricardo Jr. engage in what appeared to be two drug transactions at the home on the night of April 1, they moved in, according to an affidavit submitted by Detective Andrew J. Callaghan, an investigator with the FBI's Violent Gang and Drug Task Force, which worked the case.

According to the affidavit, Ricardo Jr. was followed as he drove away and was stopped after briefly trying to elude police. Investigators found $54,971 in plastic bags in his Ford 500. A police dog trained to sniff out narcotics had a positive reaction to the front doors and trunk of the car, the document states. Police then obtained a search warrant for the house on Federal Street. At 1:15 a.m., as the elder McKendrick walked toward his door, authorities closed in. In addition to the cocaine, police found a loaded .38 caliber handgun, $6,028 in cash, packing materials, and a pressing machine used for making kilogram "bricks" of cocaine. Most of the cocaine was stored in seven 55-gallon drums, police said. There were also several bricks.

Federal agents then obtained a search warrant for the Salem County house and Mercedes-Benz of the younger McKendrick. Authorities found $982,144 in duffle bags in the trunk of the car, which was parked in the garage of a two-story house on Rockwell Lane in Woodstown. McKendrick lived there with his wife, Dawn Edge McKendrick, a lawyer with the U.S. Equal Employment Opportunity Commission in Philadelphia. Investigators discovered an additional $9,243 in the house, which is in an upscale neighborhood around the corner from a golf course and just a few blocks from Woodstown High School. McKendrick and his wife bought the property, valued at about $400,000, in 2002, shortly after it was built. At the time of his arrest, McKendrick owned a newsstand at 54th Street and City Avenue, near St. Joseph's University, according to court documents. He held a license to operate a Pennsylvania State Lottery machine at the site.

"They were quiet, never said much," a Rockwell Lane neighbor commented last week. Like others on the block, he asked not to be identified because of the nature of the case. "They would wave and say hi, but they never socialized with anyone. No one ever knew what he did for a living," he said. "I guess now we know why."

Mayor Nutter, according to reports from the news conference when the McKendricks were charged, said the case underscored the deadly nature of their business: "It's about drugs, it's about turf, it's about money."

ROGUE COP

MARCH 23, 2009

He drove a Dodge Intrepid tricked out like a police narcotics unit undercover car, with tinted windows, lights, sirens, a police radio console, and a screen that separated the front and back seats. He had his gun. And, more important, he had his badge. Those, federal prosecutors say, were the tools of the trade for rogue Philadelphia cop Malik Snell as he targeted suspected narcotics dealers, pulled them over, and stole their cash or their drugs. Snell, who has pleaded not guilty to charges of conspiracy, robbery and witness retaliation, is to go on trial today in U.S. District Court. In October, a trial on some of the charges ended with a hung jury.

An 11-year veteran of the Philadelphia Police Department who was assigned to the 18th District in West Philadelphia, Snell, 36, was fired last year after his arrest in a Pottstown home invasion case. Two superseding federal indictments have expanded the charges against him. Among other things, he is now accused of robbing one of the biggest drug kingpins in South Philadelphia and later threatening to kill him because he was cooperating. The kingpin, Ricardo McKendrick Jr., is expected to be called as a witness for the prosecution.

McKendrick, according to motions filed in the case, has alleged that he was stopped by Snell on December 14, 2007, near Water and Dickinson Streets in South Philadelphia. Driving the Dodge Intrepid, Snell flashed the car's lights and signaled for McKendrick, who was driving a minivan, to pull over. Federal prosecutors allege that Snell "removed him from the [minivan] and placed him in handcuffs. . . . Snell then searched the [minivan] and took a diaper bag from the back of the van which contained $40,000 in drug proceeds. He put the diaper bag in the trunk of the Intrepid and left [McKendrick] handcuffed and unable to leave," according to a motion filed by Assistant U.S. Attorneys Kathy A. Stark and Leo R. Tsao, the prosecutors in the case.

Snell was arrested three days later in connection with an unrelated home invasion in Pottstown. Two men, including his brother-in-law, were charged with breaking into a house where they believed drug money was stashed. Authorities allege that Snell drove the men to Pottstown and waited outside during the break-in. He and his brother-in-law were arrested after a high-speed police chase just outside the Montgomery County borough.

Both the brother-in-law, Tyree Aimes, and a second defendant pleaded guilty before trial. Snell's trial ended with a hung jury. Federal prosecutors, apparently using information supplied by McKendrick and others, have since expanded the charges against Snell. He is being held without bail in the Federal Detention Center on Arch Street.

In the new trial, prosecutors hope to use Aimes' account of other incidents to undermine Snell's assertion that he was an unwitting accomplice, unaware that a robbery was planned on the night of the home invasion. Snell's attorney, John McMahon of Norristown, has declined to comment about specifics of the case. He is expected to attack the credibility of several government witnesses who come from the drug underworld.

According to one prosecution document, Aimes has talked about other encounters in which, he says, Snell targeted drug dealers. Aimes has said that before the Pottstown home invasion, Snell used him to stake out two houses in Philadelphia where narcotics trafficking was allegedly taking place.

After showing Aimes the Intrepid, which Snell allegedly said came from "a friend in the narcotics unit," Snell told him, "I have a job to do" at one of the suspected drug houses. One house was off the corner of D Street and Allegheny Avenue, and the other was on Callowhill Street between 63rd and 64th Streets, according to documents.

Aimes said Snell told him the house on Callowhill was frequently used by a Jamaican marijuana dealer. Aimes said he was watching when Snell, driving the Intrepid, pulled over a woman who had come from the house carrying a bag. The woman was driving a Chevy Malibu, he said.

"Snell pulled the Intrepid out behind her, activated the police lights and pulled the Malibu over," according to a prosecution motion that outlines Aimes' account. About two hours later, Snell came to Aimes' home and gave him a pound of marijuana. "He told him he had gotten 10 pounds of weed from the car stop."

Aimes told authorities that he staked out the house off Allegheny Avenue several times for Snell, but that nothing occurred there. About the same time, Aimes said, he learned about drug money being stashed in a house in Pottstown and told Snell he "had a job" there. Snell, he claimed, agreed to participate.

The Callowhill Street incident is not part of the current indictment, but prosecutors hope to use testimony about it to establish a pattern of criminal activity by Snell. The charges in the case include the Pottstown home invasion, the robbery of $40,000 from McKendrick, and allegations that Snell later threatened to kill McKendrick and another suspected witness.

McKendrick's father, Ricardo Sr., is a former member of the Black Mafia and a longtime Philadelphia drug trafficker, according to investigators who have described the duo as "suppliers to the suppliers" and key players in the Philadelphia drug underworld. The McKendricks were arrested in April after members of an FBI-Philadelphia Police Department Violent Gang and Drug Task Force raided their South Philadelphia rowhouse.

Authorities found more than 600 pounds of cocaine valued at more than $28 million in the house in Grays Ferry. It was one of the biggest drug seizures in city history. The FBI also found nearly a million dollars in cash in the trunk of the younger McKendrick's Mercedes, which was parked in the garage of his South Jersey home.

Both McKendricks entered guilty pleas to drug charges in December. Most of the documents in the younger McKendrick's court file relating to his plea have been placed under seal. McKendrick's decision to cooperate could have ramifications far beyond the current case against Snell. McKendrick's potential debut as a government witness has created a stir in both law enforcement and underworld circles. Snell allegedly made the threat to "inflict bodily harm" on McKendrick on January 30, shortly after news accounts raised the possibility that he might be cooperating.

THE FIREBOMB MURDERS

APRIL 9, 2009

Kaboni Savage, described by a federal prosecutor as the leader of "perhaps the most violent drug gang ever seen in the city of Philadelphia," was charged in a sweeping racketeering indictment yesterday that listed 12 murders, including a North Philadelphia firebombing in which six people, four of them children, were killed. Savage, a onetime professional boxer serving a 30-year sentence for drug trafficking, could be sentenced to death if convicted of the most serious charges. His court-appointed attorney, Christopher Warren, said yesterday that his client denied the allegations, which have been swirling around him since his trial in 2005. Three top associates also named in the 26-count indictment face possible death sentences if convicted.

The indictment alleges that Savage, from prison, ordered two of those associates, Lamont Lewis and Robert Merritt, to firebomb the home of Marcella Coleman in the 3200 block of North 6th Street in October 2004. At the time, her son, Eugene, an associate of Savage's in the drug business, was cooperating with authorities. Early on October 9, 2004, authorities allege, Lewis and Merritt carried out the attack. The fire killed Marcella Coleman, 54; her niece Tameka Nash, 34; Nash's daughter, Khadijah, 10; Eugene Coleman's 15-month-old son, Damir Jenkins; Marcella Coleman's grandson, Tajh Porchea, 12; and a family friend, Sean Rodriguez, 15.

U.S. Attorney Laurie Magid, detailing the charges in the case yesterday, quoted from secretly recorded conversations in which Savage allegedly threatened to kill relatives of those who might testify against him and joked about the firebombing.

"I have dreams about killing their kids . . . cutting their heads off," Magid quoted Savage as saying on one tape. On another, he said those attending the funerals of the firebombing victims should bring "barbecue sauce." The firebombing is considered one of the most vicious examples of witness retaliation in the city's history.

In all, the indictment alleges that 12 murders were carried out as part of the Kaboni Savage organization's drug-trafficking operation. The victims allegedly included rival drug dealers, potential cooperating witnesses and the family members of witnesses. Magid described Savage's group as one of the most violent ever seen in the city during a news conference called to announce the charges.

"These were not just drug dealers selling drugs, they were ruthless murderers," she said.

Janice Fedarcyk, FBI special agent-in-charge of the Philadelphia office, said the Savage organization had reached a "new level of depravity" in the drug underworld. Deputy Police Commissioner Richard Ross, a former homicide captain who worked the firebombing investigation, called the Savage organization "pure evil."

Savage has been the target of a multi-pronged investigation that began more than six years ago and that focused both on his alleged cocaine trafficking and his violence. Among other things, he is charged with the murder of North Philadelphia boxer Tybius Flowers, 32, who was killed on March 1, 2004, days before he was to testify against Savage in a Common Pleas Court murder trial. The district attorney's case collapsed once Flowers was unable to take the stand. Savage was found not guilty. The Flowers murder is one of several alleged acts of witness retaliation listed in the indictment.

Savage, Lewis, 32, Merritt, 28, and Steven Northington, 37, were named in the indictment returned yesterday. All four are in federal custody, either serving time for or awaiting trial on drug-trafficking charges or weapons offenses. Savage is charged in 11 of the murders listed in the indictment. Lewis faces seven counts of murder. Merritt was charged with six counts and Northington with two. All face related conspiracy, racketeering, weapons and witness retaliation charges.

David Troyer, one of the prosecutors, said evidence developed during and after Savage's trial in 2005 contributed to the new indictment. Among other things, authorities used conversations picked up by a listening device hidden in Savage's prison cell to gather information about his alleged plans to retaliate against witnesses and their families.

Savage took the stand in his own defense during his 2005 trial. He denied that he was a major cocaine dealer, as prosecutors alleged, but admitted that he often would rant about those who cooperated against him. He was, he said, just venting his anger and frustration, and did not intend to follow up on those threats. Savage was convicted of drug-trafficking, money-laundering and witness intimidation charges during that trial and was sentenced to 30 years in prison. At his sentencing hearing, Mark Ehlers, the federal prosecutor in the case, said he had never seen a defendant "as vicious, vindictive and hateful as Kaboni Savage."

Defense attorney Christopher Warren stated yesterday that the current charges were without foundation and were built around the tainted testimony of thus-far-unnamed cooperating witnesses. Warren said that he believed one of the co-defendants in the case had struck a deal with prosecutors and that some of the charges had been included in the earlier trial.

"I think there are some serious double-jeopardy issues here," he added. "Some of the allegations were in the last trial and are being trotted out again."

Troyer, the Assistant U.S. Attorney who is handling the case, said there had been no plea agreements. He said the investigation was continuing, but both he and Laurie Magid declined to comment further. Troyer estimated that it could be more than a year before the case comes to trial.

NO WITNESS, NO CRIME

MAY 18, 2009

The logic was irrefutable, a simple but chilling explanation of how to undermine the justice system.

"Without the witnesses, you don't have no case," Philadelphia drug kingpin Kaboni Savage said in a prison conversation secretly recorded by the FBI. "No witness, no crime."

Savage, who is accused of ordering the deaths of at least seven people in a pattern of witness intimidation designed to protect his multimillion-dollar cocaine operation, is to be arraigned in U.S. District Court this week on murder, drug-dealing and conspiracy charges. Built in part on nearly 100 conversations recorded on a listening device hidden in his prison cell at the Federal Detention Center on Arch Street, the pending prosecution could be billed as "Kaboni Savage in His Own Words."

The conversations were taped five years ago while Savage was awaiting trial on drug-trafficking charges. Convicted in 2005, he is serving a 30-year sentence in a maximum security prison in Florence, Colorado, but will be brought back to Philadelphia to face the new charges. This time, the stakes are even higher. This time, the indictment includes 12 murders. This time, Savage and three co-defendants face possible death sentences. As a result, his words carry even more import.

"Their kids got to pay for making my kids cry," he said on one tape, referring to his desire to harm not only the witnesses lining up against him but also their children. "I want to smack one of their four-year-old sons in the head with a bat."

"He's got a daughter down my way," he said while talking about another cooperator. "I gonna blow her little head off. She like five."

In another conversation, he lashed out at the captain of the prison guards, promising: "He gonna die a miserable death, and I hope I'm there. . . . I'm gonna torture his ass. I'm gonna set him on fire. Alive. . . . Watch him jump around like James fuckin' Brown." And in another tape, Savage vowed never to stop pursuing those he referred to as "rats." "The fight don't stop till the casket drop," he said.

Savage's words took on added irony last week when authorities disclosed that his nine-year-old daughter, Ciara, was killed in York, Pennsylvania, the innocent victim of a gang-related shooting. She was shot in the back while playing with friends on a street where a gang member allegedly opened fire on rivals.

Savage, 34, was once a promising junior welterweight boxer from North Philadelphia. But, authorities say, he decided he could make a better living dealing cocaine. Described by acting U.S. Attorney Laurie Magid as the leader of "perhaps the most violent drug gang ever seen in the city of Philadelphia," he was charged last month in a 26-count indictment that picks up where his previous prosecution left off.

Authorities allege that he used violence and intimidation to control the sale of cocaine on several North Philadelphia drug corners and "ordered murders of rival . . . dealers, people he deemed to be disloyal . . . witnesses, potential witnesses and family members of witnesses." The most horrendous of the charges centers on an October 2004 firebombing that killed six people, including four children. Savage was later heard on tape joking about the victims and their dog.

Transcripts of some of the tapes have already been made public. Others have been obtained by *The Inquirer*. Snippets of some conversations are also sprinkled through the 65-page indictment against Savage, Lamont Lewis, Robert Merritt and Steven Northington.

Savage is accused of ordering or taking part in 11 of the 12 murders listed in the indictment. Deputy Police Commissioner Richard Ross described him as "pure evil" at a news conference last month announcing the indictment. The Savage tapes seem to support that assessment.

"I ain't got no regrets for nothing I did," Savage said at one point on the tapes while boasting about his wealth, power and ability to buy whatever he wanted and go wherever he desired. Recognizing that there were only two ways out of the drug underworld for real players—"either you dead or in jail"—Savage said he wouldn't change anything.

"You accept what you do, and you know . . . don't nobody get no . . . free ride. . . . But I'd do it all over again. . . . I ain't complaining about my lifestyle."

Savage bragged that the "fruits of my labor" resulted in houses for his mother and wife and paid for his wife's and his sister's educations. But on another tape, he offered a less than flattering description of women, whom he referred to as "bitches." Yet he also said that women should all be licensed to carry guns.

"All my bitches, my little sister got a license to carry," he said. "My wife go and get hers in a minute. You gonna [be] with me, bitch . . . you gotta be my holster. You ain't have to worry about no shooting, babe. I'm gonna grab it and do what I gotta do, but . . . you gotta be my holster."

Savage is expected to plead not guilty at a hearing Friday. His lawyer, Christopher Warren, has argued that the new case is replete with double-jeopardy issues because so much of it echoes the 2005 prosecution. The tapes are one example. Many were played at the last trial to support witness intimidation charges. There were no murder charges in that prosecution. Savage, who testified, did not deny the statements. But he said that they had been a product of his anger and frustration, that he had been venting and never intended to carry anything further. Authorities say otherwise.

The current indictment alleges that while in prison awaiting trial in 2004, Savage ordered two of his co-defendants, Lamont Lewis and Robert Merritt, to firebomb the home of Eugene Coleman's mother. Coleman, a former associate and an admitted drug dealer, was cooperating with federal authorities and listed as a witness in the then-pending drug case. Early on October 9, 2004, Marcella Coleman's house in the 3200 block of North 6th Street was set on fire. She and five others, including four children ages 15 months to 15 years, died. The 15-month-old, Damir Jenkins, was Eugene Coleman's son. A month later, on November 4, the prison cell listening device picked up Savage joking about the funeral for the victims and the fact that Coleman had been allowed to attend the service.

"They shoulda, you know . . . took him . . . got him some barbecue sauce and poured it on them," Savage said as he and two other inmates laughed. "Pour it on them burnt bitches," he said later, adding that he did not feel sorry for the death of the infant. "Shoulda died," he said. "Pop a rat. He woulda been a mouse." The tape then recorded more laughter as Savage joked about the family dog, a pit bull, that also was killed.

"That pit bull that was in there, that was a rat in some pit bull's clothing."

Eugene Coleman testified against Savage in the 2005 drug case, but the firebombing was not mentioned to the jury. Coleman is expected to testify again when Savage, Lewis, Merritt and Northington go on trial, probably next year.

The current indictment also alleges that Savage ordered the March 1, 2004 murder of Tybius "Tib" Flowers, a North Philadelphia boxer who was scheduled to testify against Savage in a murder trial in Common Pleas Court. He was gunned down days before the trial started. Without his testimony, the district attorney's case fell apart. Savage was found not guilty.

"No witness, no crime."

Rap music impresario and cocaine dealer Alton "Ace Capone" Coles

THE TAKEDOWN OF "ACE CAPONE"

His name was Alton Coles but he called himself "Ace Capone." And of all the drug dealers to appear on the scene in the Philadelphia area in the past few years, he best epitomized the narcotics underworld at the start of the 21st century. It was an underworld of form over substance, an underworld of flash and glitter, an underworld where violence was a calling card rather than a business tool of last resort.

Coles grew up in the drug culture of Darby, a small town just outside of Philadelphia. Family members were low-level street-corner hustlers, according to cops who worked the streets and who watched him come of age. He was a barber by trade, but had big ideas and even bigger plans.

By the time Coles showed up on the radar of federal drug investigators, he had stopped cutting hair and had begun cutting records. DVDs and CDs, actually. He was a music company impresario. He had his own label, Takedown Records, that operated out of Southwest Philadelphia. Coles drove around the 'hood in a blue Bentley that had once belonged to a big New York City record company honcho. He wore lots of bling and flashed lots of cash. Audacious doesn't begin to describe him.

The stories that follow were built around a long-term investigation by the Bureau of Alcohol, Tobacco, Firearms and Explosives (ATF), the lead agency in the case against Alton Coles. The investigation stretched over two years and included hundreds of hours of wiretaps.

Coles loved to talk on the phone. He had three cell phones and sometimes had them all in play at once. Using his record company as a front, he became one of the biggest suppliers of cocaine and crack in the city. Over a six-year period, investigators estimated that Coles generated $25 million while pouring a ton of cocaine and a half-ton of crack onto the city's streets. And all the while he was promoting his hip hop record company, touting new rap artists, staging parties for entertainment and sports celebrities, and rubbing elbows with the mayor, the police commissioner and the district attorney in an anti-drug campaign that targeted the same neighborhoods that were the base of his narcotics trafficking.

With each new twist and turn in a flamboyant lifestyle, Coles seemed to thumb his nose at the investigators who were tracking him. The move that said it all, however, was his decision to make a DVD built around the rap music of his Takedown Records performers. The story line looked strangely familiar to the ATF agents working the case. It was the tale of a young drug kingpin who used fear, violence and intimidation to take over the crack distribution in Southwest Philadelphia.

The video was made on the same streets where Coles' drug network operated. The DVD starred Alton Coles as a drug kingpin named "Ace Capone." It was art imitating life imitating art. It was the drug underworld at the start of the 21st century.

THE HIP-HOP KINGPIN

NOVEMBER 11, 2007

It was a bold move by an ambitious, young rap mogul. At a time when authorities suspected he controlled a vast cocaine operation in Southwest Philadelphia, Alton Coles decided to shoot a video about that very world. *New Jack City: The Next Generation* would depict the violent rise of a fictional Southwest Philadelphia cocaine ring that used fear, intimidation and murder to take over the streets. Coles, under his hip-hop nickname "Ace Capone," would star in the 2003 rap music drama as a ruthless cocaine kingpin. It was, federal authorities now allege, a role the rap music impresario knew well.

"He was already living that life when he made that movie," says John Hageman, spokesman for the Philadelphia office of the Bureau of Alcohol, Tobacco, Firearms and Explosives (ATF). But it would take hundreds of hours of surveillance, thousands of wiretapped conversations, scores of undercover drug buys and the testimony of more than a dozen cooperating witnesses for police and ATF agents to make their case against Coles. Set in an underworld of drugs and guns, greed and power, their investigation offers insight into a violent street-corner culture that is ripping some Philadelphia neighborhoods apart.

In January, Coles is to go on trial in U.S. District Court in Philadelphia, charged with running one of the largest drug operations ever prosecuted in the city: a $25 million network that authorities say flooded the streets with crack and powdered cocaine.

"This gang was responsible for about 100,000 individual doses hitting the streets each week over a seven-year period," said U.S. Attorney Patrick L. Meehan.

The 197-count case, involving 22 defendants, includes charges of money laundering, weapons offenses and drug dealing. The organization, the indictment alleges, moved a ton of cocaine and a half-ton of crack onto the Philadelphia market between 1999 and 2005. Coles, who has been charged with heading the criminal enterprise, is named in 64 of those counts. He has pleaded not guilty. According to ATF agents, that enterprise was responsible for 21 shootings and seven murders, though only one shooting is listed in the indictment. Five co-defendants are set to be tried with Coles. Sixteen others either have pleaded guilty or are to be tried later. Several are believed to be cooperating.

"The government got a lot of people into a big case and created a conspiracy that don't exist," Coles said in a telephone interview from the Federal Detention Center in Philadelphia last week. "These are serious charges, but I'm not the guy that they allege me to be. . . . I'm not no boss of a street organization running a big, giant drug conspiracy." He called *New Jack City: The Next Generation* "a street movie."

"It's not a story of my life. . . . You wouldn't take Denzel Washington and indict him for being a drug dealer because he played one in *American Gangster*."

Prosecutors see it differently. By the time Coles, 33, started to make his video, federal authorities say, he had already blurred the lines between the make-believe world of gangsta rap videos and the take-no-prisoners street life of a cocaine trafficker.

RAP MOGUL ON THE RISE

Screenwriter Barry Michael Cooper—whose 1991 movie, *New Jack City*, starring Wesley Snipes, is regarded by some as *The Godfather* of urban gangster films—was charmed by Coles and his West Philadelphia sidekick, Tim Baukman, when they met in the fall of 2002. By then, Coles and Baukman, who went under the hip-hop name "Tim Gotti," had founded Take Down Records, a label that was promoting up-and-coming rappers in town.

Coles also was staging concerts, including a show billed as a "hip-hop explosion" at the Spectrum, and was hosting parties and after-concert events for a young, urban crowd. His weekly Friday night parties at the Palmer Social Club, at 6th and Spring Garden, attracted crowds of a thousand or more, with lines sometimes stretching around the block.

Coles drove around town in a $220,000 blue Bentley while taking care of business for his recording artists and setting up his promotional events. Dressed in baggy pants, an expensive team jersey and a matching cap, he usually wore a gold or silver neck chain with the diamond-encrusted initials TD—for Take Down—as big as a fist dangling at his chest. He was a regular at "stop the violence" anti-drug rallies sponsored by political and civic groups, never missing an opportunity, it seemed, to have his photo taken standing next to some top city official. So it wasn't surprising that in 2002 Barry Michael Cooper saw Alton Coles as an up-and-coming, well-connected, street-smart music industry entrepreneur.

The Harlem-born screenwriter, who now lives in Baltimore, had been introduced to the young rap mogul by Joseph M. Marrone, Coles' entertainment lawyer. Marrone and Cooper had hit on the idea of a reality TV series built around two guys from the streets who were trying to start a record label. It was the story of Coles, Baukman and Take Down Records: the rise of two young, savvy, independent record company executives. Cooper, 49, says he came away from their first meeting impressed.

"You know, there's that lyric from Jay-Z, 'Real recognizes real and you're lookin' real to me,'" Cooper said of the encounter. "They weren't extravagant guys," he said, before catching himself and laughing. "Besides the Bentley in the 'hood. But these guys didn't flaunt it like that." The car, the bling, the outfits were the trappings of their business, he said. The entertainment business.

"If it was a facade," he said, "it was a very good one. . . . One time, I came up to Philadelphia and they took me to a Bennigan's," Cooper recalled with another chuckle. "There were two Bentleys in the parking lot. [Allen] Iverson was there. And we sat there eating wings and watching a ball game."

Marrone came up with the name for the reality series: *Streets Inc.* Cooper started to shoot some video to pitch the idea to a network. Around the same time, Coles and Baukman began planning *New Jack City: The Next Generation.* Cooper had no involvement in that project, which was, in some ways, an homage to the original movie he had written. The video also was a takeoff on *State Property*, a full-length feature released early in 2002 starring Philadelphia rapper Beanie Sigel, a friend of Coles'.

The two video projects, which would move forward in 2003, offered different pictures of a street-hustling Alton Coles. In *Streets Inc.*, he was Ace Capone, a savvy, urban entrepreneur who saw hip-hop music as a way for young corner boys to get out of the 'hood. In *New Jack City: The Next Generation*, he was Ace Capone, cocaine kingpin. Police were leaning toward the second image as they began pursuing leads about Coles from a Darby Borough police officer. But in 2002, no one in law enforcement was exactly sure who Coles was or what role he might have been playing in the drug underworld. That spring, a killing outside the Philadelphia Zoo offered the first hints.

NEW IMAGE EMERGES

On the surface, it looked like a drug deal gone bad. Two brothers from New Castle, Delaware had arranged to buy a "quarter brick"—half a pound—of crack from Randall "Iran" Austin. They set the meeting for 7 p.m. on April 14, at their usual spot along 34th Street outside the fence by the zoo.

The brothers, arriving in a Buick LeSabre, brought $10,500 in cash. And a gun. Austin, driving a silver Mercedes, had eight ounces of crack. And a gun. Things quickly went awry. Either the brothers tried to steal the crack, or Austin tried to grab the cash. In the end, one brother ended up dead, shot in the back and lying in the street. The other, his body spilling out of the LeSabre, survived a bullet to the stomach. He told police that Austin had shot them. Then 26, Randall Austin was no stranger to narcotics investigators. By 2002, the West Philadelphia High School dropout had four drug convictions.

The police search led detectives to Austin's apartment just off Belmont Avenue, where they spotted the silver Mercedes parked in a garage. As police arrived, a man walking toward an Infiniti Q45 parked outside the apartment hit his car alarm—"an attempt to warn someone inside," according to an ATF document. The man, Terry "Taz" Walker, denied he lived in the apartment. But one of his keys opened the front door.

After obtaining a search warrant, police entered the unit. Inside Austin's apartment, they found seven guns, more than a pound of cocaine, and equipment to weigh, cut and package it. Walker, then 27, was questioned and released. Like Austin, he had had prior encounters with the law, including convictions for drug possession and aggravated assault. Investigators working the homicide were told by street sources that both Austin and Walker worked for Alton Coles and that Coles headed Take Down Records. Inside Walker's Infiniti, investigators found a Take Down Records jacket with his nickname, "Taz," inscribed on it. With that, a picture of Coles as a player in the drug underworld began to emerge.

EARLY ARRESTS

A 240-pounder who was known as "Fat Boy" before he took on the "Ace Capone" persona at Take Down Records, Coles says he grew up "rough"—largely abandoned by his parents and raised by an aunt and grandmother. The oldest of four brothers, he looked out for his siblings. "I was both their father and their big brother," he remembered. After getting into trouble for dealing drugs as a youth, he graduated from the Glen Mills School in 1992. Then, having learned to cut hair at an uncle's shop in Darby, he went on to open two barbershops of his own—Outline I in Chester and Outline II in West Philadelphia—before gravitating toward the music business and promotion.

"I like money," Coles admitted. "If an idea crosses my mind and it makes sense, I go with it. I got self-discipline. I'm just a go-getter."

Lt. Rick Gibney of the Darby Borough Police Department, which had arrested Coles "five or six times," suspected his real business was drug dealing.

"I always thought he was a knucklehead," said Gibney. "But then we started to hear that he had taken over West Chester, that he was the guy."

Gibney said at first he couldn't believe that Coles had attained status in the drug underworld. But then he noticed that defendants and informants, who allegedly were getting their coke from Coles' people, were refusing to talk about "the Fat Boy."

"They wouldn't roll," Gibney recalled. "They were afraid of what might happen to them."

Gibney said that he'd had several discussions with Philadelphia police and federal narcotics investigators about Coles late in 1999 and early in 2000, but that no one was ready to commit the manpower and resources to focus on his operation. Like many major investigations, the Coles case emerged from unconnected criminal incidents investigated by different law enforcement agencies.

The murder outside the zoo put Alton "Ace Capone" Coles on the radar screens of Philadelphia homicide and narcotics detectives and the ATF. As his name continued to pop up in seemingly unrelated cases, those agencies started files on the record company executive and those who appeared to be working for him.

A BUST NEAR TAMIKA'S

On January 21, 2003, Philadelphia police narcotics investigator Thomas Liciardello was watching Tamika's Lounge at 58th Street and Elmwood Avenue from an unmarked car, waiting for a drug deal to go down. The corner is the kind of Southwest Philadelphia neighborhood that would soon appear in Coles' *New Jack City* and in Barry Michael Cooper's *Streets Inc.*

Across the street from Tamika's is a shuttered day-care center. On the other corners are a used car lot, an abandoned deli and overgrown ball fields. Liciardello had an informant who had given up details about a pending coke deal. A guy named Ace and a guy named Taz were supposed to show up at Tamika's that afternoon with nine ounces of cocaine.

As Liciardello watched, a maroon Mercury sedan rolled up and Terry "Taz" Walker jumped out, he later testified. Walker looked inside Tamika's but apparently did not see the person he was expecting. He then walked back to the Mercury, reached inside his jacket, and handed the driver a white bag. Walker returned to the bar as the Mercury drove off, with a police backup team tailing it. A few blocks away, the driver, Hakiem "Unk" Johnson, then 42, was arrested. Johnson was Alton Coles' uncle.

Inside Johnson's hoodie, police found a white bag containing two clear plastic bags, each with four and a half ounces of cocaine. And on his cell phone, the record of incoming calls indicated that someone named Ace had called while Johnson was parked outside Tamika's Lounge.

A THRIVING BUSINESS

To his entertainment lawyer, Coles appeared to be on a roll in 2003. He was producing his version of *New Jack City: The Next Generation.* The gritty story of a Philadelphia drug czar opens with Ace Capone in a voiceover.

"Welcome to the streets of Philadelphia where niggas is scratchin' and survivin' to get that change. Only problem is, there ain't enough to go around. So we get it the best way we know how—the coke game. And believe me, it's a dirty ass game."

About the same time, the United Paramount Network (UPN) had put up $100,000 to fund *Streets Inc.*, the reality TV pilot about Take Down Records that Cooper was putting together. And Coles had a thriving business hosting parties and after-concert events for big-name rappers at area clubs. Local rappers, wannabes and others would flock to these parties, paying cash at the door to get in.

"Ace was good at that," said Joseph Marrone, the lawyer who worked with Coles on entertainment issues. "He was able to talk to people outside the city. He had contacts. To me, the guy was going places."

Lisa Natson, the popular radio personality known as "Golden Girl" from Power 99 FM, agrees. Natson said she worked as a consultant for Coles and Take Down Records and hosted his parties at Palmer, which by 2003 had become "the hot spot" on Friday nights. Coles had approached her during an NBA All-Star weekend event in Philadelphia in February 2002, she recalled.

"When I first met him, he already had the look of a hip-hop star. . . . But businesswise, he was really focused. He knew what he wanted to do. He knew about branding, about getting Take Down Records out there."

Natson said that Coles wanted to get into promotion. The parties at Palmer, she said, were his launching pad. Starting at 10 p.m. and going strong until 4 a.m., they were, she said, like no other event in the city.

"There's no one out there now promoting who knew the business the way Ace did," she said. It didn't hurt, she added, that celebrities like Allen Iverson and Donovan McNabb and rappers like Kanye West dropped by.

"It was a phenomenal thing," she admitted.

Like screenwriter Barry Michael Cooper, Natson said she never saw any signs of the drug world when she was around Coles. In fact, she said, Coles and Take Down Records sometimes sponsored her radio station's "Peace on the Streets" rallies, often providing artists who performed at the events.

"He was trying to help," which makes the charges he now faces difficult to comprehend. "I don't believe it," Natson said. "This was a guy who had everything going for him. He was making money . . . riding in a Bentley . . . living the life of a rock star."

Investigators knew about the parties, and about Coles' high-profile promotions. Informants told them that he was using the events to launder drug proceeds, that the cash spent to rent the club, pay for the liquor and provide security came from drug deals. It came back to Coles, they said, washed clean as profits from a legitimate business enterprise.

Philly Swain, 26, a rapper who'd appeared with Jay-Z, Beanie Sigel and Memphis Bleek at a Take Down Records concert at the Spectrum, often worked the door at Palmer. To him, Coles and Baukman seemed staunchly anti-drug.

"I was a nickel-and-dime dude for a while," Swain said recently, referring to his involvement in the drug trade. "I was in and out of jail. They told me I needed to get focused."

Swain said Coles and Baukman saw Take Down Records as the way to get Philly rap a national reputation.

"They were tired of seeing Philly messed up. . . . They wanted to show the 'hood there was a way out." That's why, Swain said, Coles attended and helped promote anti-drug rallies. In the summer of 2003, Swain said, "we were doing one every week."

Occasionally, Coles and Baukman would pose at the rallies with some of the city's top officials, including Mayor John Street, Police Commissioner Sylvester M. Johnson and District Attorney Lynne M. Abraham. All of them said that they did not know either Coles or Baukman. Street goes to "an awful lot of anti-violence rallies . . . and his picture is taken frequently," said his spokesman, Joe Grace. Coles would hang those photos in his Take Down Records office. As for the gangster nicknames—Capone and Gotti—they were an affectation, Swain said. Part of the rap business.

"You know how many Gottis there are?" he said. "Noriegas? It's a rap thing. . . . You can't call yourself Ace Goody Two-Shoes. Nobody would respect you." The message that rap was a way out of the 'hood was one that Cooper emphasized in the opening scene of the pilot for *Streets Inc.*

Coles and Baukman are driving around Philadelphia in a Mercedes. A cameraman is in the backseat. Coles is behind the wheel and doing most of the talking:

"Man, when you black and you from the 'hood, the odds is against you. There's only a couple of ways to get money—if you play ball, football or basketball. . . . Rappin'.

"Now rap, hip-hop takin' over. That's the only couple ways dudes is really gettin' out the 'hood, man.

"And that's why we got this record label."

CONNECTIONS AND QUESTIONS

As Coles was wheeling and dealing in the entertainment world, investigators looking into his suspected drug operation in 2003 were beginning to track businesses that he and his associates had set up and properties they owned. Coles, they knew, had founded the record company with Tim Baukman. They also believed Coles had an interest in a construction company and a possible link to an auto dealership.

They discovered that Coles had real estate holdings that were listed in the names of women who were politely described as Coles' paramours in ATF reports. There were at least three such women. One lived in a North Philadelphia apartment that authorities believed was a "stash house" for drugs and guns. Another had a home outside Woodstown, New Jersey, where Coles allegedly kept pit bulls and cash. A third lived with Coles in a posh, three-story townhouse in Newark, Delaware. Cars were also listed in their names, including Cadillacs, Jaguars, BMWs and assorted SUVs.

Agents also tracked a stream of cash deposits into and out of bank accounts held by Coles and Baukman. The transactions involved hundreds of thousands of dollars. At the same time, records indicated, neither Coles nor Baukman filed income tax returns. Both also listed some assets in the names of their underage children. Baukman, for example, was living with a woman in an apartment in the 2900 block of Schoolhouse Lane. The renter of record was his nine-year-old son.

Pulling the various threads together, investigators could now see the structure of what they believed was a drug network. Coles was at the top, they said. Baukman was his chief lieutenant. Then there were wholesalers, retailers and guys who ran the corners. "Unk" Johnson and "Taz" Walker appeared to be midlevel operatives who helped distribute drugs. Johnson had a crew of corner boys working for him, authorities believed. Walker allegedly moved "weight": large, wholesale quantities of cocaine, for the organization.

Most street sales took place in Southwest Philadelphia, around the Philadelphia Housing Authority's Paschall Homes and on several other corners, including 56th and Woodland, 71st and Greenway, and the 2000 block of Cecil Street. There was also a network operating in West Chester. One major supplier lived in South Jersey, near Salem. And there were connections extending into Baltimore and into North and South Philadelphia.

GANGSTA FOR REAL?

In the summer of 2004, as Cooper continued to pitch *Streets Inc.* and Take Down Records prepared to release *New Jack City*, a joint task force of ATF agents and Philadelphia narcotics investigators targeted the Coles organization. They stepped up surveillance, increased undercover drug buys and intensified efforts to develop informants. The operation was coordinated by the Philadelphia office of the federally funded High Intensity Drug Trafficking Area, an agency that is both a clearinghouse for drug data and a catalyst for investigations. Coles was arrested twice that year on gun possession charges but was not prosecuted while the feds quietly worked their case. If he was aware of the additional scrutiny, it did not slow him down.

In June, Take Down Records sponsored a "School Let Out/Stop the Violence Summer Jam" at the Blue Horizon, a North Broad Street venue for boxing matches, concerts and receptions.

"This will be a celebration of Philly hip-hop and a positive message for kids," Coles told the *Philadelphia Daily News*.

Also that summer, *New Jack City: The Next Generation* went on sale for $14.95 in video stores and at Take Down Records events. The cover of the DVD featured a menacing picture of Ace Capone and Tim Gotti. Each was dressed in black. A bearded Capone, a cigarillo dangling from his mouth, held an automatic pistol in each hand, one of which rested on Gotti's shoulder. Gotti, bearded and wearing sunglasses, also held a gun in each hand, his arms crossed at his waist. A parental advisory sticker warned of "explicit lyrics." A blurb on the cover touted the video as the story of a crime family "where survival depends on friends, trust and power."

54 SHOTS IN TWO MINUTES

Shortly after 9 p.m. on October 22, 2004, shots rang out along the 5700 block of Kingsessing Avenue, near Cecil Street. For a minute or two, the neighborhood was a fire zone. When the shooting stopped, a suspected drug dealer lay on the sidewalk, bleeding from gunshot wounds to a leg, hand and shoulder. He told police he had no idea who had shot him or why. Later, federal prosecutors would allege that the shooters that night included Coles, Baukman and several of their associates. But at the time, no one knew who was behind the gunfire. To many, it was another flash point of violence typical of city neighborhoods where drug gangs operate.

Residents knew the drill. One woman told police that when she heard the start of shooting, she instinctively dived onto her kitchen floor. A bullet ripped through her front door. Another neighbor had a bullet hole in her porch window, and a third complained about bullet holes in the trunk and rear windows of his 1995 Cutlass Supreme, which was parked on the street. By the time police arrived, the shooters had disappeared. On the street, investigators recovered 39 9-mm shell casings, 15 .40-caliber shell casings and one live 9-mm round.

In the span of about two minutes on a fall night in a Southwest Philadelphia neighborhood, 54 shots had been fired by men trying to gun down one another. Police suspected a shoot-out between rival drug organizations. It would take an unexpected conversation overheard on a wiretap on Coles' phone before investigators could put it all together.

Investigators were focused on Ace Capone and Tim Gotti: suspected drug dealers. Barry Michael Cooper, working on *Streets Inc.*, was focused on Ace Capone and Tim Gotti: gritty record moguls. But when executives at UPN saw a draft of his pilot, they decided to pass.

"They said it was too real," Cooper recalled.

VIOLENCE, DRUGS AND RAP

NOVEMBER 11, 2007

For the nearly 30 years that rap and hip-hop have been part of the entertainment and cultural scene, critics have complained that the lyrics are violent and misogynistic, and that they glorify drug dealing. The murders of rap stars Tupac Shakur and Notorious B.I.G., in what may have been a 1990s rap turf war, underscored the art-imitating-life component of "gangsta rap." The criminal problems of rap executive Suge Knight, a former gang member and the cofounder of Death Row Records, and the 2002 murder of rap star Jam Master Jay in his studio in Queens, New York added more grist.

Legal entanglements for local rappers Beanie Sigel and Cassidy and record executive Alton "Ace Capone" Coles have brought the issue closer to home. Sigel has federal convictions for drug possession and weapons offenses; he was acquitted in an attempted murder case. Cassidy, charged in a high-profile shoot-out that police believed was tied to a drug war, was found guilty of manslaughter.

Is rap music a cause of violence? Or does it mirror life on the streets of America's struggling cities? The questions emerge again in the case against Coles, who, authorities say, used his entertainment business as a front for a $25 million crack and cocaine distribution network. Further blurring the line, Coles produced and starred in a rap music video, *New Jack City: The Next Generation*, glorifying the rise of a Southwest Philadelphia drug gang. Both the music and the story line celebrate the power and swagger of drug dealers. Coles is scheduled to go on trial in January.

At a recent congressional hearing, rap was both defended and decried. The hearing included testimony from record company executives, recording artists, and members of African American and women's rights groups who complained of the misogynistic lyrics that belittle women.

"Not all black people and not all lovers of hip-hop endorse the materialism, violence and misogyny that characterizes commercial rap," testified Lisa Fager Bediako of Industry Ears, a nonprofit that monitors the music industry.

"Our culture has more to do with [respect]," added E. Faye Williams, chair of the National Congress of Black Women. "In our culture, the gangster . . . the thug . . . the pimp . . . the prostitute is the exception."

But David Banner, a performer and producer with SRC Recordings, who wrote the lyrics for "Like a Pimp," warned against attempts to censor or silence rap artists.

"Rap music is the voice of the underbelly of America," he told the committee. "Drugs, violence and the criminal element were around long before hip-hop existed." So, too, he added, were commercial attempts to profit from them.

"This capitalistic trend was not created nor introduced by hip-hop," he said. "It's been here. It's the American way."

TAPPED OUT

NOVEMBER 12, 2007

THE STORY SO FAR

ATF agents and Philadelphia narcotics detectives had spent two years building a case against a rap music entrepreneur who they believed was running a $25 million drug ring, one of Philadelphia's largest. People connected to drug deals, shootings and murders seemed to work for him, but investigators needed more evidence.

Shortly after 4 p.m. on January 20, 2005, Joe Smith was found riddled with bullets in the backseat of an SUV at a Getty station in Southwest Philadelphia. Smith, a barrel-chested, 30-year-old drug dealer, had been shot 20 times in the chest, abdomen, arms, legs, back and pelvis. Two shots perforated his right lung. Another shot, fired from a gun pressed against his back, sliced through his liver and right kidney. Before he died, Smith named the man who had shot him.

The homicide, one of the first of 380 that year in Philadelphia, received scant attention: one paragraph in *The Inquirer*, no mention at all in the *Philadelphia Daily News*. It was, however, big news for a group of Bureau of Alcohol, Tobacco, Firearms and Explosives (ATF) agents and Philadelphia police narcotics investigators who had been working to build a case against Alton "Ace Capone" Coles, a seemingly successful Philadelphia rap music executive whose high-flying lifestyle they had been tracking for more than two years. Coles portrayed himself then—and portrays himself now—as a businessman who was producing videos and CDs for the company he founded, Take Down Records, and promoting parties and after-concert events for big-name rap acts.

"I'm not the leader or boss of nothing besides Take Down Records, and that's that," Coles said from prison last week. "I'm not no boss of a street organization running a big, giant drug conspiracy. "

The 240-pound rap mogul drove a $220,000 Bentley, was building a $480,000 home in a South Jersey suburb, and had been a fixture at anti-violence rallies, often posing with top officials in the city, including Mayor John Street and Police Commissioner Sylvester M. Johnson.

"He was cultured. Very charming," said Barry Michael Cooper, 49, a screenwriter who had hoped to develop a reality TV pilot tracking Coles' legitimate rise in the rap music world. To federal authorities, Coles' livelihood was anything but legitimate.

HIS DYING WORDS

Joe Smith was still alive and able to speak when emergency medical technicians found him in the backseat of his van. As an EMT tried to stop the bleeding, he noticed that plastic handcuffs, called flexicuffs, were dangling from Smith's wrists. Police theorized that Smith had been the target of a drug underworld abduction—what is known on the streets as a "trunking." They figured he had been grabbed, cuffed, then thrown in the back of his own vehicle. At some point, he managed to break the cuffs. That's when the shooting apparently started.

Smith, in the ambulance, told one of the EMTs, "Terry Walker did it. Terry Walker did it." Terry "Taz" Walker, 31, was someone investigators knew. He and Coles' uncle had been arrested two years earlier on drug and gun possession charges tied to a bust at Tamika's Lounge, a Southwest Philadelphia bar. Walker also was an associate of another reputed Coles organization drug dealer who was then awaiting trial in connection with a 2002 murder outside the Philadelphia Zoo.

Smith's murder, investigators believed, was the result of a botched attempt by the Coles organization to hold him for ransom, a ploy not uncommon in turf wars involving drug gangs. Walker was a suspected enforcer for the organization, which authorities said was becoming more violent as it expanded its operations beyond Southwest Philadelphia. The trunking theory gained support as the homicide investigation unfolded.

Another Southwest Philadelphia drug dealer told police that on the morning Smith was killed, they'd had drinks together at the Gold Coast Bar at 40th Street and Lancaster Avenue. Smith had said that he was going to meet Walker that afternoon to settle a dispute over a $1500 drug debt. With that information and Smith's dying declaration, police picked up Walker and charged him with murder, robbery, unlawful restraint and firearms offenses. The case against Walker became even stronger when his DNA matched a trail of blood leading from the vehicle and blood found on the backseat.

"WHATEVER WE GOTTA DO"

At the time Joe Smith was killed, Coles' image on the streets was that of a savvy, hustling, independent record company entrepreneur. ATF and police investigative files, however, depicted him as a man suspected of calling the shots for an organization that abducted and ambushed rivals, killed competitors and moved large quantities of cocaine and crack. Ironically, that was the same picture Coles, as "Ace Capone," painted in his 31-minute rap music video *New Jack City: The Next Generation*, in which he played the role of a Southwest Philadelphia drug lord. The video featured music from rappers who recorded for Coles' Take Down Records label, a story line splattered with gangland-style assassinations, a sex scene involving nude go-go dancers gyrating to hip-hop and street-smart Ace Capone as head of the notorious "Take Down Family."

"We do whatever we gotta do," gang leader Capone says as the story opens. This is followed by a scene in which a drug rival is brought to a basement, forced to beg for his life, and then shot in the head. Investigators shook their heads at the audacity of it all. The words, the attitude and the violence were typical of what they had been seeing for months as they intensified the tracking of Coles and his associates. Surveillance and tips from informants gave them a street-level view of the organization. This helped them set up hand-to-hand drug buys from street-corner dealers. It also allowed them to more easily follow Coles, who seldom slept in one place for more than a few nights, as he moved around the city and into Delaware and New Jersey.

By the spring of 2005, investigators determined that they had to have more to make their case. They wanted to be inside the organization. They needed wiretaps. The court-authorized tapping of Coles' cell phone began on May 19, 2005. In the first 15 days, the ATF intercepted 4,300 calls, according to one affidavit. On average, Coles made or received about 280 calls a day. One of the first conversations paid immediate dividends.

Three days earlier, Jamar "Mar" Campbell, a Coles associate, had been arrested in the parking lot of an apartment complex near the Granite Run Mall in Delaware County. Tipped off by an informant, Delaware County detectives had nabbed the six-foot, 220-pound Campbell carrying five ounces of cocaine and a .40-caliber Glock handgun. He'd been released on bail, but his gold Buick Park Avenue had been impounded. On the phone, he told Coles his "work" was still in the car. Campbell was a volunteer firefighter, and among the things he wanted to recover were fire boots and pants that he kept in the trunk. The next day, he called Coles again: He now had a lawyer who was trying to get his "stuff" back.

"I didn't tell him what was in the boots," Campbell said as the ATF listened. Later that night, Coles was heard phoning a girlfriend and complaining: "Mar got locked up. . . . I took a loss on this."

By then, county detectives had inventoried Campbell's car and returned the fire pants and boots to the Green Ridge Fire Company. As a result of the wiretaps, the ATF asked to inspect the gear. An ATF agent examining the pants noticed that inside the left leg—"between the outer protective layer . . . and the inner insulation," according to an ATF report—there was a brown bag. Inside that bag was a plastic bag containing half a pound of cocaine.

Campbell's arrest provided one other dividend to investigators. The gun that police seized when they arrested him matched several of the fired cartridge casings found at a notorious shoot-out on Kingsessing Avenue in October 2004. Authorities had suspected that the firefight, in which 54 shots were fired in about two minutes, was tied to a drug dispute between the Coles organization and another drug gang. Now they had evidence to back that up.

BUYING A SECOND BENTLEY?

During the next three months, the ATF overheard Coles conducting business, talking in code, barking at underlings, and constantly cautioning others to be wary of law enforcement surveillance and informants. They also caught glimpses of Coles' personal life. To his associate, Tim "Gotti" Baukman, Coles complained about the aggravation of moving. He and his current girlfriend had vacated a townhouse in Newark, Delaware, and were building an expensive home near Mullica Hill, New Jersey. Coles was putting his clothing and furniture in storage and was camping out in an apartment until the house was ready.

"I hate this," he said. "I swear, I ain't moving no more. This is the last time." He then complained about "the crew" moving his stuff: "I gotta be here to make sure they don't break nothing."

In a conversation with another girlfriend, Coles was heard debating the pros and cons of buying a second Bentley. She argued against the $200,000 purchase.

"What the hell is the purpose of having two Bentleys?" she asked.

"One is a four-door, one is a coupe," Coles replied. Eventually, he saw the logic in her argument and asked her instead to look up information about buying a BMW.

"What's up, pimp?" was the greeting Coles typically used for male associates. And while code words were apparently used in most conversations to refer to drugs or guns, Coles occasionally seemed to let down his guard. Agents monitored more than 900 calls between Coles and a drug dealer who appeared to be conducting business even though he was in a halfway house and still on probation for a drug-trafficking conviction. They also learned that the dealer was concerned about failing a urine test for his probation officer. Agents said they heard Coles on another call tell an associate that the dealer had to be more careful while cutting and packing cocaine.

"I put the mask on, and the gloves," Coles said. "[He] didn't play his mirrors."

On June 28, 2005, agents were listening as Baltimore-based rap music promoter Gary "Dirtbike Hov" Creek set up a meeting with Coles. A few days earlier, Creek, then 23, had been released on bail after being arrested in Maryland on drug charges. His incarceration had forced him to miss a June 23 rap party he'd promoted there with Coles.

Based on the wiretap conversations, the ATF and Philadelphia police staked out a Kentucky Fried Chicken parking lot on Island Avenue in Southwest Philadelphia. They expected Creek to rendezvous there with the Coles organization to buy more than half a kilogram of cocaine. Undercover police and ATF agents, in unmarked cars, watched as a silver Lexus, driven by Creek, and a red Honda pulled into the lot around 3:15 p.m. A few minutes later, a silver Cadillac pulled in. Agents recognized the Cadillac as a car that Coles, Baukman and another suspected associate, Donte Tucker, frequently used. They watched as a woman got out of the Honda, entered the Cadillac, then carried a white paper bag back to her car. The Lexus and Honda exited the parking lot. Half a mile later, both were pulled over by surveillance police. What followed was more *Dazed and Confused* than *New Jack City.*

According to a police report, the woman in the Honda "became very nervous and began breathing heavily." A male passenger in the Lexus "became extremely agitated and began to tremble." And Creek proclaimed loudly, "Nothing in these cars is mine." After obtaining a search warrant, police discovered half a kilogram of cocaine in the Honda. Gary Creek and his three associates were arrested and charged with narcotics offenses.

Later that day, Coles appeared to abandon his usually cautious phone demeanor while talking with a woman in Baltimore. Coles complained to her that Creek had stayed in the parking lot too long and was unfamiliar with "those narc cars." Then he asked the woman whether any of the others, in particular the female driver of the red Honda, might have been undercover police.

"My man thought she was a cop," Coles said. "She never ordered nothing to eat." Later, Coles was heard saying that Creek should have been more aware of his surroundings. "Hov didn't play his mirrors. If he had, he would have been cool." Instead, he was in jail.

TIME RUNNING OUT

Early in August, about a month after the KFC bust, Alton Coles and his girlfriend, Asya Richardson, moved into their new home in South Jersey. The two-story mini-mansion was one of about a dozen built in an upscale residential community that abutted cow pastures and cornfields a two-mile drive from the quaint antique shops and restaurants of Mullica Hill. As Coles moved in, his time was running out. ATF agents Michael Ricko and Anthony Tropea, who had spearheaded the investigation, had obtained search warrants and had set up 24-hour surveillance on Coles.

"They knew where he was day and night," said agent John Hageman, a spokesman for the Philadelphia ATF office. The plan was to launch a series of coordinated "no knock" raids at dawn on August 10. More than 200 law enforcement personnel—local and county police, state police, and ATF and Drug Enforcement Administration agents—would simultaneously descend on homes and apartments in Southwest and North Philadelphia, East Falls, Chester, West Chester and South Jersey. Many of the suspects were considered armed and potentially violent, so investigators got court approval to bust in the doors without announcing their presence.

Three hours before the raids were to begin, agents monitoring Coles' phones overheard the first of eight calls he would make that morning to Monique Pullins, a girlfriend living in North Philadelphia. The calls went out between 3:07 a.m. and 3:50 a.m. Most lasted less than a minute. Agents heard the always cautious and now apparently concerned Coles tell her to get rid of the "black thing" he had left at her apartment—a gun, agents believed. First he told her to put it in a bag and drop it down the building's trash chute. After she'd done that, he told her to retrieve it in the morning and "take it to work" or "leave it over somebody else house."

"Why you telling me all this?" Pullins asked.

"Evidently it a little bit of drama, but you cool," he replied. "Just do what I ask you to do . . . . Nothing to get upset over . . . . All right?"

GUNS AND LOTS OF CASH

At 6 a.m., agents—some armed with assault rifles—launched their raids. At a modest bi-level home on Burdens Hill Road in the small town of Quinton, New Jersey, they came through the front door looking for James Morris, suspected of being a major cocaine supplier for the Coles network. He was asleep in the master bedroom. Also in the house were two young children and their mother, Thais Thompson.

Cash was stashed everywhere. It was on the floor and in a purse in the master bedroom where Morris had been sleeping, in a dresser drawer and in a bag in the closet of another bedroom, in the pockets of a pair of men's jeans in the living room, in a New York & Co. shopping bag in the attic, in two duffle bags and a Gap shopping bag stashed behind a loveseat in the basement, and in a suitcase in the storage shed behind the home. Agents also found an electronic money counter, a 9-mm Smith & Wesson semiautomatic pistol and bullets.

According to an ATF report, as agents left, Morris noted that "it's not illegal to have a money-counting machine." He also wanted to know how he could get his money back. A final count of the cash seized in the house that day: $559,396.21. In all, authorities grabbed more than $800,000 during the raids. This included $114,780 found bundled in rubber bands in a floor safe in a home just outside Woodstown, New Jersey, where another one of Coles' girlfriends lived. Agents also seized an arsenal of weapons: 31 handguns, rifles and shotguns and nearly 500 rounds of ammunition.

The biggest cache was found in an apartment in the 300 block of East Essex Avenue in Lansdowne that was rented by Tim Baukman. It included:

A Ruger rifle
A Mossberg 12-gauge shotgun
A 9-mm High Point rifle
A 9-mm Intratec semiautomatic handgun with its serial number obliterated
A 9-mm Leinad semiautomatic handgun and a magazine with 32 live rounds
A .22-caliber Stogeger Arms semiautomatic handgun loaded with 11 live rounds
A .357 Magnum Dan Wesson revolver loaded with six live rounds
A 9-mm Smith & Wesson handgun
A .22-caliber Magnum Davis Industries handgun
A 9-mm Feg semiautomatic handgun
An additional 483 live rounds of ammunition

Also found in the apartment was a heavy-duty hydraulic press typically used to form cocaine powder into kilogram "bricks."

THE ATF AT COLES' NEW HOME

A few minutes before sunrise on a muggy summer morning, a team of more than a dozen ATF agents moved in on Alton Coles' home. It sat on about a half-acre along Dillon's Lane in Harrison Township. Stands of trees lined both sides of the property and stretched across the backyard.

An all-window, high-ceilinged sun porch was attached to one side of the house, and a two-car garage was on the other. Coles' $220,000 Bentley was parked in one of the bays. The agents, armed with shotguns, rifles and pistols, moved quickly toward the ornate, wooden front door. Others covered back and side entrances. All wore standard-issue blue uniforms with "ATF Agent" in large, yellow letters across the back of each shirt. Many had bulletproof vests. A team trained in surreptitious entry breached the front door, and the agents poured into the house.

Coles and Richardson were asleep in the master bedroom when the raid began. According to one ATF report, as he emerged from the bedroom in his underwear, Coles appeared more perplexed than surprised to see a group of armed agents swarming through the house.

"How did you guys find me?" he allegedly asked. "I've only been here, like, a week."

A 197-COUNT INDICTMENT

Coles was arrested that morning on gun possession charges. During the next several months, the case was expanded to include charges of drug dealing, money laundering and conspiracy. Denied bail, he has been in the Federal Detention Center in Philadelphia since that summer morning.

"This is beyond a nightmare. It's torture," Coles said last week. "These charges are not who I am."

Coles, Baukman, Richardson, Pullins, Morris and Morris' girlfriend Thais Thompson are scheduled to go to trial January 7 in the first case to come out of the 197-count, 22-defendant federal indictment. Among other things, Monique Pullins is charged with conspiracy to distribute cocaine and weapons offenses. The police recovered a Glock 9-mm semiautomatic handgun in the trash bin when they raided her apartment on August 10.

One defendant, Gary Creek, has pleaded guilty. Several others are believed to be cooperating. The rest are awaiting trial, including Terry "Taz" Walker, who was convicted in March and sentenced to life in prison for the murder of Joe Smith. If found guilty of the major drug-dealing, money-laundering and weapons charges, both Coles and Baukman could be sentenced to life in prison.

The evidence that is expected to be presented by Assistant U.S. Attorneys Richard A. Lloret and Michael J. Bresnick will include hundreds of secretly recorded conversations; testimony from more than a dozen witnesses who allegedly had dealings with the drug network; testimony from the agents and investigators who conducted the probe; financial and real estate records, including deeds, mortgages, bank statements, loan documents and lists of automobiles that were bought and sold; and the guns and drugs seized during the raids. The jury is also expected to be shown *New Jack City: The Next Generation.*

THE HUSTLE DIARIES

Screenwriter Barry Michael Cooper says he still cannot reconcile the Alton Coles and Tim Baukman described in the indictment with the two street-smart record company executives he met in 2002 when he began filming *Streets Inc.*, the reality TV pilot that was to tell the story of their rise in the music industry.

"I understand they had to present a certain kind of image," said Cooper. "But I think they were a lot more complex than people will give them credit for." Coles, he added, "sounded like somebody from a Fortune 500 company."

Cooper now hopes to resurrect *Streets Inc.* as *The Hustle Diaries.* Coles' trial and related publicity could help promote the project that he now says focuses on "how Ace and Tim misinterpreted the American dream."

A snippet from the new version appeared briefly on YouTube earlier this year. It opens with a dark screen. Then a scroll reads: This is not *The Wire.* This is not a rap video. Next is a montage of Philadelphia street scenes with a voiceover that intones:

"Hello, America. Meet your two newest corporate superstars, Ace Capone and Tim Gotti, the CEOs of Take Down Records.

"These are two venture capitalists who understand two things: The shortest distance between the street corner and the board room is a Bentley. And the only difference between a gangster and a record executive is an expense account.

"Streets Incorporated!"

A WOMAN'S STORY

JANUARY 24, 2008

The trial of Alton "Ace Capone" Coles turned personal yesterday when a former girlfriend testified about her life with the onetime rap music impresario who is accused of using his record company as a front for a $25 million, Southwest Philadelphia-based cocaine-trafficking network. Kristina Latney, the mother of two of Coles' children, told a U.S. District Court jury that she made illegal gun purchases for him, lied on loan applications for luxury car purchases, collected cash from reputed drug associates, and was once asked to beat up a woman suspected of stealing drugs from the organization.

"There were no questions asked, I just did what he said," Latney, 32, said at one point during nearly four hours of testimony.

Speaking in a monotone and often responding with one- or two-word answers, Latney was questioned at length by Assistant U.S. Attorney Richard Lloret, one of two prosecutors in the high-profile case. One of the few times she flashed any emotion was when Lloret showed her a picture of a $500,000 home in South Jersey where Coles was living with another woman at the time of his arrest in August 2005.

"I knew he lived with a female," Latney said, adding that she had "tricked" a friend of Coles into telling her where the house was. "Alton kept lying and said he wasn't cheating," she contended.

Coles' defense attorney, Christopher Warren, who will cross-examine Latney when the trial resumes today, is expected to portray her as a woman scorned who has agreed to cooperate because Coles ended their relationship. Warren has a series of angry, expletive-laden letters Latney wrote to Coles in prison after his arrest.

Dressed in striped slacks, a short-sleeved, scoop-necked sweater and with a floral tattoo on her right arm, Latney was the first key government witness to take the stand in the week-old trial. To date, most of the testimony and evidence have focused on guns, drugs and handwritten business ledgers seized during a series of raids in August 2005 when Bureau of Alcohol, Tobacco, Firearms and Explosives investigators closed in on Coles and his top associates. Several other cooperating witnesses are expected to take the stand during the course of the trial, which is likely to last about eight weeks. Prosecutors also plan to play hundreds of wiretap conversations in which Coles was secretly recorded, allegedly conducting his drug business.

Kristina Latney, who has pleaded guilty to a money-laundering charge, was one of three women described as "paramours" of Coles in ATF investigative affidavits that are part of the case. She said she met Coles outside a North Philadelphia nightclub in 1997 and they soon began living together, first at her grandmother's home in Philadelphia and later in a home outside of Woodstown, New Jersey. She said she had two children with Coles: a son, Naseem, eight, and a daughter, Sajae, five.

Latney agreed to cooperate after ATF agents raided her Woodstown home and discovered $114,000 in cash that allegedly belonged to Coles. Latney said that while the home was in her name, it was purchased in 2001 with cash provided by Coles. He later moved out. She also described how she bought two handguns for him with money he supplied and how he used her to purchase luxury automobiles, including a 2001 Mercedes-Benz for $74,000 and a 2002 Cadillac Escalade for $54,000. Coles, she said, would provide cash for the down payment and then give her money each month to cover the loan payments. Those transactions formed the basis for the money-laundering charges against Latney. She said Coles eventually traded the two cars to Philadelphia rapper Beanie Sigel for a Bentley. ATF investigators often tracked Coles driving the $200,000 luxury automobile around Philadelphia.

Alton Coles, 34, is on trial along with his alleged top lieutenant, Timothy "Tim Gotti" Baukman, and four others. Coles and Baukman founded Take Down Records in 2002, a local record label that focused on rap and hip-hop. Coles also built a reputation hosting parties at social clubs and other venues in the city and made frequent appearances at anti-drug, stop-the-violence rallies. All the while, authorities said, he was heading an organization that brought a ton of cocaine and a half-ton of crack into Philadelphia.

Others on trial include reputed drug supplier James Morris; Morris' girlfriend, Thais Thompson; and two other girlfriends of Coles, Monique Pullins and Asya Richardson. Coles was living with Richardson in a newly built mansionette outside of Mullica Hill at the time of his arrest. It was a photo of that home that drew the most emotional reaction from Kristina Latney yesterday.

TAKING THE STAND

FEBRUARY 10, 2008

They have heard from admitted drug dealers who said they had worked for him. They have listened to an angry former girlfriend, the mother of two of his children, who said he had given her money to buy him a Mercedes-Benz and a Cadillac Escalade and to finance the purchase of their home in South Jersey. They were shown photos and videos and were played hundreds of wiretapped conversations that depicted his high-flying lifestyle and the alleged drug dealing that supported it. Now the jurors in the federal narcotics trafficking trial of Alton "Ace Capone" Coles are scheduled to hear from Coles himself. The Southwest Philadelphia rap music impresario and reputed drug kingpin is expected to take the stand tomorrow as the trial against him and five co-defendants enters its fifth week. Coles, 34, is accused of using his company, Take Down Records, as a front for a $25 million cocaine-trafficking network.

"Alton wants the chance to tell the jury his side of the story," said his lawyer, Christopher Warren. In an interview from prison in November, Coles denied the charges against him. "I'm not the guy they allege me to be," he said.

Smooth-talking and street-smart, Coles will get his chance to sway the jury during what is likely to be a full day of testimony. His appearance on the stand opens the defense phase of the case. Coles, not surprisingly, is expected to put a decidedly different spin on what jurors have heard and seen to date. He will be pressed to refute the wiretapped conversations that seem to put him in the middle of drug deals, the testimony that appears to tie him to the drug underworld, and the financial records and bank statements that indicate he had access to tens of thousands of dollars in cash despite little documented income.

Personal photos seized during a series of raids in August 2005 enhance the picture that federal prosecutors Richard Lloret and Michael Bresnick have painted during their four-week presentation. It is one thing to offer the jurors charts and graphs of money flowing into and out of accounts controlled by Coles and his live-in girlfriend and co-defendant, Asya Richardson, as the prosecutors have done. It is something else to show those jurors a photo of Richardson, 27, smiling on a couch with a wad of $50 and $100 bills fanned out like a deck of cards in her hand and more cash strewn over her lap. That shot was one of dozens that captured Coles and his associates in decidedly happier times, before agents for the Bureau of Alcohol Tobacco, Firearms and Explosives (ATF) brought the hammer down in their investigation of Coles' reputed $25 million cocaine-trafficking network. The personal photos included a shot of Coles and former girlfriend Kristina Latney smiling at a New Year's Eve party.

Latney, who has pleaded guilty to money-laundering charges, rarely smiled when she testified for the prosecution early in the trial. During two days on the stand, she provided information about her life with Coles, the flow of cash into and out of their homes, and the drug dealing she said she had witnessed. She also offered a bitter account of how Coles had left her and their two young children to begin an affair with Asya Richardson. The breakup began, she said, on Valentine's Day in 2003, when she learned Coles was having an affair with Richardson.

Latney also provided details about Coles' lifestyle, including vacations in Miami and Las Vegas; a posh, newly built home just outside Mullica Hill in South Jersey; and lots of luxury cars. Latney testified that Coles had provided the cash for the down payments and had given her money for the monthly payments for a Mercedes and an Escalade. She bought the vehicles in her name, she said, but he drove them. Coles later traded the cars to popular Philadelphia rapper Beanie Sigel in exchange for a Bentley that Sigel was driving. Latney said Coles also had used her as a straw buyer for properties, including a home outside Woodstown, New Jersey, where they lived before he moved into the mini-mansion with Richardson. Those purchases were the basis for the money-laundering charges against her.

More personal photos, these coming at the request of the defense, are likely to be introduced when the trial resumes. Confiscated during the August raids, they show Coles and his co-defendant Timothy Baukman at anti-drug and stop-the-violence rallies in Philadelphia. The two men are pictured with, among others, Mayor John Street, Police Commissioner Sylvester Johnson and District Attorney Lynne Abraham.

Coles, raised in rough neighborhoods in Darby and Southwest Philadelphia, is prepared to acknowledge that he has had several brushes with the law and some minor drug and weapons convictions, his lawyer said. But he will contend that his involvement in the music and video business led him away from the drug underworld. The money that fueled the lifestyle portrayed during the trial, he is expected to tell the jury, came from his success as a record and hip-hop party and concert promoter, not from the sale of cocaine.

Christopher Warren hopes to play for the jury a 31-minute rap video drama called *New Jack City: The Next Generation*. The video was produced in 2003 by Take Down Records, which distributed and sold tens of thousands of copies, Warren said.

"I think it was very professionally done, and it shows that he obviously knows what he's doing," the lawyer added.

Prosecutors had hoped to introduce the video as part of their case, but Judge R. Barclay Surrick ruled that it might be prejudicial. Warren now contends that the video is one example of Coles' ability to produce, promote and make money in the rap and hip-hop world. What the jury will see if the video is allowed as evidence is the fictional story of a Southwest Philadelphia drug gang that used fear, intimidation and murder to take over crack distribution in the neighborhood.

The video, awash with murders, drug deals and other violence, was taped on and around the same street corners that federal authorities allege Coles and Baukman used for their drug network. Coles stars in the video as Ace Capone, drug kingpin and leader of the Take Down Family. Baukman, as Tim Gotti, is his top lieutenant. Coles contends that tens of thousands of copies—at $14.95 apiece—were sold at rap concerts, hip-hop events and weekly parties that he promoted before his arrest.

"We shot that movie over, like, two weekends," Coles said in a telephone interview from prison. "It's a street movie. It's not a story of my life." But ATF investigators tracking Coles at the time the video was circulating saw it as an example of his street-corner audacity and underworld arrogance. If the video is shown to the jury, prosecutors are expected to argue at the end of the trial that *New Jack City: The Next Generation* is art imitating life.

"CAPONE" TELLS HIS STORY

FEBRUARY 12, 2008

He made money running a barbershop, a water-ice stand and a day-care center in Chester. He generated cash by hosting parties, and by raising and fighting pit bulls. But he never sold kilograms of cocaine. That was the message Alton "Ace Capone" Coles delivered to a jury yesterday after taking the stand in his federal drug-trafficking trial. Wearing an orange, cable-knit sweater with a highly starched white dress shirt and a white skullcap, Coles spent about two hours quietly offering a thumbnail sketch of his life and times.

Alton Coles portrayed himself as a small-time drug dealer who had spent about nine months in prison on minor drug charges before his arrest in the current case. When he was released from a Delaware County jail in August 1997, he said, he stopped "hustling" and started to concentrate on legitimate ways to make money.

"I didn't want to go back to jail," he told the jury.

Coles, who will be back on the stand when the trial resumes this morning, said he was making more than $10,000 a month in cash from his various enterprises. He added that he never paid taxes. Federal authorities, however, allege that Coles, 34, made millions dealing large quantities of crack and cocaine. They contend that he used his Southwest Philadelphia-based Take Down Records as a front for a $25 million cocaine and crack distribution network, and that during an eight-year period he was responsible for putting a ton of cocaine and a half-ton of crack onto the Philadelphia drug market. Five others, including Timothy "Tim Gotti" Baukman, 31, who cofounded the record company and whom authorities have described as Coles' top lieutenant in the drug conspiracy, are also being tried. The case is now in its fifth week.

Coles' decision to testify in his own defense is an attempt to refute the allegations against him. He has insisted that he is not the kingpin authorities have made him out to be. Smiling occasionally and talking in a matter-of-fact manner that was in sharp contrast to some of his tirades picked up on wiretaps played during the trial, Coles said he was born in Darby and grew up there and in Southwest Philadelphia. He said he got the nickname "Ace" because he was a card player and gambler. At the casinos, he said, his games of choice were blackjack and craps. Was he good at it? his lawyer, Christopher Warren, asked.

"Great at it," Coles responded without missing a beat.

Coles claimed that he developed significant income selling high-quality "cut" to drug dealers who hung out at his barbershop. Cut, he explained, was an additive dealers use to dilute and expand a quantity of cocaine. Coles said he had a supplier in North Philadelphia from whom he bought a cut known as "fish scale" for about $800 a kilogram. He said he would sell it, often in smaller quantities, to dealers, generating a profit of $1,000 to $2,000 for each kilo he purchased.

Coles also outlined his relationships with three women, two of whom are the mothers of four of his children. One of those women, Kristina Latney, has testified for the government in this trial. Two other women who have also been identified as girlfriends are on trial with Coles. One of his first drug arrests, he said, came as he and a girlfriend were heading for the Feather Nest Inn in Cherry Hill for a tryst. They had rented a "theme room" after returning from a night of gambling in Atlantic City where he had won $5800, he said. Coles was driving a friend's car and was stopped by police in the parking lot of the hotel because he was spotted drinking a beer. Inside the car, police found 14 small, individual-sale bags of crack cocaine. That drug case was pending, he said, when he was jailed in Delaware County on unrelated drug-dealing charges also involving small quantities of crack and marijuana. He eventually spent about eight months in prison.

Coles said he went to barber school after graduating in 1993 from Glen Mills School, a residential facility in Delaware County for court-adjudicated male delinquents. He said he opened his first shop, Outlines, in Chester in 1997 after he was released from prison. It quickly became a neighborhood hangout and attracted drug dealers. Coles said he was making about $1500 a week cutting hair himself and $600 a week renting chairs in the shop to other barbers. A day-care center he opened next door that was run by one of his girlfriends netted about $3,000 a month, he added. In addition to the sale of cut to the dealers who hung at his shop, he said, he had a steady income from his dogs—pit bulls that he bred and raised for fighting.

"I couldn't even count it," Coles replied when asked how much money he had made gambling on and raising fighting dogs. "I made a lot of money in dog fights." Coles said he formed Take Down Kennels to breed his dogs. He said he considered them "athletes" and insisted that he took good care of his animals. He claimed never to have seen a dog killed.

"To me, it was no different than a boxing match," Coles said of the dog fights he would attend and often sponsor. He said he had seen matches where gamblers bet from $2500 to $93,000 on a fight. He said his dogs were trained, exercised and well-fed. He acknowledged that he would inject them with steroids prior to a match. Steroids, he added, "enhanced their speed, their agility and their bite."

Coles was asked by his lawyer if he knew Michael Vick, the former Atlanta Falcons quarterback convicted in an illegal dog-fighting case in Georgia. Coles said he did, but before he could say more, federal prosecutor Richard Lloret objected and Judge R. Barclay Surrick upheld the objection. Coles had just begun explaining how he got started as a rap music promoter and independent record label owner when the trial recessed for the day. The jury is expected to be shown a rap music video, *New Jack City: The Next Generation*, that Take Down Records produced.

Alton Coles and Tim Baukman face potential life sentences if convicted. Also on trial are James Morris, 33, a reputed cocaine supplier from Salem County, New Jersey; Morris' girlfriend, Thais Thompson, 32; and Monique Pullins, 24, and Asya Richardson, 27, who have been described as Coles' girlfriends.

ART IMITATING LIFE:
THE VIDEO

FEBRUARY 13, 2008

Over the last five weeks, evidence and testimony at the cocaine-trafficking trial of rap music impresario Alton "Ace Capone" Coles has provided a federal court jury with an unvarnished look at what prosecutors say is a Philadelphia drug underworld awash in guns, cash and crack. Self-acknowledged drug dealers, jilted girlfriends and expletive-laden wiretapped conversations have been used by the government to tell a story that at times sounded like the script from a grade-B gangster movie. Yesterday, those jurors got the soundtrack.

For nearly 30 minutes, the jury watched and listened to a rap music video produced by Coles' Take Down Records. Called *New Jack City: The Next Generation*, it is a fictional account of a drug kingpin, played by Coles, who takes over crack distribution in Southwest Philadelphia. The video, produced in 2003, was filmed on many of the same streets where prosecutors alleged Coles and his associates ran a multi-million-dollar cocaine network. In the video, Coles stars as a violent drug kingpin named "Ace" whose organization shot its way to the top of the drug underworld.

The narrative is interspersed with rap music videos performed by artists from Coles' independent Take Down Records label. Among the songs jurors heard while guns blazed and bodies dropped were "New Jack Hustler," "Cocaine America," "Everything a Go," "Crackhouse Landlord," "Eye 4 an Eye" and "Love of Money." Coles, testifying in his own defense for a second day, offered commentary and explanation as his lawyer, Christopher Warren, periodically stopped the video.

Warren introduced the video as evidence in an attempt to show that his client was a sophisticated producer capable of making money in the rap and hip-hop entertainment world. Sometimes self-effacing—"I can't rap. I just talk a lot of trash," he said at one point—and at other times businesslike, Coles, 34, spent nearly six hours on the witness stand talking about the video and other business ventures. As he had on Monday afternoon, he once again offered what he hoped were plausible explanations for the tens of thousands of dollars in cash that flowed through his various bank accounts. Coles has said that the cash came from legitimate businesses he ran.

Dressed in a dark suit, peach-colored dress shirt and color-coordinated striped tie, Coles said Take Down Records, which he founded in 2002, generated income through the sale of CDs and videos. He also said he earned tens of thousands of dollars hosting weekly parties at Philadelphia nightspots, including Palmer's Social Club and the Eighth Street Lounge.

Coles described Take Down Records as an independent label that offered recording opportunities to local rappers and rap groups. At different times, he said, Philadelphia-area groups that recorded for him included the Young Assassins, the Untouchables, the Delinquents and Plead the Fifth. Artists included "Bugsy," "Snake," "Philly Swain," "Caution" and "Nino Brown." "Scratchin' and Survivin'" by Bugsy and Snake was one of Take Down's biggest hits, he stated. When he was arrested, he added, the company was trying to negotiate with a major record label a production and promotion deal for some of its artists.

"We were this close to a record deal," Coles said, holding his thumb and forefinger less than an inch apart. "This close to getting two to three million dollars."

Coles acknowledged that he did not keep good financial records, in part because he did not want the IRS to know about his cash income. He said the *New Jack City* video cost about $25,000 to produce and was filmed "over two weekends." He claimed that he had 10,000 copies made by a firm in California and that he and his associates sold them on street corners, on consignment at local stores, and at rap parties and promotional events.

While the jacket listed the video for $14.95, Coles said he usually sold it for $10 and estimated that he generated about $100,000 in gross profit on the original 10,000. After that, he said, he "bootlegged" about 15,000 additional copies. Based on a two-year investigation by the Bureau of Alcohol, Tobacco, Firearms and Explosives, authorities allege the money was drug profit.

For the second day of testimony, Coles also offered details about his drama-filled romantic entanglements that have provided a back story to the money-laundering charges that are also part of the case. One former girlfriend, the mother of two of his children, has testified for the government. Two others are on trial with Coles, and his relationships with two additional women have also been mentioned repeatedly. He has at least five children. Coles said at the time of his arrest in August 2005 that he was still paying to maintain a South Jersey house where he once lived with Kristina Latney, who testified earlier in the trial for the prosecution.

"I still had a relationship with Kristina," he said at one point. "I just didn't go home at night." At the same time he claimed to be "engaged" to co-defendant Asya Richardson.

Coles said he got "caught" having an affair with Richardson on Valentine's Day in 2003. And after Latney and Richardson confronted one another in angry phone calls, he "made them both change their phone numbers so they couldn't call one another." He also said that in March 2005, he met Monique Pullins, another co-defendant, and spent time with her in a North Philadelphia apartment on which he paid rent. Coles was arrested on August 10, 2005, less than two weeks after he and Richardson had moved into an almost $500,000 home they had built in a posh residential development near Mullica Hill, New Jersey.

Authorities allege that the money Coles used to finance his high-flying lifestyle came from his drug dealing. They contend that the Coles organization brought a ton of cocaine and a half-ton of crack onto the Philadelphia drug market between 1998 and August 2005.

Coles is expected to finish his direct testimony when the trial resumes this morning. He will then face cross-examination by Assistant U.S. Attorney Richard Lloret, one of two prosecutors in the case. Coles is on trial along with Pullins, Richardson and three other co-defendants. The case is likely to go to the jury sometime next week.

GUILTY AS CHARGED

MARCH 5, 2008

Rap music impresario Alton "Ace Capone" Coles was convicted yesterday of using his record company as a front for a multi-million-dollar drug distribution network that brought massive amounts of cocaine and crack onto the Philadelphia market between 1998 and 2005. Five other defendants, including Timothy "Tim Gotti" Baukman, Coles' business partner and cofounder of Take Down Records, were also found guilty by a U.S. District Court jury after nearly seven days of deliberations.

"This kind of crime is literally evil," said Assistant U.S. Attorney Richard Lloret, who prosecuted the case. Coles' network, prosecutors allege, was responsible for putting 100,000 doses of crack per week on city streets. In all, the jury of eight women and four men delivered guilty verdicts in 123 of the 137 criminal counts contained in the case. Coles, 34, was convicted of 37 of the 43 charges he faced, including conspiracy to distribute cocaine and heading a continuing criminal enterprise. He faces a mandatory life sentence, according to federal prosecutors.

The verdicts capped a six-week trial that included testimony from drug dealers, investigators and Coles himself, who spent nearly six hours over two days on the witness stand denying the allegations. Richard Lloret, who prosecuted the case along with Michael Bresnick, called the verdicts "gratifying." Lloret, a veteran prosecutor who has won convictions against several notorious drug kingpins, said the charges underscored the kind of impact drug dealing has on the city's neighborhoods.

"There are neighborhoods in Philadelphia that are just degraded by crack and cocaine," he stated. "We're glad we did something positive."

Coles showed little emotion during the 50 minutes it took the jury forewoman to deliver the verdicts in the case. He sat quietly at the defense table, occasionally conferring with his attorney, Christopher Warren.

"He was kind of stoic," Warren said afterward. "We were prepared for it. But until the jury announces its verdict, there's always hope."

Warren said Coles had no second thoughts about testifying. The extensive use of wiretaps in the case—more than 1,000 conversations were recorded during the investigation and more than 300 were played for the jury—required Coles to speak, Warren contended. Prosecutors alleged that the tapes showed Coles and his associates setting up and carrying out drug deals. The only way to overcome the wiretap evidence, Warren added, was for Coles "to get up there and explain what he meant" in the conversations played for the jury.

The onetime barber from Darby was soft-spoken and articulate on the witness stand. But his explanation that he knew drug dealers but was not a dealer himself, and that he generated income from both legitimate and illegitimate sources but not from cocaine trafficking, apparently fell flat. Yesterday's convictions capped a detailed investigation by a task force set up under the federally funded Philadelphia-Camden High Intensity Drug Trafficking Area program. The probe was headed by agents with the Bureau of Alcohol, Tobacco, Firearms and Explosives and included IRS agents and narcotics detectives with the Philadelphia Police Department.

Before his arrest in August 2005, Coles was well known on Philadelphia's rap music scene, staging weekly parties at clubs, hosting after-concert parties for rap stars who performed in the city, and promoting CDs and DVDs featuring rappers who performed for Take Down Records. He drove around the city in a blue Bentley that he obtained in a trade with rap star Beanie Sigel. And he starred in a music video called *New Jack City: The Next Generation* that investigators said underlined Coles' audacious, almost insolent attitude. The video, which was played for the jury, told the story of a Southwest Philadelphia drug ring that used violence, intimidation and murder to take over crack distribution.

Coles and Baukman played the roles of drug kingpins in the video, which, authorities alleged, was an example of art imitating life. Prosecutors contended that at the time the video was produced in 2003, Coles and Baukman had, in fact, taken over crack distribution in the same Southwest Philadelphia neighborhoods where the video was made.

Evidence at trial included testimony from more than 40 witnesses, including two admitted drug dealers who said they routinely bought kilogram quantities of cocaine from the Coles network. The jury was also shown drugs seized during the investigation as well as 30 weapons and more than $800,000 in cash confiscated during raids on August 5, 2005.

A former girlfriend, Kristina Latney, also testified for the prosecution, admitting that Coles used her as a frontwoman to buy properties and luxury automobiles purchased with drug proceeds. Latney was one of five women linked romantically to Coles during the trial. Two other girlfriends, Asya Richardson, 27, and Monique Pullins, 24, were co-defendants. They were convicted of related charges yesterday.

Pullins, whose bail was denied after the verdicts were announced, was convicted of the most serious crime: conspiracy to distribute cocaine. She faces a sentence of from 10 years to life. She was also convicted of maintaining a stash house where Coles kept drugs, and of using the telephone for drug trafficking. Richardson was convicted of two counts of laundering money in connection with the purchase of a nearly half-million-dollar house near Mullica Hill that she shared with Coles for just two weeks before his arrest in August 2005. Authorities charged that Coles used drug proceeds as a down payment for the property.

James Morris, 33, a reputed drug supplier, was convicted of conspiracy to distribute cocaine. Like Coles and Baukman, he faces a life sentence. His girlfriend, Thais Thompson, 32, was convicted of two counts of perjury but acquitted of three other related charges. When agents raided Thompson's home outside Salem, New Jersey, where Morris was staying on August 5, 2005, they found $559,321 in cash stashed throughout the house. Thompson was convicted of lying to a grand jury about the source of that money and about the source of a $25,000 cash payment made to a defense attorney. She and Asya Richardson remain free on bail. As she left the courthouse yesterday afternoon, Thompson, who has three children with Morris, said, "Now I have to go home and explain to my kids their father won't be coming home."

Judge R. Barclay Surrick set sentencings for the week of June 9. In all, 22 defendants were indicted in the case. Six have pleaded guilty. The others are awaiting trial.

LIFE PLUS 55 YEARS

APRIL 17, 2009

Alton "Ace Capone" Coles, the rap music impresario who used his hip-hop Philadelphia record label as a front for a major cocaine distribution network, was sentenced yesterday to life plus 55 years in federal prison. U.S. District Court Judge R. Barclay Surrick imposed the sentence during a brief hearing in which the 35-year-old Coles, his voice cracking, said he did not believe he deserved to spend the rest of his life behind bars.

"I never thought it would come to this. I don't think life is deserved for selling drugs."

But Assistant U.S. Attorney Richard Lloret, one of the prosecutors in the case, said Coles "amply demonstrated" that he deserved such a sentence. Lloret added that the amount of cocaine distributed by the Coles network and the "destruction" it brought to the city justified the maximum sentence. Based on what Lloret called "conservative" calculations, authorities believe that between 1998 and his arrest in August 2005, Coles headed a drug network that brought two and a half tons of cocaine and crack into the Philadelphia drug underworld. In imposing sentence, Surrick said that "the amount of drugs is staggering and the money involved was even more staggering."

Coles, who has been held without bail since his arrest, enjoyed a lavish lifestyle, according to testimony at his trial last year. He lived in a luxurious home just outside Mullica Hill, New Jersey, drove a Bentley, and owned several other high-priced cars and properties. Authorities confiscated more than a million dollars in cash during the investigation. The money and the properties are now subject to federal forfeiture actions.

Once a burly 240 pounds, Coles appeared thin under his green prison jumpsuit when he was escorted into court in handcuffs yesterday. A former barber from Darby, he told Surrick that he was a "product of his environment" and had been raised "by the streets."

"My father was a crack dealer," he said, his voice breaking. "My mother kicked me out when I was 12 . . . . I became a man on my own."

Surrick said the crimes of which Coles was convicted were "horrendous" and required "extreme punishment." He called Coles a "high-profile drug dealer," and said his sentencing should serve as a warning and a lesson for anyone else thinking about getting involved in the drug trade.

"Everyone in the area knew Ace Capone" and what he did, Surrick added.

Coles and five co-defendants, including two former girlfriends, were convicted last year after a six-week trial in U.S. District Court. Coles was found guilty of 37 of the 43 counts he faced, including conspiracy to distribute cocaine and heading a continuing criminal enterprise. The convictions capped a two-year investigation by agents with the Bureau of Alcohol, Tobacco, Firearms and Explosives (ATF) and detectives with the Philadelphia Police Department narcotics bureau. The investigation included hundreds of secretly recorded conversations and information provided by nearly a dozen cooperating witnesses, including another former girlfriend. In a sentencing memo filed last week, Lloret said the investigation documented "tens of millions of dollars generated during the course of the conspiracy and the lavish lifestyle led by the defendant."

Coles founded Takedown Records, a rap music company that produced CDs and DVDs. Adopting the trappings of a rap star himself, Coles drove around Philadelphia in his blue Bentley, hosted after-concert parties for rap and hip-hop stars who performed in the city, and produced and starred in a rap music video that investigators said underscored his bold, in-your-face attitude.

The video, called *New Jack City: The Next Generation*, was a fictional account of a violent drug gang that used murder and intimidation to take over the crack cocaine trade in Southwest Philadelphia. Coles, as "Ace Capone," and his business partner Timothy Baukman, as "Tim Gotti," starred as the drug kingpins in the video, which was shot on the streets of Southwest Philadelphia. At the same time, investigators alleged, Coles and Baukman were in fact taking over the crack trade in that area. Baukman, 34, was one of the five co-defendants convicted along with Coles last year. He also faces a possible life sentence.

In a series of raids executed in August 2005, authorities seized cash, drugs and guns while arresting Coles, Baukman and most of their top associates. Coles was living in a home he had moved into only two weeks earlier when he was arrested on August 10. Authorities alleged the $100,000 down payment on the home, which Coles shared with co-defendant Asya Richardson, came from his drug operation. His Bentley was parked in the garage.

Investigators found $114,780 in the New Jersey home of another girlfriend near Woodstown and discovered $559,000 in a home shared by co-defendants James Morris and Thais Thompson just outside Salem. After the conviction, $200,000 in cash was found in a bank safe deposit box belonging to Coles, Richard Lloret reported yesterday. Ten weapons and nearly 400 rounds of ammunition were found in an apartment in Lansdowne, Pennsylvania, maintained by Baukman.

Authorities attributed seven murders and nearly two dozen shootings to the Coles drug ring, although none of the murder charges was listed in the federal drug case. Two of the murder cases were tried in Common Pleas Court and resulted in convictions for two Coles associates. At its height, the U.S. Attorney's Office estimated, the Coles drug operation was putting 100,000 doses of crack on the streets of the city each week.

"It is very difficult to overstate how damaging the defendant's conduct was to the city of Philadelphia and surrounding area," Lloret wrote in his sentencing memo.

Alton "Ace Capone" Coles and Timothy "Tim Gotti" Baukman posing on the cover of their DVD, *New Jack City: The Next Generation*.

Frank "Frankie the Fixer" DiGiacomo and Louis "Bent Finger Lou" Monacello

COSA NOSTRA 2000

Thirty years of intense prosecution, wanton violence and turncoat testimony have crippled the American Mafia. Once the dominant player in the underworld, the mob is a shell of its former self. It's like a corporation that has been through a bankruptcy reorganization. It's been downsized. It no longer sets the agenda. But it's still in business. The Philadelphia crime family is prototypical in that regard. What's happened here is a microcosm of what's happened throughout the country.

The stories that follow offer a snapshot of La Cosa Nostra at the start of the 21st century. Its resilience is captured in the person of Joe Ligambi, the alleged Philadelphia mob boss. Uncle Joe spent more than 10 years in prison for one of the more notorious—and senseless—murders that occurred during the bloody reign of Nicodemo "Little Nicky" Scarfo in the 1980s. Ligambi was charged with being one of the shooters in the slaying of Frank "Frankie Flowers" D'Alfonso.

Ligambi, Scarfo and half a dozen other wiseguys were convicted and sentenced to life in prison. But the convictions were overturned on appeal and a new trial ended with acquittals all around. Ligambi, however, was the only guy to come home. Scarfo and the others were serving—and continue to serve—lengthy federal jail terms on racketeering charges from another case.

From an underworld perspective, Ligambi seems to have made the best of a second chance, running the family the way Angelo Bruno once did: Staying in the shadows, keeping a low profile, making money, not headlines.

Ligambi's tenure as boss has been sorely tested, as several of the stories in this section demonstrate. (See the saga of Bent Finger Lou Monacello and Frankie the Fixer DiGiacomo as a prime example.) As of this writing, Ligambi and most of his top associates are the targets of an ongoing FBI racketeering investigation.

NATALE ON TAPE

SEPTEMBER 25, 2000

He thought Atlantic City was a can't-miss proposition. He said he had the inside track on government contracts in Philadelphia and Camden. He threatened to use a baseball bat and a ball-peen hammer to instill discipline. He dismissed informants as gutless "rats." From September 1995 to October 1996, mob boss Ralph Natale bragged, blustered and talked street-corner philosophy—"in life you got to do the right thing and be a man"—to friends and associates. All the while, the FBI was listening. Now tapes of those conversations are being turned over to defense attorneys preparing for cases—including those of Camden mayor Milton Milan and former Natale ally Joseph "Skinny Joey" Merlino—in which Natale is expected to testify as a prosecution witness. The attorneys are looking to use the 69-year-old mob boss' own words against him, and a review of nearly 1,000 pages of court documents and partial transcripts from more than 100 conversations indicates that the defense has a lot to work with.

What emerges from the conversations, secretly recorded with listening devices planted in Natale's posh penthouse apartment at the Cooper River Plaza in Pennsauken and at a restaurant at the Garden State Park racetrack in Cherry Hill, is a verbal self-portrait of a mob boss who talked a better game than he played. Natale, for example, once disdainfully said of mob informant Philip Leonetti that he ought to "do his time like a man." Now Natale is, like Leonetti, cooperating in order to avoid spending the rest of his life in prison.

The Natale recorded by the FBI was also a man full of braggadocio and bluster whose grandiose plans were long on form but short on substance. In the Camden case, for example, Mayor Milan is accused of accepting gifts and money from a Natale associate in exchange for help in awarding contracts to mob associates or their companies. Milan denies the charge. But while the indictment alleges such a conspiracy, it provides no details about actual contracts that were awarded to mob-tainted companies. Likewise, sources say, the talk about contracts in Philadelphia and Atlantic City was, in large part, talk.

"This was Ralph being Ralph," one defense lawyer said. "He was a legend in his own mind."

At times, Natale sounded almost philosophical, preaching the values of hard work, nobility and honor.

"There's no mystery to life or to being a success in business," he said during a discussion in which he emphasized the importance of working hard. In another, when the topic of Merlino and his young associates came up, Natale complained, "Nobody wants to go to work. . . . They want to be gangsters. And they can't even be that."

But Natale, who has also admitted his role in several mob murders, often sounded petty and vindictive, ranting about perceived slights and the failure of his associates to generate income. Offended when the secretary of an associate had put him on hold during a phone call, he said he would set the woman on fire.

"Don't think I won't. I'll come in with a fucking gallon of gasoline. I'll pour it all over her." And when a gambling operation was coming up short financially, he complained: "Nobody knows how to count. . . . I'm going to start carrying a fucking bat around."

Everyone comes to him with complaints, he said at another point, but "nobody brings me a little happiness," an apparent reference to the failure of certain associates to make tribute payments. When several associates ignored his advice, he threatened to use a ball-peen hammer to get their attention.

"I got to get that ball-peen hammer," he said. "Then, when they talk, you give them the circle right in the forehead."

In dozens of conversations, Natale discussed plans to win government construction contracts in Philadelphia and Camden. Of Camden, he said, "We can have the city. . . . Don't seem too extravagant." He also talked about opportunities to make money in Atlantic City, telling an associate, "If we don't become successful in Atlantic City . . . we ought to put weights around our necks and jump in the river."

Natale said he had connections to casino officials; talked about opening an Atlantic City strip joint "with the finest broads," discussed deals to supply cigars and produce to the gaming halls, talked about setting up an "independent" union for the billion-dollar casino-hotel Steve Wynn was planning, and tried to get his youngest daughter a job through a Wynn executive. Yet indications from state and federal law enforcement sources are that the mob made no significant inroads into New Jersey's gambling capital while Natale ran the crime family.

Instead, the FBI heard discussions such as the one recorded in May 1996 after an unidentified associate of Natale's had met with an unidentified casino executive. The associate had little to say about any business deals, but a lot to say about the executive who had joked that he, the associate, looked like actor Joe Pesci.

"No," the associate told Natale. "Joe Pesci looked like me. I was Joe Pesci a long time before that fucking guy. When I was a kid, I was a tough motherfucker. But no more. I'm a businessman now."

In another conversation, Natale complained that he couldn't be the businessman he wanted to be—"can't talk to casinos . . . can't talk to construction"—because federal authorities were all over him.

"Everywhere I go, I'm being watched by Uncle Sam," he said. "I can't even talk on this thing anymore," he told an associate, correctly surmising that the phone in his penthouse apartment was tapped. The FBI also was listening and taping when Natale and two associates took the phone off the hook and tried to determine whether it was bugged.

"Turn it the other way. . . . Go back, go back. . . . OK, you're dead. That's good," they said as the FBI bug picked up the sounds of the phone being twisted and turned.

In fact, few of the business deals discussed on the phone and in meetings at Natale's apartment and the racetrack's Currier & Ives restaurant, which Natale dubbed his "office," ever got past the talking stage. The only business that generated significant income, it appears, were the drug deals that led to Natale's arrest and indictment in June 1999. Natale, who had served 15 years in jail on drug-trafficking and arson charges brought in the late 1970s, was facing the prospect of life in prison when he decided in August 1999 to begin cooperating. Now he is the "rat" that he and his associates claimed to despise in several of the FBI tapes.

Though the defense hopes to use many of those conversations to undermine and challenge Natale's credibility, one rambling discussion recorded in March 1996 could work in the government's favor. In that conversation, Natale, the highest-ranking American mob figure ever to turn government witness, went on at length about informants.

"I hate them. You hate them," he said to an associate. "Everybody in the world [hates them]. Because what they did to themselves shouldn't be done to a man. But very seldom does an informant lie [because] if it's proven, they lose their deal of immunity." Cooperating witnesses, Natale grudgingly acknowledged, "have no need to lie."

"They tell the truth so they can keep their deal of immunity and put another man in jail."

ANGELO LUTZ, NO REGRETS

AUGUST 2, 2001

No regrets. That's what Angelo Lutz said yesterday as he prepared to surrender to federal authorities to await sentencing for racketeering and extortion.

"I spoke my mind at the trial," said the South Philadelphia mob associate. "I told the truth. Maybe I didn't do it in the most sympathetic, humble way, but I told it." And, he said, he would do it again.

Lutz, 37, whose bail was revoked after his conviction on July 20, is scheduled to surrender tomorrow at 2 p.m. He is expected to join reputed mob boss Joseph "Skinny Joey" Merlino and five co-defendants in the Federal Detention Center at 7th and Arch Streets pending sentencing hearings in December. He faces a minimum of five years in prison. Outspoken to the end, Lutz said that he did not second-guess his decision to take the witness stand in his own defense, even though several members of the anonymously selected jury panel said in post-verdict interviews that they thought it was a bad idea.

"I believe in speaking my mind," he said.

Lutz also said that while he understood the media attention that surrounded the case, and that he willingly took part in it, he was hard-pressed to understand why the *Philadelphia Daily News* has been running a daily "Fat Ange" watch, requesting readers to report "sightings" of the five-foot-five, 400-pound Lutz. He said he did not understand the almost gleeful, pulling-wings-off-a-fly tone of the uncorroborated reports.

"Why is what I do now news?" he asked. But, in fact, almost everything Lutz has said and done over the last four months (the trial began on March 29) has been news.

Because he was the only defendant free on bail—he was and still is required to wear an electronic ankle bracelet and has been placed under restricted house arrest—Lutz became the "face" of the mob during the trial. He did little to discourage that. Each day, as he arrived and left the courthouse, he was swamped by the media. That, coupled with his penchant for quips, one-liners and asides, provided reporters with a guaranteed sound bite from the defense camp whenever a twist or turn in the marathon trial warranted it. After a 15-week trial, he was convicted, along with Merlino and the others.

The still-controversial verdict included a split decision. All seven defendants were found guilty of racketeering charges related to gambling, extortion, the collection of unlawful debts and the receipt of stolen property. But Merlino and five co-defendants were found not guilty of murder and attempted murder charges that were at the heart of the case. (Lutz was not charged with murder or attempted murder.) Merlino was also acquitted of a drug-trafficking charge.

As he sat yesterday in the living room of the home he shares with his mother, Helen, 70, in South Philadelphia, Lutz said he thought his outspoken nature might have been misinterpreted as arrogance, particularly by the federal prosecutors and FBI agents who built the case against him.

"Look, I'm an entertainer," said Lutz, who has marched with string bands for most of his life. "I like being in the forefront." An accomplished chef and musician, Lutz insisted throughout the trial that he was not a mobster. A native South Philadelphian and a street-corner raconteur, he tried to portray himself as a cook, not a crook; a Mummer, not a gangster.

Any crimes he committed, Lutz stated from the stand and again in interviews this week, he committed for his own benefit. He admitted to bookmaking and collecting unlawful debts but denied extorting anyone. And he insisted he did nothing on behalf of La Cosa Nostra. The government, on the other hand, described Lutz as a loquacious wannabe wiseguy, a Mafia sycophant who drew his identity from his affiliation with the Merlino organization. He was willing to do the mob's bidding, prosecutors contended, even after he was brutally beaten and belittled by his longtime friend and mob mentor, George Borgesi, another defendant in the case.

Lutz said he has spent his last week trying to "put my affairs in order" and arranging for his mother to have people to help her in his absence. This week, for example, he said he has visited his doctor, discussed his case with his lawyer and spent time in the dentist's chair. While stung by the verdict, Lutz said he has been most troubled by the reported comments of one of the anonymous jurors who told a television reporter that Lutz did not seem to have any shame or remorse when he testified.

Lutz described himself as a degenerate gambler whose frequent debts forced his mother and late father to mortgage and remortgage their home and other properties to cover his gambling losses. Lutz's father died about a year ago. His mother uses a walker, needs an oxygen tank nearby, and is afflicted with heart, respiratory and spinal problems.

"The juror said I had no shame for what I did," Lutz recalled. "I know what I did. . . . What remorse I have is here in this house with my mother. Actions speak louder than words. Do the jurors see me help my mother get to the bathroom? Do they see me cook for her? Clean the house for her?" Helen Lutz, sitting next to her son, nodded and smiled. But she said she didn't want to talk about the future.

Lutz has invited some friends to the house tonight for a party to mark his last night of quasi-freedom. He said he may grill some chicken; one of the news stories during the trial was a profile that included his recipe for "Chicken Angelo." His trial testimony also included a description of Merlino's favorite dish, a pork chop casserole Lutz calls "Pork Chops Joey-Style." Tomorrow afternoon, Lutz said, he will turn himself in to federal marshals as U.S. District Judge Herbert Hutton has ordered.

"I'm going to do my time, whatever it is," Lutz said philosophically. "I hope to turn a negative into a positive." Among other things, he added, he hopes to read, write and lose some weight.

"I'll be fine," he stated, saying again that he would not have done anything differently during the trial. Then he checked himself.

"Maybe the tone could have been different. Some of the jurors said I treated it like a joke. I didn't think it was funny, but that's the way I tried to deal with it. In a way, it was a joke, me being charged with being a gangster." But, he added, he never thought it was anything to laugh about.

ROGER VELA, NO JUICE

JULY 27, 2003

He has been described as a wannabe wiseguy and a gofer with little common sense and limited intelligence. "A mental midget," said one former associate who predicted he will wilt under the pressure of a strong cross-examination once he takes the witness stand. But Roger Vella, the mob associate who once idolized jailed Mafia boss Joseph "Skinny Joey" Merlino, may be the key to the next major case built against the beleaguered Philadelphia organized crime family.

More than two years after Vella, 31, first agreed to cooperate, an outline of what he is telling authorities is taking shape. Some details were contained in a racketeering conspiracy charge filed against the wiry, dark-haired Merlino sycophant on July 18. More are contained in federal documents that are surfacing in an unrelated double-homicide case in which Vella is scheduled to testify this week.

Among other things, Vella is providing information about:

The unsolved murder of mobster Ronald Turchi Sr. whose bullet-riddled body was found in the trunk of a car parked in the 900 block of East Passyunk Avenue on October 26, 1999.

Attempts to intimidate witnesses in the 2001 racketeering trial of Merlino, Georg Borgesi and five other defendants.

A series of drug deals, including a heroin transaction involving a Newark, New Jersey-based drug dealer in 1994 and cocaine deals in Philadelphia in 1996, ones that he claims were approved by Merlino.

The systematic extortion of bookmakers, numbers writers and drug dealers by the mob between 1993 and 2000.

Vella will plead guilty to a conspiracy charge, admitting that he played a role in two gangland murders, took part in the collection of a mob "street tax," engaged in drug trafficking and was involved in attempts to intimidate witnesses. All of it, according to the charge filed earlier this month by federal prosecutors, was part of a conspiracy to advance the goals of La Cosa Nostra.

No one else has been charged, but it's no secret that authorities made a deal with Vella in exchange for his possible testimony. He also has been allowed to plead guilty to a third-degree murder charge in a case now pending in Common Pleas Court. Whom he will implicate and how damaging his testimony will be remain open questions. But it is clear from the documents already on file that the targets include several mobsters who are currently in jail, such as Merlino and Borgesi, and others who are still on the street, such as reputed acting boss Joseph Ligambi and several of his top associates.

"I'm not so sure he's strong enough [as a witness] to indict somebody based on what he's told them," said Joseph Santaguida, a former Merlino attorney who also has represented Vella in the past. "He's a real shaky witness."

"Anything that Mr. Vella says is not worthy of comment," added Ligambi's attorney, M.W. "Mike" Pinsky.

Ligambi has been identified in court testimony as a target in the Turchi investigation, one of two mob murders in which Vella has said he played a role. The other was the 1995 slaying of William Veasey. In addition, Vella has confessed to being part of a crew of armed mobsters sent to a bar in Delaware County in 2000 in an attempt to intimidate witnesses scheduled to testify against Merlino and Borgesi in a then-pending racketeering trial. What is unclear from the documents filed thus far, however, is how much firsthand knowledge Vella has of anyone else's involvement in the crimes to which he has confessed.

A high school dropout who never held a job but who drove a fancy car and appeared to live well, Vella was part of a group of wannabe wiseguys who gravitated to Merlino in the 1990s when "Skinny Joey" was the city's celebrity gangster. Vella, a South Philadelphia corner boy, would ferry Merlino around in his black Cadillac Seville. He became part of an entourage of mobsters and associates who frequented the bars and clubs in Old City and along Delaware Avenue where Merlino's appearance was considered an event.

At the time, Vella was heavily involved in cocaine trafficking and had a ready supply of cash that investigators say Merlino was happy to tap into. Vella has told authorities about a series of meetings he, Merlino and others had with a group of young African American drug dealers who were trying to resurrect the Junior Black Mafia in the mid-1990s, according to one FBI investigative report. The meetings, in which Vella said drug deals were discussed and money sometimes changed hands, took place at the Eighth Floor and Rock Lobster, two popular Delaware Avenue clubs where Merlino was a regular.

Vella, who spent nearly three years in prison after pleading guilty to a cocaine-trafficking charge in 1996, was arrested in October 2000 for the murder of Ralph Mazzuca. Mazzuca, whose body was found hog-tied and set afire near the South Philadelphia Food Distribution Center on February 24, 1995, had been shot in what authorities say was a dispute over drugs and money. George Borgesi also was a suspect in that murder, but has never been charged. He has denied any involvement in the slaying.

Vella is likely to make his debut as a government witness in Common Pleas Court where Trent Pickard, a suspected drug dealer, is to be tried for a double homicide authorities have linked to the drug trade. Jury selection is to begin in that case tomorrow. The trial itself, however, will begin on September 2. Vella has alleged that Pickard discussed the murders and the possibility of killing a witness in the case when they were both in prison in 2001. Vella has told authorities that he was introduced to Pickard and Pickard's late brother, Julius, in 1994 by Merlino. He said Merlino subsequently approved drug deals that Vella set up with the two brothers, including a heroin deal that included a New Jersey drug trafficker known as "Money." Vella contends that Merlino took a cut of the profits from those transactions.

Gregory J. Pagano, Pickard's attorney, will be the first defense attorney to cross-examine Vella. He said last week that his client denies all of Vella's allegations. And, in what is likely a preview of his cross-examination, Pagano questioned Vella's motives and credibility.

"He's coming into court with an awful lot of baggage," said Pagano, ticking off Vella's admissions to the murder of Mazzuca, to his involvement in two other slayings and to assorted acts of racketeering. Pagano said he thought it somewhat ironic that the District Attorney's Office is seeking a first-degree murder conviction and possible death sentence for Pickard while using the testimony of a confessed murderer who hopes to get out of jail by cooperating. Those same credibility issues are expected to be raised if Vella is called to testify against the mob.

"Roger Vella is unusual in terms of others who were similarly situated," his attorney, Nicholas Nastasi, said while comparing him with other cooperators. "He's not really a tough guy. He's somewhat immature." But he is not the incompetent his detractors have made him out to be, said Nastasi, who negotiated Vella's plea agreement with authorities.

Vella faces a sentence of twelve and a half to 25 years for the Mazzuca murder and a related weapons offense to which he has pleaded guilty. He faces a maximum life sentence in the federal racketeering conspiracy case. But his plea agreement indicates that he hopes for a substantial reduction in those sentences as a result of his cooperation.

"He's genuinely remorseful for what he's done," said Nastasi, who added that his client is ready to testify whenever he is called. Mob figures, sitting either on a South Philadelphia street corner or in a prison cell, are waiting to see what Vella says and how well he holds up while saying it.

"They're squeezing an orange with no juice," one jailed mobster mused several years ago when authorities first tried to get Vella to cooperate. "He don't know nothing."

RON PREVITE:
SITUATION WANTED

AUGUST 31, 2003

He had the clams casino and a shrimp and pasta dish, washing it down with two small bottles of San Pellegrino water. He was dressed casually in slacks, open-collared shirt and a black Adidas baseball cap. Calmly hiding in plain sight, Ron Previte, one of the most effective mobsters ever to turn government informant, sat in a restaurant outside of Philadelphia one afternoon earlier this month talking about where he had been and where he hoped to go.

The first part was easy. It had been outlined in his own court testimony, in FBI memos and in more than a dozen interviews over the last two years. For emphasis, it was underlined at a federal court hearing on August 7 where Previte was sentenced to five years' probation after federal prosecutors touted his life-threatening undercover work as unparalleled in the FBI's long and highly successful battle against the Philadelphia mob.

But that was in the past. The future, Previte is quick to admit, is a puzzle. He is, in one way at least, like a corporate executive downsized out of a job. He got his golden parachute—a bonus payment of $250,000 from the feds, on top of more than $500,000 in pay and expenses he received while working undercover—but he no longer has anything to do. At 59, he says he is too young to retire. But after living on the edge for the better part of 40 years, he says he is bored with the leisure life a new identity and relocation have brought him.

"I'm used to doing things," he says. "All my life I worked. Usually I worked at crime, but I worked. I can't sit around. It makes me nuts."

For more than three decades Ron Previte roamed the underworld, making deals, busting heads, setting his own agenda. When he was on top of his game, the six-foot, 300-pound wiseguy moved easily in gangland circles that stretched from Philadelphia to Boston, from New York to Atlantic City. Pick any mob scam or gambit—drugs, prostitution, bookmaking, extortion—Previte had a piece of it. His life was crime, organized or disorganized, petty or high-profile.

"Every day was a different felony," he says nostalgically.

First as a member of the Philadelphia Police Department in the 1970s, then as a freelance underworld entrepreneur, and finally as a "made" member and *capo* in the Philadelphia-South Jersey mob, Previte left his fingerprints on millions of dollars. As a cop he was corrupt. As a mobster he was brutal. But it was in his final underworld role, as confidential informant and government witness, that Previte was deadly.

His work for the FBI brought down the Philadelphia mob, leading to the arrests and convictions of mob bosses John Stanfa, Ralph Natale, Joseph "Skinny Joey" Merlino and a dozen other prominent wiseguys. His story, a violent, sometimes funny and always surprising saga of an underworld mercenary, provides a definitive explanation of how and why the American Mafia has come undone. In the end, Previte was the mob's worst nightmare: a wiseguy wearing a wire. But even before he reached that point, Previte was a gangland wild card. Opinionated, outspoken and fearless, he was a mobster whose only allegiance was to the individual he saw looking back at him in the mirror each morning. Arrested but never convicted, targeted but never shot, he was the quintessential underworld survivor.

"I've always looked out for myself," he said during one of several candid conversations in which he explained his philosophy of life. "Nobody else is going to. Look, you do serious things, there are serious consequences. I always knew that. But I also knew if you wanted to make money, you had to take risks. Fortune favors the bold.

"If I fell out of this chair right now with a heart attack, I'd have no regrets. I lived my life the way I wanted to live it.

"Didn't make all the money I wanted to make," he added with a laugh, "but I made a lot."

It was not, Previte admitted during his sentencing hearing on August 7, "an exemplary life." And, he told Judge Stephen Orlofsky, he hoped the work he had done for the FBI "made up" for some of it. Orlofsky agreed. So did the federal prosecutors and FBI agents who showed up in support at Previte's hearing. The risks that Previte took—he literally put his life on the line each day for the decade he worked as a mob informant—warranted probation and a chance to start again. Defense lawyers, not surprisingly, found it "outrageous."

"This is an incentive plan for career criminals," said Christopher Warren, whose client, Angelo Lutz, was convicted in a mob racketeering trial in 2001 in which Previte was a key witness. "The incentive is to say what the government wants to hear," added Warren, who now represents Merlino. Previte is used to the criticism. He just shakes his head and smiles.

"I told the truth," he says. "They know it and I know it."

Previte's testimony and his tapes tied Natale to a major methamphetamine distribution ring and put Merlino in the middle of a gambling, loan-sharking, extortion and stolen property operation. As for the "sweet deal"—the probation and the cash—Previte says he doesn't understand what the fuss is about.

"Let them do what I did," he says. "You think that was easy? Let them try it."

What Previte did for the FBI was, in the words of one prosecutor, "unprecedented." As a confidential informant during a bloody mob war in the early 1990s, he was described as "the eyes and ears" for the FBI inside the Stanfa crime family. Then, in the late 1990s, with Stanfa in jail and with Previte managing to align himself with Natale and Merlino, he strapped on a body wire and recorded more than 350 conversations.

The tapes were candid discussions about drug deals, stolen property scams, gambling, extortion and, in one instance, the effectiveness of Viagra. ("You know you can go for two days with them things. You think you're 12 years old, man," said one wiseguy.) Played in court and backed up by Previte's direct testimony, they were devastating.

A mercenary who once said, "Everything I've ever done was for money," Previte is quick to point out that he worked hard at his trade, that he knew how to "grind out" a living from the bookmaking, loansharking and extortion rackets at the heart of a criminal enterprise. He estimates that even before he became a formally initiated wiseguy, he was earning about a million dollars a year.

"I was everything in one," he has said on more than one occasion. "I was a GP, a general practitioner of crime."

A blue-collar John Gotti, Previte is free today, he says, because he was smarter, shrewder and more savvy than Natale, Merlino and the cast of characters that surrounded those high-profile mob bosses. Previte made his deal. And he delivered. Now he's living with the consequences. His was a mob stripped of the glamour and honor so prevalent in popular books and movies. He moved in a world of violence, treachery and greed—succeeding, he frankly admits, because he was often more treacherous and more violent than those around him. Previte was always thinking, always planning, always evaluating his options and looking at his alternatives.

One of the reasons he was able to get a much better cooperating deal than high-profile informants who came before him—such wiseguys as Nick Caramandi, Phil Leonetti and John Veasey—is that he became a cooperator while still on the streets. This allowed prosecutors to argue that he risked his life for the government. Another is that, despite all his bad acts—and Previte admits he cannot remember them all—he claims never to have been involved in a murder. It was, again, a business decision.

"I spent my whole life trying not to kill people," he says. "I had a good thing and that would ruin it. Murder is bad for business. You create problems for yourself, plus you don't get paid. How's a dead guy gonna pay ya?"

A victim's fear of being murdered, or of being badly beaten, was often more effective than the act itself. Previte knew that.

"I had a better time intimidating people," he says. "And I usually got my money."

Talk with Previte at length and he will inevitably begin to wax almost philosophical about his life in the underworld. He will joke, for example, about the time he jammed a .38-caliber pistol into the mouth of a deadbeat gambler who owed him $20,000.

"Of course I took the bullets out beforehand," he says. "I didn't want to have an accident. Sometimes in that situation, a guy will jump and the gun could go off." The hapless victim, however, thought the gun was loaded.

"He threw up," Previte says with a laugh. "I guess I put the gun too far down his throat."

There was also the time when he and two associates grabbed another deadbeat—this over a $10,000 debt—and terrorized him by sticking his head under the hood of a late-model Lincoln Continental.

"We had his head, like, two inches from the engine fan," Previte says. "We had it jammed in there. Then we'd rev the engine."

Once, twice, three times they went through the routine, laughing, cackling and threatening as they brought the victim up for air, then shoved his head back under the hood where he could feel the fan, smell the engine oil, and breathe in the smoky soot and fumes. In both instances, Previte said, the gamblers had claimed they didn't have the cash to satisfy their debts. Within two days of each confrontation, Previte said quietly, they came up with the money.

There was a different Ron Previte on display in court for sentencing earlier this month. Low-key and understated, dressed in a blue blazer, tan slacks and white shirt and tie, Previte spoke briefly, thanking those in law enforcement—FBI agents and New Jersey State Police detectives—who he said had helped him turn his life around. Other than that, he let prosecutors and his work speak for him.

Now divorced with two grown daughters, Previte grew up in West Philadelphia, where he attended Our Lady of Lourdes grammar school and served as an altar boy. To please his grandmother, he spent his first year of high school in a local seminary.

"She wanted me to be a priest," he says. "But that wasn't going to happen."

Previte then attended Hammonton High School in Atlantic County, where his family had moved. From Hammonton he enlisted in the Air Force, doing a two-year stint in the mid-1960s that included several brushes with authority.

"Me and a buddy used to rob stuff," he says, pointing out that leather flight jackets and aviator glasses moved particularly easily on the black market. A botched attempt to break into the credit union on the base where he was stationed resulted in some time in the brig and a session with an Air Force psychiatrist.

"They had me take these tests, then I went to see this doctor," Previte recalls, smiling. "I think it's going to be some kind of counseling session. Instead, he looks at my test scores and says, 'Son, there's nothing I can do for you. You have a criminal mind.'"

In retrospect, Previte says it was a concise and accurate description. For the next 20 years, first as a Philadelphia police officer and then as a security guard at the Tropicana casino in Atlantic City, he enforced the law even as he took every chance he could to rob and pillage.

"I was good at my job," he says. "But I was also a crook."

One of Previte's favorite expressions—"Fortune favors the bold"—captures his approach to life. It is, he now realizes, also a basic tenet of Machiavelli's classic story of political intrigue, treachery, power and control. Previte, it is clear, understands the Machiavellian philosophy intuitively. His decision to cooperate with law enforcement while still actively involved in the underworld was a gambit right out of *The Prince*. So was his agreement in 1997 to wear a body wire—a move that he knew meant the end of his life in the underworld.

"The mob was a losing proposition, plain and simple. You'd have to be Ray Charles not to see that. . . . I didn't want to leave, but the bad outweighed the good."

While Previte had generated tens of thousands of dollars for Merlino and Natale, he didn't respect them. He found them to be shortsighted and greedy. A master at setting up and carrying out rackets that generated steady income, Previte was turned off by the business approach of both his mob bosses. Merlino, young and spoiled, was interested only in today.

"Joey's agenda on Monday was to get to Tuesday," Previte says disdainfully.

Natale, who had spent 15 years in jail, was blinded by a desire to make up quickly for all the time he had lost.

"One of the reasons I was able to get close to them was because I brought them money," Previte says. "Remember, I was with Stanfa. I was against them during the mob war. But after Stanfa went away, I got a call. Ralph wanted to see me."

Despite the fact that he could have been killed, Previte went to see the new mob boss. Instead of a bullet to the head, he was embraced. The message was clear: Come up with the cash and you're welcome in the fold. All is forgiven. Within a year, Natale made him a *capo*, putting him in charge of a crew that operated throughout South Jersey.

Previte used to bristle at the "Fat Rat" moniker that his former associates slapped on him after they learned he was cooperating with the FBI. Now he laughs.

"Where are they?" he asks. "And where am I?" They, of course, are in jail. Previte is still around. Literally. He has rejected an offer to enter the Witness Security Program. He has been relocated twice since his role as an informant was made public, and he has been given a new identity. But he still surfaces occasionally in the area. That, he says, is not an act of bravado. Rather, it is a reflection of his own self-confidence.

"It's over," he says of the mob.

As he looks back on it now, Previte realizes he came along about 30 years too late. His mentality, his demeanor, his attitude were much more suited to the mob of the 1950s and '60s, the glory days of the organization when "real gangsters" ran the families. Of course, back then an individual like Natale or Merlino would never have risen to the top of an organized crime family. And an ex-cop like Previte would never have gotten close enough to a mob boss to record his conversations.

"Today it's Ali Baba and the Forty Thieves," he says. "They want to rob everybody, even people that are with them. There's no honor anymore."

Honor, of course, is a relative term. Previte is speaking in an underworld context. In fact, he would be the first to admit that he is a less than honorable individual. Even before he became a "made" member of the mob, he had stolen millions of dollars in scams, quasi-legitimate business deals and extortions. He was the "godfather" of Hammonton, holding court each night in the same booth at the Silver Coin Diner while directing a small but loyal crew of associates.

"If you wanted to see Ronnie, that's where you went," says an associate from those days. "And if you didn't want to see him, you didn't go there."

"Crime was not a hobby for this guy, it was his life," says another. "He studied it every day. He was the real deal." Consider one of his scams while working as a security supervisor at an Atlantic City casino.

"High rollers would come in and they'd get comped," he explains. "They'd get rooms, free meals. That kind of stuff."

Sometimes the high roller would leave early. Previte and a desk clerk had a deal worked out. They'd "sell" the room for the remainder of the time the high roller had been assigned it. The "buyer" would order up whatever he wanted from room service, on the house: food, liquor, "entertainment." The entertainment might include hookers and drugs supplied by Previte. The casino would unknowingly pick up the tab. Previte would pocket the cash. The Atlantic City casinos, he says, "were open-air markets . . . I could buy or sell anything there. "Among other things, he stocked a friend's entire bar/restaurant with supplies stolen from a casino warehouse.

"Stools, chairs and tables, silverware, crystal, linens," he says. "I got it all."

He and his casino associates routinely rifled hotel safes and security boxes where patrons stashed their cash, jewelry and other valuables. "I had a guy on the inside who made sure the security cameras were turned off when we hit a safe," he says. Most of the thefts were not reported because the casino feared negative publicity. It made more economic sense just to reimburse the patrons. On more than one occasion, Previte noted, patrons claimed they had lost more than he and his friends had actually taken, reinforcing Previte's worldview that everyone looks for an angle.

At the same time he was working security at one casino, Previte was gambling heavily at another. He'd leave his security job late in the afternoon, changing out of his uniform into slacks, a sweater and sports jacket. Usually he'd have a large gold chain around his neck, a Rolex watch on his wrist, and a huge diamond pinky ring flashing on his left hand. Then a limo sent from the other casino would whisk him away for a night of gambling at the craps tables where, on a regular basis, he won and lost tens of thousands of dollars. His $15,000-a-year salary as a security guard was chump change, pocket money.

"There was this mob guy from Newark, Bobby Cabert [Gambino crime family *capo* Robert Basaccia], who would come down all the time," Previte says. "I'd set him up in a room, get him girls, whatever. One time he says to me, 'Why don't you come up and work with us?' I said, 'You can't pay me as much as I'm stealing from this joint.'"

Ten years later, Previte was a made guy himself, moving up the ladder of the Philadelphia-South Jersey crime family even as he worked to bring it down. His testimony has exposed the mob for what it is, he says—a treacherous, cutthroat group of individuals who have no sense of honor or loyalty.

"*The Godfather* movie was probably the greatest movie of all time," Previte said while testifying before the New Jersey State Commission of Investigation back in June. "But it was fiction. Believe me, total fiction."

COOPERATING WITNESS

JUNE 20, 2005

Steven Carnivale says he was involved in extortion, loan-sharking and the video-poker machine business with the wiseguys from downtown. The Bucks County drug dealer claims that he was part of a mob murder plot, but that the hit never took place. Now a cooperating federal witness, he alleges that he got his orders directly from the late Joseph "Joey A" Altimari, a mob bookmaker from Bensalem, and indirectly from Gaeton Lucibello, a reputed mob *capo* in South Philadelphia.

Last month, Carnivale helped the feds convict a Trenton mob figure in a cocaine-trafficking case. But will his information lead to more organized crime charges? Is the handsome, articulate, 30-year-old cocaine dealer talking a better game than he played? Or is his information a building block in an emerging organized crime racketeering case?

"The investigation is continuing," said Erik L. Olsen, chief deputy prosecutor in the Organized Crime Section of the Pennsylvania Attorney General's Office. "That's all I can say."

Olsen and Assistant U.S. Attorney Barry Gross have used Carnivale to win convictions or guilty pleas from more than two dozen drug dealers, including members of a North Philadelphia cocaine ring that filled multi-kilogram orders for Carnivale and a group of Mexican suppliers in California who shipped cocaine to Carnivale via Federal Express. Carnivale, who began cooperating after his arrest in December 2002, has admitted dealing more than 500 kilograms of cocaine and more than 6,000 pounds of marijuana between 1994 and 2002. At a going rate of about $22,000 per kilogram, the cocaine alone accounted for more than $11 million in gross sales. That was serious money for a kid from Bristol who started selling marijuana at age 19 while working for an electrical supply company. Facing a possible life sentence, Carnivale hopes his guilty plea to drug trafficking and his cooperation under his plea deal will earn him a substantial reduction in jail time.

Carnivale's dealings with La Cosa Nostra are detailed in a nine-page report filed in April 2003 by Mike Carlson and Chris Galetti, investigators with the Pennsylvania Attorney General's Office who built the drug case against him. The report has become part of the case file in several of the federal drug trials in which Carnivale has testified. Carnivale said that he had met Joseph Altimari in the summer of 2000 at an Italian Day festival in Bristol, and that he was soon in business with the mobster. He told investigators he had made protection payments to Altimari and, later, to Gaeton Lucibello as insurance for his illegal poker machine and drug businesses.

"As long as he gave Lucibello a percentage of the narcotics proceeds, he could sell in South Philadelphia without the threat of any repercussions," the report reads in part. Carnivale said Altimari had introduced him to Lucibello at Michael's Diner in Bensalem in March 2002. Altimari vouched for him by telling Lucibello that he was a "good earner." During that meeting, Carnivale recalled, Lucibello complained that jailed mob boss Joseph "Skinny Joey" Merlino had "screwed up" the organization's lucrative bookmaking business "by not paying when individuals won their bets." Also at that meeting, he said, he was introduced to Trenton mob associate Anthony "Tony Gags" Gagliardi.

Carnivale said he had been assigned to assist Gagliardi in "shakedowns" in Lower Bucks County: attempts by the mob to grab cash from individuals involved in bookmaking or poker machines. Later, he said, they were ordered to plot the hit of a poker machine distributor who was refusing to pay. Carnivale said he was told that South Philadelphia mobster Raymond "Long John" Martorano had been killed for the same reason. He also claimed a Lucibello associate had bragged to him about being the getaway driver the day of the Martorano hit.

Martorano had been gunned down in January 2002, a few weeks before Carnivale's meeting at the Bensalem diner. The murder is one of three unsolved mob hits authorities hope to put in a racketeering case, law enforcement investigators say. Altimari died of natural causes in March 2004. Lucibello and reputed mob boss Joseph "Uncle Joe" Ligambi have been the focus of federal and state investigations for four years, according to trial testimony and other investigative documents. Gagliardi, 52, was convicted of cocaine-trafficking charges last month based on Carnivale's testimony. During the trial, Carnivale called "Gags" his mob mentor.

"Tony's a veteran," he replied to a question posed by Barry Gross, the federal prosecutor in the case. "He was teaching me. . . . I was under his wing."

Among the lessons Gagliardi tried to instill, according to the investigative report, was the art of extortion. While they were trying to shake down bookmakers and poker machine operators, Carnivale said, he was told there was a fine line between scaring someone enough to make him pay and frightening him to such a degree that he shut down his business. Or as Carnivale recalled Gagliardi explaining: "It's no good conquering Rome if there are no Romans."

THE BROTHERS MASTRONARDO

JUNE 11, 2006

Joe and John Mastronardo, the bookmaking brothers from Montgomery County, have made a fine living over the years taking bets and playing the odds. Their fancy homes in Meadowbrook and Blue Bell, their expensive cars and their comfortable lifestyles are testaments to their success. But last month, with $2.7 million on the line, the self-described professional gamblers folded. They decided to walk away rather than take a shot at getting their money back.

In a deal negotiated with the Montgomery County District Attorney's Office, the Mastronardos have agreed to plead guilty to misdemeanor gambling charges and not to contest the seizure of the cash District Attorney Bruce Castor claims came from their "multi-million-dollar" gambling network. In exchange, Castor has agreed not to file more serious felony charges against the two.

The case offers a glimpse inside the world of high-stakes sports betting, a world where Joseph "Joe Vito" Mastronardo, 56, is a legend. In that regard, the $2.7 million hit is an indication of how lucrative his bookmaking operation is. Call it a cost of doing business. But there was a second element at play in the case: family.

"Some things are more important than money," said attorney Dennis Cogan, who represents Joseph Mastronardo and who is a friend of Joe and John, 50.

The Mastronardos decided not to fight the charges or try to recoup the cash seized during a series of raids on April 24, because Castor's office was threatening to arrest several other family members. The list of potential targets in the investigation included the Mastronardos' elderly parents, Joseph and Lucy; their businesswoman sister Cindy; and Joe Mastronardo's wife, Joanna, and their 23-year-old son, Joey. Joanna Mastronardo is the daughter of the late Mayor Frank Rizzo. Joey Mastronardo is Rizzo's only grandchild.

Whether there was enough evidence for the charges to stick was immaterial. The Mastronardo brothers didn't want to risk setting off the media frenzy such allegations could have generated. Think of the headline: "Rizzo's daughter and grandson charged in bookmaking probe."

"I think this was a good deal for everybody involved," said Castor, who by law can spend the $2.7 million on law enforcement activities that otherwise would require taxpayer dollars.

In an interview Wednesday, Castor stated that the case against the Mastronardos was solid, built primarily around wiretapped conversations. But he also conceded that the threat of charging family members may have helped negotiations along: "There was some value in not having your wife and family members arrested."

Free on bail, the Mastronardos face possible jail terms when sentenced, although probation is also a possibility. Their business, for now, appears to be shut down. A Web site they used—with ties to a gambling operation in Costa Rica—was not in service last week.

At a hearing following their arrests, both brothers described themselves as "professional gamblers." Dennis Cogan said that has never been in dispute. But what he does dispute is the insinuation that the Mastronardo operation was somehow tied to a Vietnamese gambling ring and a series of assaults that were the catalyst for the county investigation. In fact, a member of the Vietnamese ring was bringing gambling bets to an associate of the Mastronardos. A wiretap on the associate's phone led investigators to the brothers. Both Castor and First Assistant District Attorney Risa Vestri Ferman said in response to Cogan's complaints that there was no indication that the Mastronardos were involved in or even had knowledge of the alleged beatings.

Joe Mastronardo's reputation always has been that of the quintessential nonviolent businessman gambler, a sports betting entrepreneur whose use of the Internet is a sign of how he has adapted with the times. Fifteen years ago, Mastronardo was cutting-edge with his use of toll-free phone lines, recorded betting orders and computerized billing statements. Now, according to the current investigation, he's got off-shore betting through a Web site accessed by passwords issued to customers.

Then, as now, Cogan emphasized, customers were never harassed. Those who failed to pay their debts in years past were simply denied the right to bet with the Mastronardos. On the Internet, those who didn't bring enough action, the investigation showed, simply had their passwords canceled. The bottom line, however, was this: While the technology may have changed, the game and the action were still the same. In just three weeks of wiretapped conversations that began on April 5, detectives in Montgomery County heard discussions about payouts and collections of significant sums of cash: $190,000 in one instance, $201,000 in another and $279,000 in a third, according to documents in the case.

On the day Joe Vito was arrested, he was returning from Florida. In his Cadillac, authorities seized $500,000 in cash. A raid on his home netted a million dollars, and raids at other locations, including John's home, turned up $1.2 million more. That's the money the brothers are willing to walk away from. It may be one measure of their success. Another is found in Montgomery County property records, where Joe Mastronardo's home is assessed at $1.1 million. The two-story, tan and green European-style villa is on a corner lot in the exclusive Meadowbrook section of Huntingdon Valley. John Mastronardo's home in Blue Bell is a somewhat more modest property for which, records show, the former Villanova University football star paid $491,845 in 1997.

Both brothers apparently have rebounded from federal gambling convictions back in 1987 that landed Joe in jail for 18 months and John for three. In fact, in gambling circles the perception has always been that the Mastronardos were open for business.

"They've been booking for the past 20 years," mob associate Angelo Lutz noted in a telephone call from a federal prison last week. Lutz, serving an eight-year sentence on gambling and extortion charges, claimed he'd happily trade his legal problems for those facing the Mastronardos.

"For me, they make gambling a federal offense," the rotund former street-corner wiseguy said. Then he paused and added, "Maybe that's because I didn't have two million dollars to give up."

LIFE ON THE RUN

APRIL 9, 2007

Tony Soprano swung back into action on TV last night. But HBO's long-running story of the fictitious New Jersey mob boss and his dysfunctional crime family would be hard pressed to top the life and times of reputed Garden State wiseguy Michael "Trigger Mike" Coppola. The latest chapter in that real-life gangland saga will play out today in a Somerset County courtroom, where lawyers will argue the fate of the reputed two-gun hit man who spent more than a decade on the run before his arrest in New York City last month.

Coppola, 60, is now back in New Jersey, where he faces a first-degree murder charge in connection with the 1977 shooting of John "Johnny Coca Cola" Lardiere. But for nearly 11 years it appears he was hiding in plain sight, living the life of a well-heeled gangster, maintaining apartments in New York and San Francisco and generating income through gambling, extortion, loan-sharking and, possibly, murder. The fact that federal and state law enforcement agencies were looking for him did not appear to slow him down.

"It was business as usual," said one law enforcement official familiar with Coppola's background. And the business was sometimes deadly.

Authorities allege that Coppola, then a young up-and-comer in the Genovese crime family, was the triggerman who blew away Lardiere in the parking lot of the Red Bull Inn in Somerset County on Easter Sunday morning 30 years ago. The hit did not go down smoothly. According to an organized crime informant, Coppola's gun jammed as he took aim, prompting Lardiere, a wiseguy in his own right, to ask: "What are you gonna do now, tough guy?" With that, Coppola allegedly reached for another gun he had in an ankle holster and pumped five bullets into Lardiere.

In 1996, after the informant fingered Coppola in what was then a 19-year-old unsolved murder, the New Jersey Attorney General's Office sought a court order requiring Coppola to supply samples of his DNA. Investigators had recovered a baseball cap and the ankle holster not far from the shooting scene. Microscopic hair samples were taken from both. Rather than show up for the court hearing in which the DNA issue was to be argued, Coppola took off. Over the next 11 years he became something of an underworld legend, with speculation that he was living in various exotic locales.

"He's in the wind," said the late George Fresolone, a North Jersey mobster who was a Coppola contemporary. Fresolone said the best way to find Trigger Mike was to stake out the Super Bowl each year. He said Coppola never missed a game. Investigators at one point tracked another mobster to an airport and found a set of what they believed were Coppola's golf clubs in the trunk of the gangster's car, but the trail went cold there.

Coppola also was featured on a segment of *America's Most Wanted.* Coppola watched the report while living in hiding and apparently was not pleased with a scene depicting New Jersey investigators serving him with a warrant requiring his appearance in court for the DNA argument back in 1996. In the reenactment, the actor portraying Coppola spits at the investigators.

According to court documents filed after his arrest, living on the lam did not have a negative impact on either Coppola's lifestyle or his criminal career. He and his wife, Linda, had a comfortable, bicoastal living arrangement with apartments in San Francisco and the Upper West Side of Manhattan.

When Michael was finally arrested, Linda was charged with attempting to obstruct the investigation. At the time of the arrests, detectives discovered plane tickets in their Manhattan apartment, indicating that they were planning to fly back to the West Coast in the near future. Authorities also recovered documents showing that the couple used three or four aliases and that Coppola remained involved in the workings of the Genovese crime family, where he had reached the rank of *capo* before disappearing.

Coppola generated cash from bookmaking, extortion and loan-sharking operations, authorities now believe. They also allege that he and his son were involved in another notorious mob hit, the murder of North Jersey union official Lawrence Ricci in 2005. Ricci's body, shot in the back of the head, was found in the trunk of his car parked behind the Huck Finn Diner in Union, not far from the fictional haunts of Tony Soprano and his associates.

Two issues will be argued in New Jersey Superior Court today. The state Attorney General's Office has asked that Coppola's bail, set at a million dollars after he was arrested last month, be increased to $20 million. Not surprisingly, the state contends that Coppola is a serious flight risk. The Attorney General's Office has also argued that the 1996 court order requiring Coppola to supply saliva and blood samples for a DNA test should be enforced. Coppola's attorney, Thomas Cammarata, contends the order—issued in absentia after Coppola failed to appear for the 1996 hearing—is unenforceable because Coppola was never formally served. The Attorney General's Office, in a written argument filed last week with Superior Court Judge Paul W. Armstrong, said that Coppola should not be "rewarded for intentionally absconding."

If Coppola goes on trial for the murder of John Lardiere, mob informant Thomas Ricciardi is expected to be the key witness against him. Ricciardi, who began cooperating after being convicted in a 1993 Toms River murder case, told authorities of a conversation he had in which Coppola recounted the details of the Lardiere hit, including the story of the gun's jamming and Lardiere's mocking his would-be assassin, not realizing he had a second gun.

"He was a tough guy," Coppola allegedly said of his victim. "He died like a man."

Coppola was arrested on March 9 after leaving a Broadway shoe store where he had purchased a pair of socks, according to an account of the arrest included in the document filed by the New Jersey Attorney General's Office. When asked for identification, he produced a New York driver's license in the name of "José Quiñones." But when one of the detectives making the arrest called him "Mike," Coppola asked the detective where he was from. The detective identified himself and said he was with the New Jersey Attorney General's Office.

"C'mon, you're Mike Coppola and we gotcha," the detective said. "It's over." Coppola then conceded.

"OK, you got me," he said.

But Coppola wanted to set the record straight, according to court papers filed in his case. A few hours later as he was being fingerprinted in the presence of two New Jersey detectives, Coppola told them *America's Most Wanted* had gotten it wrong. He had never spit at any investigator.

HE'S BACK IN TOWN

AUGUST 9, 2007

He's back. And he's in business. Nicodemo S. Scarfo, son of jailed Philadelphia mob boss Nicodemo D. "Little Nicky" Scarfo, has returned to the Atlantic City area—a move that has raised eyebrows in both law enforcement and underworld circles. Although his lawyer says he's simply working for a cement contractor in Atlantic County, some law enforcement sources believe the younger Scarfo could be making a move to take control of the crime family that his father ruled through fear, intimidation and violence in the 1980s.

"He is trying to make a life with a legitimate business and avoid all illegal contacts," said attorney Donald Manno, who declined to identify the contractor because of the notoriety surrounding his client. Scarfo, 42, is "not interested in getting involved with organized crime in Philadelphia or anywhere else," added Manno. He returned to the area with his wife and young child, the lawyer noted, to be close to his mother and invalid younger brother, who live in Ventnor.

The FBI, the New Jersey State Police and organized crime investigators with the Philadelphia Police Department have been tracking Scarfo's presence since he relocated to South Jersey about five months ago. Scarfo had been living in North Jersey after finishing a 33-month federal prison sentence for a 2002 gambling conviction. Several law enforcement sources, who would speak only anonymously, said federal authorities had received reports that the younger Scarfo had the "backing" of the New York crime families and that his father, from prison, was also supporting his move to take over the local organization.

The Philadelphia crime family is now reputedly headed by Joseph "Uncle Joe" Ligambi, a longtime member of the Scarfo mob. Ligambi was convicted with Scarfo and several others of the notorious 1985 gangland murder of Frank "Frankie Flowers" D'Alfonso. He served nearly 10 years in prison before that conviction was overturned and a second trial ended in a not guilty verdict.

Whether Ligambi would step aside for the younger Scarfo is a question law enforcement authorities say they cannot answer. Some investigators believe Ligambi, who turns 68 today, would be happy to "retire" to Florida. Others say a long-rumored federal indictment, with Ligambi as the lead defendant, could make any argument about his stepping aside moot.

Another key question is whether South Philadelphia wiseguys still loyal to jailed mob leader Joseph "Skinny Joey" Merlino would oppose a move by Scarfo to take control. Bad blood between the Merlino and Scarfo families is no secret. Merlino, 45, who is serving a 14-year sentence for a 2001 racketeering conviction, has long been the suspect in a brazen 1989 Halloween night murder attempt on the younger Scarfo. Scarfo was gunned down as he sat eating a plate of spaghetti and clams with friends in Dante's & Luigi's, a popular South Philadelphia restaurant.

The shooter arrived at the restaurant wearing a mask and carrying a trick-or-treat bag. Inside the bag was a machine pistol that he used to spray Scarfo's table. Miraculously, Scarfo survived the hit, leaving the hospital just a few days after being rushed there with multiple gunshot wounds of the torso and arms. New Jersey State Police investigators subsequently picked up wiretap conversations in which Scarfo and his imprisoned father discussed the murder attempt, identified Merlino as the shooter and plotted to kill him in revenge. "Little Nicky" Scarfo, 78, is serving a 55-year sentence on federal racketeering-murder charges. It is unlikely he will be paroled.

In an attempt to protect his son after the Dante's & Luigi's shooting, the elder Scarfo reportedly formed an alliance with Victor Amuso, boss of New York's Lucchese crime family and an inmate in the same federal prison in Atlanta. The younger Scarfo, while living in North Jersey prior to his arrest on gambling charges in 2002, was aligned with a New Jersey faction of the Lucchese organization, according to Robert Buccino, an organized crime expert and chief of investigations for the Union County Prosecutor's Office.

"He's been associated with the New Jersey factions of the Lucchese and Gambino families," said Buccino. He added that authorities believe the younger Scarfo was formally initiated into the Lucchese organization and is the "skipper" of a crew operating in the Atlantic City area.

According to an organized crime source in South Jersey, the younger Scarfo's name surfaced in a gambling and labor racketeering case that targeted members of the Gambino and Lucchese families in North Jersey back in May. Wiretaps established an association, the source said, but did not provide enough information to warrant a criminal charge.

While Donald Manno insists that his client has been spending his time helping to build up a cement contracting business, other sources say he and a group of associates have begun to flex their underworld muscles at local clubs, strip joints and bars in the Atlantic City area. Scarfo's father was notorious for shaking down quasi-legitimate business operators, demanding a "street tax" from bar owners, restaurateurs, bookmakers and drug dealers who were not directly affiliated with the organization. Labor racketeering and extortion were big money-makers for the organization while he was in charge.

The elder Scarfo was also in the cement business. He and his nephew, Philip "Crazy Phil" Leonetti, headed Scarf Inc., an Atlantic City cement contracting company that did work on at least six casino-hotel projects in the early days of casino gambling at the Shore. Leonetti, who was Scarfo's underboss, later became a government witness. He testified at more than a dozen trials and is considered one of the most devastating Mafia informants ever to take the stand. In a telephone interview several years ago, Leonetti, who has established a new life with a new identity supplied by federal authorities, lamented the fact that his cousin, the younger Scarfo, had not broken with his father and the mob.

"My uncle is going to get my cousin killed," Leonetti said at the time.

Robert Buccino said that while there is a danger that the younger Scarfo could "end up in a box," there is precedent in the American mob for sons to be handed leadership positions almost as a birthright. John Gotti's young and inexperienced son, John A. Gotti, rose to power in New York's Gambino crime family after his father was jailed. The Taccetta brothers, leaders of a North Jersey faction of the Lucchese organization, handed their positions to their sons, Buccino noted.

"Unfortunately, these guys let their kids get into the business," he added. "In the end, they all end up in jail."

THE QUIET MOB BOSS

DECEMBER 2, 2007

Joseph Ligambi, the reputed mob boss of Philadelphia, is an early riser, often out of the house by six in the morning. But unlike his predecessors—who, not coincidentally, are in jail—Ligambi spends most of his nights at home.

"He's a quiet family man," said an associate without a trace of irony in his voice.

"He's more interested in making money than in making headlines," adds Captain Charles Bloom of the Philadelphia Police Department's Criminal Intelligence Unit.

Low-key, circumspect and happy to stay in the shadows. That's the picture of the onetime bartender and bookmaker as he marks an unofficial anniversary as the alleged head of what used to be the most dysfunctional crime family in America. It's a picture painted both by law enforcement officials and by several associates who, because of Ligambi's desire for privacy, would speak only anonymously. Ligambi, 68, has quietly brought stability back to the troubled Philadelphia-South Jersey branch of La Cosa Nostra with a business approach that is a reflection of his personality, they say.

Gone are the nights of wiseguys carousing at bars and clubs along Delaware Avenue, an entourage of hip gangsters out to see and be seen. Gone, too, are the high-profile parties, media-oriented charity affairs, and celebrity-like appearances at sporting events and social gatherings. And gone, at least over the last four years, are the wanton acts of violence that attracted investigators, spawned informants and tore the organization apart.

"He's interested in two things," said a former wiseguy. "Peace . . . and money." He appears to have both.

Ligambi lives comfortably in a $275,000 brick corner rowhouse in an upscale South Philadelphia neighborhood. The neatly appointed home includes a carport and deck out back and a small patio in front. The house is in the name of his wife, Olivia, according to tax records. He has three sons, two of whom are reportedly attending college. The third is believed to work in the building trades.

Ligambi spends most summers at a rental home in a posh section of Margate at the Jersey Shore. He drives nice cars, most recently a black Cadillac STS. And since November 2003, there hasn't been a serious act of violence attributed to the organization. Even his nickname, "Uncle Joe," is benign.

Through his attorney, M.W. "Mike" Pinsky, Ligambi declined to comment last week. The usually loquacious Pinsky said he could not respond to questions about his client, including several inquiries about employment and sources of income. Police say Ligambi claims to be "retired."

"He's very low-key," said Captain Bloom. "That's the way he runs the organization. . . . They're not as big and strong as they once were, but . . . they're doing business."

Bloom's unit, along with the FBI, has been tracking Ligambi since his return to South Philadelphia in 1997, after serving 10 years for a gangland murder conviction that was later overturned. Police say Ligambi eschews the celebrity gangster style of his predecessor, Joseph "Skinny Joey" Merlino, and the volatile, take-no-prisoners approach of his onetime underworld mentor, Nicodemo "Little Nicky" Scarfo. Merlino, serving a 14-year sentence on federal racketeering charges, was the John Gotti of Passyunk Avenue, whose comings and goings were chronicled in front-page stories and gossip columns.

Young, brash and media-savvy, Merlino garnered headlines by hosting an annual Christmas party for homeless children, sponsoring Thanksgiving turkey giveaways in low-income housing projects, and pitching for a South Philadelphia softball team whose games attracted fans and police surveillance cameras. Ligambi is Scrooge-like in comparison. And very circumspect.

Conscious of informants and wiretaps, Ligambi seldom discusses business on the phone or with groups of individuals, investigators say. His closest confidant is Anthony Staino, his former driver and the man authorities believe is now running the organization's South Jersey operation. Staino lives in a stylish house in an upscale development outside Swedesboro in Gloucester County, but he is sometimes an early-morning visitor to Ligambi's home. The two have been spotted walking around the block together, deep in conversation.

"When you see Ligambi, you see Staino," said one investigator.

Ligambi is thought to have become acting boss when Merlino was jailed in 1999. After Merlino was sentenced on December 3, 2001—six years ago this week—Ligambi's position became permanent. His management style is compared most often to that of Angelo Bruno, whose relatively peaceful, 21-year reign ended abruptly when he was killed in

March 1980. Under Bruno, murder was a negotiating tool of last resort. When Scarfo took over, it became a calling card.

Ligambi was convicted along with Scarfo and several others of the 1985 murder of Frank "Frankie Flowers" D'Alfonso, a conviction that was later overturned. The murder was one of more than two dozen that occurred during the Scarfo era. Scarfo is serving a 55-year sentence on federal racketeering charges. Ligambi, said one associate, learned from the past.

"People respect him, they don't fear him," the associate noted. Nonetheless, Philadelphia homicide detectives continue to work three unsolved mob killings that have occurred during Ligambi's watch. And the FBI is actively gathering evidence in an ongoing mob racketeering investigation.

Testimony at Merlino's trial in 2001 linked Ligambi to a lucrative illegal video poker machine network that authorities say remains one source of income. Bookmaking, loan-sharking and extortion also are moneymakers for the crime family, according to Charles Bloom. Two associates were recently charged in a $22 million sports betting operation being run out of the Borgata Hotel Casino & Spa in Atlantic City. To date no one has put all the pieces together in the type of multi-pronged prosecution that led to jail time for Philadelphia's last four mob leaders: Joseph Merlino, Ralph Natale (now an informant), John Stanfa and Nicodemo Scarfo. However, bits and pieces of different investigations have become public.

Informants Peter "Pete the Crumb" Caprio and Roger Vella have provided information about the October 1999 slaying of mobster Ron Turchi, according to court records. But their credibility, particularly that of Vella, is suspect. Another informant has tied members of the Ligambi organization to the killing of Raymond "Long John" Martorano in 2002. And three associates of the crime family are suspects in the slaying of John "Johnny Gongs" Casasanto, shot to death in his South Philadelphia rowhouse in 2003.

After seeing a federal jury reject a half-dozen murder counts that were part of the Merlino racketeering case, prosecutors apparently have decided that hard evidence, not just informant testimony, is needed to make those types of charges stick. Thus far, investigators haven't found that evidence. In the interim, law enforcement sources say, the FBI continues to build a gambling, loan-sharking and extortion case. And Ligambi continues to live a quiet, unassuming life.

"He's a problem-solver," said a friend who called Ligambi the antithesis of the hot-tempered, paranoid and irrational Scarfo. "He's not going to have somebody whacked because they didn't come to a Christmas party and kiss his ring."

RACKETEERING, JERSEY-STYLE

DECEMBER 24, 2007

The New Jersey Division of Criminal Justice provided the outline for a new Garden State mob saga last week when more than two dozen reputed wiseguys, including three alleged leaders of the Lucchese organized crime family, were charged in a $2.2 billion gambling, money-laundering and racketeering case. Based on a 16-month investigation in which hundreds of conversations were secretly recorded, the probe offered an inside look at what authorities allege was one of the biggest gambling operations ever uncovered.

The conversations, from wiretaps on phones and from listening devices planted in homes and cars, also provided a personal view of La Cosa Nostra more typical of New Jersey's best-known, albeit fictitious, mob family, the Sopranos: Who's in and who's out? Who can see the boss and who can't? Whose word can you trust and who will stab you in the back?

That kind of unguarded talk provided a rich backdrop for investigators as they put together a massive case that tied the mob to an international gambling operation with a wire room in Costa Rica, and included what New Jersey Attorney General Anne Milgram called an "alarming alliance" between traditional wiseguys and a member of the Bloods street gang to smuggle drugs and cell phones into a state prison.

Piles of cash, fancy cars and luxury homes were seized when authorities shut down the high-tech bookmaking ring that allegedly generated tens of thousands of dollars in profits weekly for some crime family members. But though passwords, Web sites and the wire room in Central America defined the new age gambling operation, old-school intimidation and threats of violence were still part of the collection process.

"Go and find this kid . . . and make an example now . . . bust his head." That's how one reputed wiseguy suggested they deal with a gambler called "Boo" who was balking at paying a $12,000 debt. Later, he suggested they lay in wait outside Boo's house.

"I don't give a fuck if it's three in the morning. . . . I don't care if you gotta break his front fucking door down to get this little fucker. . . . You get him out of his fucking house . . . and you bring him to me."

The conversations were just two of dozens cited in a 195-page affidavit filed by Christopher Donohue, an investigator in the case, to support the arrest warrants. The affidavit included two Philadelphia references. One involved mob associate Michael Ramuno, who is charged with providing thousands of dollars in bets per week to the organization, even though he was living in a prison halfway house in Philadelphia in the fall, working off the final months of a 10-year drug sentence. The other was an account of how Nicky Scarfo Jr., son of jailed mob boss Nicodemo "Little Nicky" Scarfo, was "demoted" within the Lucchese organization because of media reports about his alleged underworld operations at the Jersey Shore. Scarfo has not been charged in the current case.

Dubbed "Operation Heat," the investigation targeted what Attorney General Milgram termed the "command structure" of the organization. Those arrested included reputed New York mob leaders Joseph DiNapoli and Matthew Madonna, both 72, who were described as part of the ruling triumvirate of the Lucchese organization. Also charged was Ralph V. Perna, 61, a *capo* who allegedly supervised the New Jersey branch of the organization. Perna's three sons, Joseph, 38; Ralph M., 35; and John, 30, also were arrested. Wiretaps on phones used by the Pernas, bugs placed in one of their homes, and a listening device and global positioning system hidden in Joseph Perna's black Infiniti M35 provided details of the criminal activity alleged in the arrest warrants.

On November 10, authorities were watching and listening when Joseph and John Perna were formally initiated into the crime family during a "making ceremony" at Joseph Perna's home in Toms River, New Jersey. Most of the ranking members of the organization, including DiNapoli and Madonna, attended the ceremony, according to the affidavit. Afterward, investigators heard Joseph and John discussing mob protocol while riding in the car. At one point, Joseph explained that made members refer to one another as *amico nostro*, "a friend of ours." Some members, Joseph said, use the English, but DiNapoli "likes it in Italian, so do it that way." Perna also told his brother not to put too much trust in DiNapoli.

"People have their ways," he said. "Don't ever believe for one second that if it's something serious that Joey will always protect you." The two brothers then discussed the hierarchy of the organization, their father's position and the fact that no one in the New Jersey faction could go to see the leaders in New York "without Daddy's knowledge."

Ralph V. Perna's rise to the top spot and Scarfo's demotion were the topic of conversations the brothers had in August, according to the affidavit. Investigators were watching on August 9 when Ralph Perna and his son, Joseph, met at a diner in the Bronx with DiNapoli. And authorities were listening minutes later when Joseph called his brother John to tell him that their father had been tapped to replace Scarfo as head of the New Jersey branch of the crime family.

"He's the new captain," Joseph Perna told his brother, adding, "Tomorrow I'm going down to tell the other kid he's demoted." John, laughing, said, "I bet you're all broken up about that."

The brothers then referred to media reports raising the possibility that the younger Scarfo might make a move against those controlling the Philadelphia crime family his father once headed. That was part of the reason he was being demoted, they said. Two days later, investigators used the GPS hidden in Joseph Perna's Infiniti to track him to a meeting on the Garden State Parkway with Nicky Scarfo. During that meeting, according to the affidavit, Scarfo was told he was being demoted.

Asked to comment about the references to his client, the younger Scarfo, lawyer Donald Manno said last week, "Obviously, there is no criminal involvement by him and everything else is just outlandish speculation."

Criminal charges of gambling, extortion, loan-sharking, money-laundering and racketeering were filed against most of those arrested. Those charged in a jail contraband scam also face drug charges. In addition, authorities moved to seize real estate, freeze bank accounts and confiscate automobiles owned by several of those charged.

Joseph Perna's finances offered a typical example of a cash flow that appeared to exceed legitimate income, authorities said. His targeted assets included five bank accounts in which cash deposits totaling $329,531 were made between July 2005 and August 2007. This, the affidavit noted, was during a period when Perna and his wife claimed income of $63,836.

Authorities placed liens against 16 properties, including Perna's $712,500 house in Wyckoff, New Jersey and the Toms River house where the making ceremony allegedly took place. The cars subject to seizure orders included Perna's Infiniti M35, a 2007 Jaguar, a 2008 Mercedes-Benz SUV, a 1993 Chevrolet Corvette, a 2006 Lincoln Navigator, a 2007 Cadillac STS and a 2007 Cadillac CTS. All were allegedly purchased with what authorities called "a torrent of illicit income" from the gambling operation.

GLITZ, GLITTER AND HIGH ROLLERS

JUNE 22, 2008

It looked more like a casting call for *Guys and Dolls* than an arraignment. Twenty-four lawyers and an equal number of defendants crammed into a small courtroom in Atlantic County Superior Court here Monday to answer gambling and racketeering charges tied to "Operation High Roller," a New Jersey State Police investigation that has attracted national attention.

The lawyers wore expensive tailored suits, starched shirts and patterned ties. The defendants favored striped polo shirts or floral print Tommy Bahamas with just a hint of bling—a Rolex here, a thin gold neck chain there. And despite the fact that it was not yet summer, most had deep tans. All 24 (22 men and two women) entered not guilty pleas, their lawyers answering in unison at the request of Judge Michael Donio. Aware of the publicity the case had already generated, Donio cautioned that he didn't want a "dog and pony show." But if it goes to trial, that may be just what he gets.

Based on a review of law enforcement testimony and a wiretap affidavit, the investigation reads in part like an electronically enhanced, 21st-century Damon Runyon short story. It's a saga of low-lifes and high rollers played against the glitz-and-glitter backdrop of the Borgata Casino Hotel & Spa. Hundreds of secretly recorded conversations provide an inside look at an alleged multi-million-dollar bookmaking operation run illegally—and audaciously—out of the luxurious casino's high-stakes poker lounge.

Records seized at a South Philadelphia wire room and from two offshore Internet sites offer accounting statistics that placed the action during a 20-month period at nearly $100 million. Profits from one of those Internet sites, investigators say, amounted to two million dollars. There was a coding system to disguise the size of the bets, and nicknames to shield the identities of the customers. One group of gamblers used the names of fancy cars, so each week thousands of dollars in bets were placed by Audi, Lexus, BMW and Mercedes.

Then there is the lifestyle of the two reputed leaders of the operation: Jack Buscemi, a 50-year-old South Jersey resident described as one of the biggest bookmakers in the Philadelphia area, and Andrew Micali, a 32-year-old former South Philadelphian who sometimes depended on his mother, Marianne, or his girlfriend to tally up records and keep track of payments. Buscemi lives in a $500,000 home just outside Mullica Hill. Micali has a $400,000 home in Ventnor and takes frequent trips to Las Vegas. Both drive expensive cars. Yet neither appears to have a legitimate source of income. Finally, there is Anthony Nicodemo, the short, bull-necked, 36-year-old reputed mob hit man who, investigators cryptically allege, "exercised leadership authority" over the gambling ring.

"Traditionally, with bookmaking operations this large, you always have a mob liaison," New Jersey State Police Detective David Feldstein told a grand jury. "Anthony Nicodemo was that liaison."

Feldstein, an investigator with the state police Organized Crime Casino Intelligence Unit, testified earlier this year before the state grand jury that returned a six-count indictment charging racketeering, conspiracy, gambling, loan-sharking and money-laundering. His testimony and the sworn affidavits he filed to obtain court-authorized wiretaps offer a detailed account of the gambling operation and paint a picture of several of its principal players.

Investigators learned the organization tried to hide the volume of its action by listing bets at only 10 percent of their value. A bet listed at "500," for example, was actually a bet of $5,000. In a wiretapped conversation, Micali told an associate that Buscemi designed the system as a precaution.

"He thinks if something ever happens with the government or somebody gets the computer, it looks like they're little bets," Micali said.

Detectives also learned of a lucrative loan-sharking operation run in conjunction with the sports betting ring. Gamblers unable to pay off their debts could arrange loans from Micali at staggering interest rates. In one case, a gambler borrowed against his 401k to pay off the principal rather than continue making the weekly payments. In another, investigators tracked the less-than-chivalrous conduct of a deadbeat gambler saddled with an $8,000 loan that required weekly interest payments of $250 to $300.

"He . . . was just paying interest, nothing went to the principal," Feldstein explained, "and he would just pay that $250 to $300 per week that would go on forever." The gambler finally got out from under the debt, the detective said, when "his girlfriend . . . took a home equity loan out . . . so he could . . . pay that $8,000 off in the lump sum." A short time later, the gambler "broke up with the girlfriend and never gave her the money back."

According to Feldstein, Micali conferred with Buscemi whenever a major decision needed to be made about the business. But it was clear from the wiretaps and surveillance that Nicodemo, the reputed mob soldier, was someone Micali deferred to on a more personal level. Investigators were listening to an October 5, 2007 phone call in which an angry Nicodemo told Micali to "tone down."

Andrew Micali routinely did business from one of the poker tables in the Borgata's plush high-stakes lounge. He'd drive over from Ventnor each afternoon in a silver 2007 Mercedes valued at about $130,000 that Feldstein claimed he bought "with cash." He wore a one-carat diamond in each ear and a diamond necklace bearing a five-inch cross around his neck. He'd settle in for "work" with about $50,000 in cash and chips in front of him. All of this was picked up on casino surveillance cameras after the investigation began in March 2006.

After the October phone call from Nicodemo, Feldstein said, Micali started driving to the casino in a 10-year-old Acura, seldom wore the necklace or earrings, and never had more than a few thousand dollars in cash or chips in front of him. Asked if this indicated that Micali was complying with Nicodemo's suggestion that he tone things down, the detective replied, "Right. Or else, you know, he would face repercussions."

During the investigation, Micali spent time in Ventnor, where he lived with his girlfriend, a casino dealer, and South Philadelphia, where his mother had a home in the 2500 block of South Adler Street. Feldstein said that the gambling operation also had a wire room in a rowhouse next door to Marianne Micali's residence and that "sitters" would man the five phones installed there to take bets from "traditional" gamblers who couldn't or wouldn't use the Internet.

"You still have people who aren't comfortable with computers," Feldstein explained. Or banks, it would seem.

In one phone call, Micali told a gambler who was doing some repairs on his mother's home to leave the cash he owed him "in the freezer" in his mother's kitchen. In two other phone calls, detectives heard Micali and his mother arguing over money. At one point she threatened to take one of the gamblers "to court."

Marianne Micali, 63, one of the 24 defendants in the case, is charged with conspiracy, money-laundering and promoting gambling. While authorities allege the wiretapped conversations between her and her son support those charges, at least one offers another side of her. In the opening of a conversation recorded on July 13, 2007, she sounded like a typically frustrated South Philadelphia mother still caring for a son in his 30s.

"All right, number one, first of all, I'm not cooking today."

FRANKIE THE FIXER

AUGUST 24, 2008

There are a lot of people down in South Philadelphia looking for Frankie the Fixer. And not all of them are suspected wiseguys arrested in the organized crime case in which he is a witness. A plumber by trade, The Fixer was also a gambler and a wannabe underworld tough guy. Now he's the latest in a long line of mobsters and mob associates who have cut deals with investigators, strapped on body wires and testified before grand juries. A key informant in a Delaware County investigation, "Operation Delco Nostra," the burly 44-year-old hasn't been seen around the neighborhood in a month. Most believe he's in protective custody, beyond the reach of bookmakers, loan-sharks and angry customers who want their plumbing work done.

"People are coming in here all the time asking for him," said Joe DeSimone, one of the owners of Grumpy's Tavern in the 1500 block of South 9th Street, where The Fixer—real name Frank DiGiacomo—used to hang out. "Either he owes them money or they gave him a down payment on a job and he ran out on them."

The story of Frankie the Fixer is a contemporary chapter in the saga of the Philadelphia mob, which has proved again and again to be one of the most dysfunctional crime families in America. According to authorities in the pending criminal case, DiGiacomo was a sometime enforcer who leaned on gambling customers when they were late with their payments. That he had problems keeping up with his own loans and gambling debts adds a bit of underworld irony to the tale.

Late last year, when he was a target of an investigation, DiGiacomo began cooperating with state police. He recorded dozens of conversations, including one in which his reputed boss, Louis "Bent Finger Lou" Monacello, plotted to kill a ranking South Philadelphia mob figure, and another in which Monacello and a lawyer coached him on how to lie to a grand jury.

DiGiacomo, who in the 1990s hung at a Passyunk Avenue coffee shop/clubhouse run by mob boss Joseph "Skinny Joey" Merlino, reported to Monacello, a South Philadelphia mob associate, authorities say. Monacello, in turn, answers to jailed mob leader George Borgesi, a close Merlino ally. Those connections make investigators more than a little interested in a flap between Monacello and Marty Angelina, a "made" member of the organization and the mobster Monacello allegedly threatened to kill. DiGiacomo has provided most of the details, including some tape recordings.

First, authorities allege, Monacello said he wanted Angelina dead, but later decided he just wanted him "beaten so badly that he would have to be hospitalized." Not surprisingly, the allegations and recorded comments have created criminal problems for Bent Finger Lou. What is unclear is whether his ranting has had any repercussions in the underworld.

In theory at least, a mob associate cannot threaten a formally initiated, or made, member of a crime family. In the 1980s underworld of Philadelphia mob boss Nicodemo "Little Nicky" Scarfo, that kind of behavior could have resulted in someone's getting whacked. But today's mob, decimated by two decades of turncoat testimony and a staggering series of high-level convictions, seldom goes by the rules. The threats, the shakedowns, the gambling and the obstruction-of-justice allegations linked to DiGiacomo were detailed in grand jury presentments last month.

Seventeen defendants have been charged, including Louis Monacello, 41, and two major underworld money-makers: reputed Delaware County bookmaker Nicholas "Nicky the Hat" Cimino, 49, and alleged South Philadelphia bookmaker Vincent Manzo, 47. One of the presentments alleges that Cimino, who kept a photo of himself and reputed mob boss Joseph "Uncle Joe" Ligambi hanging on his wall, ran a casino in the basement of a business on MacDade Boulevard in Folsom. There were card games and betting on horse races and boxing matches.

During one match, "Cimino provided women from a local gentlemen's club to act as ring girls and cocktail waitresses," according to information provided by DiGiacomo, who also alleged that the women had provided "sexual services to patrons for money." That's just one of many inside stories DiGiacomo has provided investigators. But none shed any light on why he agreed to cooperate. What is clear from the documents is that he began wearing a wire in December and was still recording in June. A month later, when the arrests came, he was gone.

Left behind are an estranged wife who did not respond to requests for comment, customers who paid for plumbing work that will never get done and loan sharks The Fixer owes cash. Monacello, for example, was still collecting vig—interest—on $25,000 DiGiacomo owed him when he was arrested, authorities say. Ligambi and Borgesi, who is the reputed mob boss' nephew, are mentioned prominently in one of the presentments, but are not charged. Chief Deputy Attorney General Erik Olsen, who is coordinating the case, declined to comment last week.

Other law enforcement sources said the FBI hoped to add some of the evidence gathered in the Delco Nostra probe to a federal racketeering investigation. Monacello, according to the presentments, is the link to Borgesi and Ligambi. Investigators allege that he routinely visited Borgesi at a federal prison in West Virginia and gave some of the cash from the gambling operation to Borgesi's wife.

What, if anything, Frank DiGiacomo could add to the federal probe is another unanswered question. Investigators say that while his reputation and character might be suspect, the tapes that he made speak for themselves. Still, in South Philadelphia there are those who have a problem reconciling Frankie the Fixer with the reputed "enforcer" described in the presentments.

"Look, maybe in Delaware County they thought he was a tough guy from Downtown," said one source who asked not to be named. "But Downtown we knew who Frankie was. He was nobody." At Grumpy's Tavern, the assessment is not as harsh.

"I liked the guy," Joe DeSimone said as he sat at a table in his bar one afternoon last week. "He was funny. If you sat here talking with him, you'd be laughing. But you could never believe anything he told you." DeSimone said he knew nothing about the investigation but described DiGiacomo as someone who had always played fast and loose with his business and gambling debts.

"I think in four years he changed the name of his company six times," DeSimone recalled. "He owed a lot of people money."

If nothing else, then, DiGiacomo's law-enforcement-assisted disappearance may have solved some of his financial problems. Tony Tran, the owner of T&T Hairstyling at 8th and Moore, is one of the customers The Fixer left hanging. Tran said he had paid DiGiacomo $1500 this summer to repair the air conditioning in his shop. When DiGiacomo failed to show up to do the work, Tran began to complain and threatened to go to the police. Last month—apparently a few days before the Delco Nostra arrests—DiGiacomo showed up at Tran's shop to return the money, giving him $500 in cash and a check for the remaining thousand.

"He told me not to cash it for a week," Tran said. "I waited a couple of days, then went to the bank. They told me there was no money in the account."

BENT FINGER LOU

FEBRUARY 2, 2009

Bent Finger Lou saw it all coming. He knew the state police were planning to squeeze him and he knew the feds were waiting in the wings, hoping they could take parts of a gambling and loan-sharking investigation unfolding in Delaware County and put it into a broader organized crime racketeering case. Louis "Bent Finger Lou" Monacello, 41, knew he was the guy authorities hoped to pressure in order to build a case against jailed mobster George Borgesi and Borgesi's uncle, alleged mob boss Joseph Ligambi. What he didn't know was that one of the guys he was talking to was wearing a body wire and working for the Pennsylvania State Police.

"They'll try and come and box me in and say, 'Look, tell us what you were doing with Georgie and the other guy . . . or you're going to get 10 years,'" Monacello remarked in a conversation secretly recorded back on January 14, 2008. But Bent Finger Lou, displaying a street-corner swagger that belies his courtroom image as a suit-and-tie-wearing businessman-entrepreneur, said he was unfazed by the threat.

"I'll say I was hoping for 20," he claimed on the tape, one of several made during a state police investigation dubbed "Operation Delco Nostra."

Transcripts of conversations recorded on January 7 and 14, 2008 in lawyer Gregory Quigley's South Broad Street office offer the first inside look at the case which has resulted in the arrests of Monacello and 16 others, including Quigley on an obstruction of justice charge. The conversations were two of dozens secretly recorded by Frank "Frankie the Fixer" DiGiacomo, a burly Monacello associate who began cooperating with authorities in November 2007. DiGiacomo, who is now living in protective custody, made his debut as a witness on Thursday, testifying at a hearing in which Monacello was accused of plotting to have mob rival Marty Angelina beaten.

Based on DiGiacomo's testimony and portions of three tapes, Judge Bradley Moss ruled that Monacello should stand trial on assault charges in Common Pleas Court. He also faces gambling, loan-sharking and obstruction of justice charges in Delaware County. Until the Delco Nostra case broke with arrests in July, Monacello was a little-known mob associate who authorities say was tapped by Borgesi to oversee his gambling interests in Delaware County.

Louis Monacello lives in a neatly appointed rowhouse in the 3100 block of South 18th Street, an upscale South Philadelphia neighborhood that several other reputed mobsters, including Joseph Ligambi, call home. For his court appearances, Monacello has shown up in a tailored, pinstriped suit, shirt and tie, with his thick black hair neatly coiffed. During Thursday's hearing, he quietly conferred with his defense attorneys, Robert Mozenter and Joseph Santaguida, but showed little emotion. He offered a brusque "no comment" as he left the 10th-floor courtroom.

Monacello has an interest in two fitness centers that train personal trainers, and authorities say he owned Gavone's, a now-shuttered bar-restaurant at 10th and Wolf Streets. This is in keeping, they add, with Ligambi's attempt to legitimize his organization by insisting that members and associates have jobs and legal sources of income. But the tapes played in court on Thursday and transcripts from conversations back in January offer a different picture of the reputed mob associate. On those there is talk of bookmaking and extortion, of threats and beatings.

In one January conversation, Monacello readily acknowledged that law enforcement's interest in him was tied to their interest in George Borgesi. Authorities were "hot," he said, to build another case against the jailed mobster. He also complained that state police, who were investigating Delaware County bookmaker Nicholas "Nick the Hat" Cimino, were "asking more questions about me than him.

"They offered him a deal. They took 90,000 in cash from his house. . . . They said, 'Look, we know Georgie Borgesi put Louie Monacello on you. Tell us about it, we'll let you go and give you all your money back, all your properties . . . no charges.' " Cimino, Monacello claimed, turned down the offer: "Nick said, 'I don't know what you're talking about.'"

Cimino, 49, and his girlfriend are facing gambling charges in the Delco Nostra case. Among other things, investigators allege Cimino ran an illegal casino in the basement of a storefront business in the town of Folsom. DiGiacomo, according to court records, has provided details about both the gambling operation and Monacello's ties to Borgesi. He has told authorities that Monacello regularly visited Borgesi, currently serving 14 years on racketeering charges in a federal prison in West Virginia, and returned with word that the jailed crime family consigliere was pleased with the way things were going in Delaware County.

On the January 14 tape, Monacello predicted "a federal roundup down the road" in which he, Borgesi and Ligambi were likely to be charged. In a conversation recorded one week earlier, Monacello said an associate who had been subpoenaed to testify before a state grand jury told him, "Lou, you're the guy they want." He went on to say that investigators considered him "the leader . . . of one of the biggest bookmaking operations in Philadelphia."

Monacello said increased law enforcement attention was the reason he was not going to reopen Gavone's. He also referred sarcastically to Deputy Chief Attorney General Erik Olsen, the prosecutor in the Delco Nostra case, as "a big fan of mine . . . real big fan." The January 7 and 14 tapes are, in fact, the basis for the obstruction of justice charges in the Delco Nostra case. On them, both Monacello and Quigley are heard coaching DiGiacomo on what to say when he appears before a grand jury. Both were concerned about what might happen if he were offered immunity.

"He can just lie," Monacello suggested.

"Take the immunity and then lie," Quigley added. DiGiacomo went along with the discussion.

Nicknamed "The Fixer" because he worked as a plumber, DiGiacomo noted that he had professional training as a liar.

"You don't need a gun and a mask to rob people," he said. "You get a Philadelphia registered [plumber's] license."

CAUGHT ON A WIRE

APRIL 5, 2009

It was a wiseguy lesson in street-corner economics, a how-to-succeed-in-business speech that you won't hear at the Wharton School. Reputed mob soldier Anthony Nicodemo was explaining about the "sharks" and the "lions" and the "lambs" to bookmaker Andrew Micali, who was running an illegal multi-million-dollar sports betting operation out of the poker room of the Borgata Hotel Casino & Spa in Atlantic City. Nicodemo, 36, "exercised leadership authority" over the $60 million betting enterprise, according to New Jersey authorities who used the secretly recorded 13-minute conversation to support that allegation in a gambling indictment. He faces sentencing this week for his role in the operation.

"I'm always in your corner, so you don't have to worry about no sharks at all," said Nicodemo, apparently referring to unnamed individuals who were trying to get a piece of Micali's action.

"You don't have to worry about no one. Anyone comes up, it could be . . . John Gotti's son could come up to ya, anybody. I don't give a fuck."

His voice rising, Nicodemo then told Micali to contact him at his real estate office on Federal Street in South Philadelphia if anyone caused a problem.

"Anyone in . . . the world's atmosphere comes up to you, come to 1246 Federal Street."

The conversation was recorded on March 5, 2007 as part of a New Jersey State Police investigation dubbed "Operation High Roller." Investigators used court-authorized wiretaps to record hundreds of conversations during the 20-month probe.

Last April, 24 defendants, including Nicodemo and Micali, were indicted on gambling, money-laundering and loan-sharking charges. Most have pleaded guilty. In February, Micali, 33, and Jack Buscemi Jr., 51, the leaders of the operation, were sentenced to five years in prison. Nicodemo, who has pleaded guilty to a gambling conspiracy charge, is to appear Thursday before Atlantic County Superior Court Judge Michael Donio. He could get up to three years in prison. Authorities are expected to point to the conversation with Micali to argue that the bookmaking ring was tied to the mob and that Nicodemo was the organization's point man.

The investigation also has shed light on an ongoing FBI investigation that is believed to target Nicodemo and reputed South Philadelphia mob boss Joseph "Uncle Joe" Ligambi. A state police affidavit in the Borgata case states that the FBI considers Nicodemo a "prime suspect" in the gangland murder of John "Johnny Gongs" Casasanto in 2003. It is one of three unsolved mob hits included in an ongoing FBI racketeering probe.

The phone call also provided an underworld perspective on the never-ending game of cat and mouse that pits law enforcement against wiseguys and their associates. At one point, Nicodemo referred to an investigation in Delaware County that had targeted bookmaker Nicholas "Nicky the Hat" Cimino. Law enforcement, Nicodemo told Micali, was building cases around the fringes of the organization because it was unable to get at "the whales," an apparent reference to Ligambi and the other reputed leaders of the crime family.

"Everything's been so quiet that . . . the real whales that they want, they can't get. If you notice, they're bothering a lot of fringe people. Nicky from Delaware County's in trouble."

Last summer, Cimino and a dozen others were arrested in "Operation Delco Nostra," a Pennsylvania State Police investigation into a mob-linked gambling ring in Delaware County. Another prime target of that probe was Louis "Bent Finger Lou" Monacello. Monacello is a close associate of jailed mobster George Borgesi, Ligambi's nephew.

"They're bothering the fringe people," Nicodemo said in the conversation that took place more than a year before those arrests. "That's who they're starting to torture."

Because of technical problems, the taped phone call only captured Nicodemo. Micali's voice was not picked up. Investigators, however, had little trouble reading between the lines as Nicodemo counseled Micali to "tone down" his flashy appearance and free-wheeling style because it might attract unwanted attention and it sparked jealousy among other mobsters who wanted to get their hooks into his business.

"Tone it down a little bit," Nicodemo told Micali. "The people that we always talk about, they're going back and they're throwing bait into the ocean and telling the sharks things like, 'Ooooh, this guy did this.' . . . They're throwing jealousy and innuendo. . . . 'Oooh, you should see the piles of money they got in front of them when they play cards.' . . . So, you go play with lesser chips."

Then Nicodemo offered a lesson about the underworld's haves and have-nots: "Like I always say, the lions are on top of the hill and the lambs are down in the valley. When the lions got meat and the lambs got meat, everything's fine and dandy. When the lambs got meat and the lion's up there on the hill and he don't have nothin', what's gonna happen?"

Things had changed in the underworld, Nicodemo told Micali: "Back 30 years ago, all the lions were fully fed. They didn't care about the lambs, you know what I mean? Today, the lions are starving."

Micali should stop wearing "diamonds on your neck" in the poker room, Nicodemo counseled. And it would be smarter if he drove his Honda to the casino, he said. Authorities said Micali spent several hours each day in the poker lounge taking bets and collecting from or paying off customers. He usually drove from his condo in Ventnor to the Borgata in his $130,000 Mercedes.

Nicodemo again emphasized that he would back up Micali in any dispute: "Ya ever have a problem . . . come and see me. . . . I don't care if it's...Carlo Gambino's son. . . . Don't worry about none of that stuff."

He told Micali that everyone knew he was "doing the right thing." That was a reference, it was believed, to the fact that Micali was working with organized crime figures in his business. Then, in what investigators interpreted as an offer to expand that relationship, Nicodemo told Micali that if he would "tone it down . . . they're going to want you to do more of the right thing. You understand what I mean?"

MARRIED TO THE MOB

SEPTEMBER 12, 2009

It was *Married to the Mob* without the humor: a dark story out of a soap opera that offered a rare look inside a woman's relationship with a notorious organized crime figure. There was mental and physical abuse: beatings, black eyes and threats of gun violence, including a forced game of Russian roulette. There were financial problems: for years after their breakup there was no child support, and she struggled on her own to raise their five children. And there was—and, most important from her perspective, still is—guilt by association, a mob-connected label that haunts her, her children, and, she worries, perhaps even her grandchildren.

That's the personal portrait Phyllis Merlino, 60, painted yesterday as she testified before a Casino Control Commission hearing examiner considering whether she, her son and their construction products company should be licensed to work on casino projects. Twice, first in 1987 and again in 1996, Bayshore Rebar Inc. of Pleasantville, New Jersey has been denied a license because of suspected mob associations. Whether those ties exist is at the heart of the current licensing hearing, which is expected to continue at least two more weeks.

For three hours yesterday, Phyllis answered questions, first from her lawyer and then from Assistant Attorney General Anthony J. Zarrillo of the New Jersey Division of Gaming Enforcement. Though the focus was on potential mob ties, the story itself was part Oprah, part Jerry Springer.

"I was married at 16, had five children by the time I was 22, and was separated by the time I was 23," Phyllis said of her relationship with the late Lawrence "Yogi" Merlino, a mob *capo* who died in 2001. The Merlinos divorced in 1977.

"He was abusive," she told her attorney, John Donnelly, as he led her through her story. "He gave me a black eye." Asked whether her husband had ever threatened her with a gun, she paused, then, biting her lip, said, "he forced me to play Russian roulette."

When Phyllis left her husband, she took her five children, all under age seven. They included her oldest son and current business partner, Joseph, now 43; daughter Kimberly, 42; son Nicholas, 40; and twins Marco and Monique, 38. Four of her five children were at yesterday's hearing.

Phyllis Merlino testified that she raised her children on her own, often struggling to pay bills, sometimes staying in a house without electricity, and seldom receiving any help from her former husband, who by the early 1980s was an up-and-comer in a mob family dominated by Nicodemo "Little Nicky" Scarfo, one of the most violent mob bosses in Philadelphia history. Phyllis said she knew very little "about that nonsense" and was not fully aware of her ex-husband's role in the mob until he agreed to pay the mortgage on a house in Margate where she moved with her five children in 1982.

"When I got married, he was a butcher and his brother was a bartender," she said.

Phyllis stated that over the years she had little to do with her husband's "side of the family." She described a rocky relationship with her former sister-in-law, Rita, wife of mobster Salvatore Merlino and mother of mob leader Joseph "Skinny Joey" Merlino.

"It was a peculiar relationship," she recalled. "For about five years, they didn't talk to us at all."

Phyllis said that she had known of her nephew Skinny Joey's mob ties from "reading the papers," but that until his conviction on racketeering charges in 2001 she had not been fully aware of how deeply he was involved.

"I never knew him that way," she claimed, explaining contacts now being cited by the Division of Gaming Enforcement, including the fact that Bayshore had offered Skinny Joey a job when he was seeking parole in 1995 and that Skinny Joey and his wife were sometimes house guests and attended parties at the Merlino home in Ventnor in the late 1990s.

Phyllis Merlino said that she and her family had decided to sever all ties with that side of the family in 2000 or 2001 because of the notoriety. Among other things, the division has cited phone records that Phyllis supplied showing calls between Bayshore and Skinny Joey's side of the family, including calls from Skinny Joey while he was in prison awaiting trial in the 2001 racketeering case.

According to phone records, there also were several calls from top Merlino associate Martin Angelina. Phyllis had become a friend of Angelina's wife, Lauren, who, she said, was going through the same kinds of problems in her marriage. Asked whether she had ever discussed Angelina's mob activities with his wife, Phyllis replied: "We never discussed what her husband did, only what he did to her." Martin Angelina's attorney did not return a call last night seeking comment on Phyllis Merlino's testimony.

Phyllis said the last time she spoke to her former sister-in-law, Rita, was in November 2001. By that point, Lawrence Merlino, who had been in the witness protection program in another part of the country, had died of cancer. Phyllis said she and her children decided to have his body brought back for burial because it was the right thing to do. Rita, whose husband, Salvatore, is still serving a 45-year prison sentence, didn't see it that way.

"Rita called me and said we were assholes for burying him," Phyllis remembered. "I said, 'I'm not asking for your permission,' and then I hung up the phone."

Phyllis Merlino ended her testimony yesterday insisting that she, her son and their company have had nothing to do with organized crime.

"We're like branded," she said. "Is this life without parole?" She stated that if it were up to her, they wouldn't even be in front of the Casino Control Commission. Their company, she added, has enough work and doesn't need the license. They are living well. They don't need the aggravation that the hearing brings: the testimony, the rehashing of old allegations, the retelling of a family saga that sounds more and more like a soap opera as it ages.

"My son, he wants his name cleared," she summed up.

So Phyllis agreed to try one more time for a license, for her children and her grandchildren. This despite the fact that when they were denied a license in 1996, she said she would never try again.

"I told my kids then, 'If Jesus Christ came down from the cross and defended us, we still wouldn't get licensed.'"

THE "OTHER" JOEY MERLINO

SEPTEMBER 20, 2009

Joseph N. Merlino—the "other Joey Merlino"—tried to make a point last week as he testified before a Casino Control Commission hearing examiner. The New Jersey examiner is being asked to determine whether Merlino and his construction company are, in gangland parlance, "mobbed up."

"Everybody in South Philadelphia knows everybody," said Merlino, 43, who is sometimes called "Fat Joey" to distinguish him from mob kingpin Joseph S. "Skinny Joey" Merlino, his cousin. But knowing a wiseguy, he argued, even a relative, doesn't make you a wiseguy. That's a pivotal issue in the debate over whether Merlino and the construction reinforcement materials company he and his mother own, Bayshore Rebar of Pleasantville, New Jersey, should be granted a casino service industry license.

The state Division of Gaming Enforcement (DGE) has opposed the request, citing the same suspected mob ties that led to Bayshore's being denied a license twice in the past. Merlino is due back on the stand when the hearing resumes tomorrow. Testimony and evidence have turned the protracted legal proceeding into an underworld nostalgia trip built around a gangland version of a question once posed by Shakespeare: "What's in a name?" Merlino contends that he and his company have been denied the license because his late father, Lawrence, and "Skinny Joey" were well-known mobsters.

"We've never done anything wrong," Merlino testified Tuesday. "We go to work every day."

He and his mother have insisted that any ties they and their company had to the mob were familial, not criminal, and were severed years ago. It will be up to William T. Sommeling, the casino commissioner who is sitting as the hearing examiner, to sort through the arguments. The hearing, which began August 25 and has included sessions once or twice a week, is expected to conclude by the end of the month.

Deputy Attorney General Wendy Way and Assistant Attorney General Anthony Zarrillo have built the DGE's case in part around dozens of surveillance reports, most more than 10 years old, compiled by the Philadelphia Police Department. These include detailed accounts of surveillance at christenings, weddings, wakes and funerals. The prosecutors used the information to establish associations that they say tie Joseph N. Merlino to the mob. They also allege that those associations continue, pointing to Anthony Giraldi, a South Philadelphia plumber who has been a friend of Joseph N. Merlino's since 2001.

The DGE alleges that Giraldi is a mob associate, although even one of its witnesses, a Philadelphia Police Department intelligence unit supervisor, said neither he nor the department had any direct knowledge of Giraldi's being tied to the mob. A retired FBI agent, called as a witness for Bayshore, has said Giraldi is a "neighborhood plumber."

The ex-agent, James Darcy, spent three days on the stand during the first two weeks of the hearing, mostly under grueling cross-examination by Zarrillo. Using surveillance reports, the assistant attorney general took Darcy through nearly two years of intelligence gathering that, among other things, underscored how dramatically the face of the Philadelphia mob has changed over the last decade.

Typical was a report from May 1997. Philadelphia police were on hand to record the names of those showing up at the Airport Ramada Inn, where mobster Steven Mazzone was hosting a christening party for his daughter. The list of guests was a who's who of mobsters and mob associates and included then-mob boss Ralph Natale, "Skinny Joey" Merlino, Martin Angelina, George Borgesi, Gaeton Lucibello, Anthony Accardo, Daniel Daidone, Damion Canalichio, Ronald Turchi, Roger Vella and Ron Previte. Anthony Giraldi also was there. James Darcy and John Donnelly, Merlino's lawyer, pointed out that many other people attended that party and the wakes and funerals that ended up in surveillance reports. Attendance at an event does not, in itself, connote a mob affiliation, they argued.

The list of attendees at the christening party also demonstrated how things have changed in the underworld in the 12 years since. "Skinny Joey" Merlino, Mazzone, Borgesi, Angelina, Accardo and about a dozen other mobsters have been jailed for racketeering, and Merlino and Borgesi are still in prison. Although it was not known at the time, Previte was cooperating with the FBI when the party took place and, in all probability, was wearing a body wire.

Ralph Natale, charged with drug dealing as a result of Ron Previte's cooperation, later became a government witness. So did Roger Vella after he was tied to a murder and a drug case. Ronald Turchi, a Natale loyalist, was killed after Natale began cooperating in 1999. While Zarrillo has argued that the surveillance reports and other evidence support the DGE's allegations of mob ties, Donnelly has said none of the historic data have any relevance in 2009.

Bayshore Rebar was first denied licensure in 1989, when the Casino Control Commission found that the four-year-old company was a front for another rebar company, Nat-Nat, owned by Lawrence "Yogi" Merlino and Salvatore "Chuckie" Merlino. The Merlino brothers, ranking members of the Scarfo crime family at the time, were convicted of racketeering in 1988. Lawrence Merlino became a cooperating witness. He died in 2001 while in the witness protection program. Salvatore Merlino is serving a 45-year sentence. The brothers each named their first-born son after their father. "Skinny Joey" is Salvatore's son.

In 1996, the Casino Control Commission turned down a second Bayshore application, citing associations with "Skinny Joey" Merlino, who, like his father, had become a high-profile mob figure. Joseph N. Merlino, his lawyer has argued, took a different path. Testifying last week, the "other Joey Merlino" did not deny that he knew many of the mob figures on the surveillance reports. He also acknowledged that he and his mother had attended funerals, christenings and other social events where mobsters were present. But mother and son say that what the DGE sees as potentially nefarious connections are common South Philadelphia neighborhood and family ties.

"Many of these people I know from growing up as a kid in South Philadelphia," Merlino said from the stand last week. "We don't label anybody. But," he added, "we're being labeled right here."

Danny Provenzano on the set of *This Thing of Ours* with James Caan and Frank Vincent

REEL TO REAL

Most people's frame of reference when it comes to the mob is the movies. In that regard, the 30-year demise of the Philadelphia branch of La Cosa Nostra can be quite easily explained in cinematic terms. The Bruno years were *The Godfather* and *Godfather II.* The turbulent and wantonly violent Scarfo years that came after Bruno were part *Goodfellas* and part *Donnie Brasco*, for my money two of the best and most realistic mob movies ever made. Then came the craziness that was John Stanfa, Ralph Natale and Joey Merlino. Make that a dark comedy, a blend of *Pulp Fiction* and *Analyze This*. That, in movie shorthand, is the history of the Philadelphia crime family.

The Sopranos, of course, brought the mob into everyone's living room. And that classic HBO series deserved most of the acclaim it received. It accurately depicted the conflict now going on in the American underworld, a conflict that embodied both a struggle to survive and a desperate attempt to retain an identity.

Simply put—and I've said this before—second- and third-generation Italian Americans don't make good gangsters. The best and the brightest in our community are now doctors, lawyers, teachers and artists. Today the Mafia is scraping the bottom of the gene pool. That wasn't always the case.

You could make the argument that in another time and place, a guy like Angelo Bruno or Carlo Gambino could have been the CEO of a company. Each had the innate intelligence and sophistication to succeed at whatever he chose to do. But both men came to this country as immigrants at a time when many doors were closed to them. The career path they chose was the Mafia. That's not to justify what they did, but to explain it.

While it was no doubt true that Bruno, Gambino and immigrants from their generation experienced bias and prejudice, it would be difficult to make that case today. Think about it. Other than President of the United

States, the most prestigious office in this country is a seat on the U.S. Supreme Court. There are only nine Supreme Court justices. In 2010, two of them are Italian American.

Today the characters attracted to the American Mafia lack the style, wit, grace and brain power of previous generations. The results are detailed in the various RICO indictments handed up by grand juries in all the major cities where La Cosa Nostra once flourished. But that hasn't stopped the new generation of wiseguy from playing the part. For many of them, the classic mob movies mentioned above have become training films. They know how to act like gangsters, but what they really want to be, it seems, are celebrities.

The Mafia is now part of American pop culture. The organization is hardly what it used to be, but it has become a brand, like Dolce & Gabbana or Prada. It's got a marketing niche, a genre. Old timers like Bruno and Gambino would be aghast. Where are the men of honor? What about *omertà*? This is a secret society?

The fact of the matter is that many of today's wiseguys have taken an entrepreneurial approach of the business. They're cashing in on their associations and connections. Free enterprise. The next new thing. The first three stories in this section look at that phenomenon.

The Mafia remains part of the Italian-American experience, but with each passing decade, its impact and influence wane. Once an institution to be feared, it is now one to be parodied. To be sure, there was always some of that. But to understand how it has changed, take a look at the fourth and final piece in this section, a story about Frank Sinatra, an iconic Italian American, and his associations with what was, at the time, one of the most exclusive men's clubs in the world.

DANNY PRO AND *THIS THING OF OURS*

MAY 6, 2002

Danny Provenzano wants to be in the movies. State prosecutors want him in jail. Both could happen before the year is over.

"I might be on trial when the movie comes out," said Provenzano, a reputed mobster and erstwhile filmmaker, smiling as he sat in the hallway of the Bergen County Courthouse in Hackensack last week. He was there for a status conference in his criminal case. The saga of Danny Provenzano is quintessential art imitating life imitating art, set—where else?—in New Jersey, where mobsters are often larger than life and their stories often better than fiction.

The trial, in which Provenzano is charged with racketeering, is tentatively set for September. The movie, which had a screening at an independent film festival in Hoboken last month, could be showing in theaters this fall. Provenzano, 38, cowrote, directed and stars in *This Thing of Ours*, which takes its title from the English translation of La Cosa Nostra. Heavy on Mafia macho and mayhem, it includes one scene in which a businessman is brutally beaten in a dispute over a debt to a printing company and another in which a mob associate's thumb is crushed with a hammer.

Provenzano also has the lead in the criminal case, in which he is accused of heading a mob crew that extorted hundreds of thousands of dollars through fear, intimidation and violence. One of the charges is that a businessman was severely beaten in a disagreement over a $182,000 debt. Another is that a mob associate's thumb was smashed with a hammer because he balked at making a payment.

"They say you write what you know," an investigator quipped.

"I really don't want to get into that," said Deputy Attorney General Robert H. Codey, rolling his eyes and smiling as he walked out of the Hackensack courtroom Tuesday. Provenzano, who has pleaded not guilty and denies that he is "mobbed-up," said the movie came from the heart. It is not, he insisted, an act of arrogance or bravado.

"I'm just trying to make a living," he said. "I want to be a director. I want to be an actor." In fact, Provenzano believes that who he is, rather than what he has done, has shaped the case against him.

Provenzano is a great-nephew of the late Anthony "Tony Pro" Provenzano, a legendary New Jersey Teamsters Union boss and wiseguy. Among other things, Tony Pro was the primary suspect in the disappearance of Jimmy Hoffa.

"My uncle was a dynamic person," Provenzano said last week. "I never really knew too much about his business. My parents never said much. . . . But I can remember big family dinners, and afterwards me and all my cousins would be playing. Our mothers would be in the kitchen, and my uncle and the other men would be sitting at the dining room table talking. . . . I always wanted to be at that table."

State prosecutors allege that he eventually got there, that he is linked to the same Genovese organized crime family as his uncle, and that the extortions were part of a mob-linked enterprise.

"If a guy owes me money and I go after it, am I an extortionist or a guy who just wants what's his?" Provenzano asked. "These were legitimate debts." Provenzano and longtime friend Daniel Farash, one of the producers of the movie, point to the charge that alleges extortion of $182,103.85.

"They got it down to the 85 cents," Farash said. "Does that sound like an extortion or an account receivable?" That, along with the alleged "manner and means" by which the money was collected, will be issues put before a jury. Provenzano said he is willing to take his chances in court.

"I'm not afraid," he said with the same cool confidence that his character, Nick Santini, exudes on the screen.

In real life and on film, the dark-haired actor and alleged mobster has an edgy charisma. Many of those who crammed into the Hudson Street Cinema in Hoboken on April 25 to view *This Thing of Ours* came away talking about Provenzano's "presence." The movie was featured on the first night of a film festival sponsored by the Hudson Waterfront Film Society.

James Caan and comic Pat Cooper have cameo roles. Vincent Pastore of *The Sopranos* and Frank Vincent, a veteran character actor who has appeared in *Goodfellas*, *Casino* and *Raging Bull*, have substantial parts. Vincent plays a mob leader who is the uncle of Provenzano's character.

The film, produced for about two million dollars, according to Provenzano and Farash, copped the festival's awards for best picture and best director. Provenzano, who was raised in Fort Lee but now lives with his wife and two young children in Upper Saddle River, Bergen County, said he had gotten the idea for the script "from things I've seen and experienced . . . and from things I read right out of the indictment."

"That doesn't mean they were true," he quickly added.

Financing for the movie came from "friends," Provenzano said, including John "Sonny" Franzese, a notorious *capo* in the Colombo crime family.

"I don't ask my investors where they get their money," Provenzano stated. "But, yeah, I know who Sonny is. He's a friend of mine."

Distribution is still being discussed, but Provenzano and Farash conceded that timing it to the trial would be a publicist's dream.

Provenzano was indicted in 1999 after a probe into a printing company he had owned and the alleged extortion of business associates. He said that he had built the business up from scratch, and that when he sold it in 1997, "we were doing $20 million a year in sales." The money from the sale, he said, has allowed him to embark on a film career, something he had wanted for years. Two of his earlier, straight-to-video films, *The Regenerated Man* and *Vampire Vixens from Venus*, earned money, Provenzano noted, but are not works that he is particularly happy to have in his filmography.

"They were schlock," he admitted.

This Thing of Ours, on the other hand, is something Provenzano says he believes in and can be proud of. Then he smiles. And the question that hangs in the air is whether he is talking about the movie.

MAFIA:
MORE CARTOON THAN COSA NOSTRA

AUGUST 28, 2005

It was all there in a federal courtroom in Lower Manhattan last week: a moment in time that perfectly captured what has happened to the American Mafia. La Cosa Nostra, the "honored society" that spawned Mario Puzo's classic saga, has become the stuff of comic books and supermarket tabloids. "This thing of ours" is now a caricature of itself. *The Sopranos* writ large.

So here was Curtis Sliwa, the flamboyant founder of the Guardian Angels and a local morning radio personality, on the witness stand pointing a finger at a mobster who allegedly pumped two bullets into his belly back in 1992. And there was John A. "Junior" Gotti, son of the late mob boss John J. Gotti, at the defense table, accused of ordering the kidnapping that led to the shooting. And in the back of the crowded courtroom was the defendant's older sister, Victoria, the tart-tongued Mafia princess, stopping by after a morning television appearance that touted the start of the third—and they said it wouldn't last—season of her show, *Growing Up Gotti*. Reality TV meets talk radio. That's the mob of the 21st century.

The Gotti racketeering trial, about to enter its fourth week, is just one example of how La Cosa Nostra has come apart at the seams. Up in Westchester County, New York, three prominent doctors are facing charges of supplying drugs to a Gambino family *capo* in exchange for favors from the mob. The drugs? Viagra, Cialis and Levitra. The favors? Free repairs at mob auto body shops, bootleg DVDs and an impossible-to-get reservation at Rao's, the popular and tiny East Harlem restaurant where wiseguys and celebs hang out. Clearly, this is not your father's Mafia.

And that doesn't even take into account the case now pending in federal court in Brooklyn, in which two highly decorated and retired New York City police detectives have been indicted on charges that, between 1986 and 1990, they moonlighted as hit men for the Lucchese crime family while on the job. That indictment puts nine bodies on the ex-cops, Louis Eppolito and Stephen Caracappa, who have pleaded not guilty.

Most of the victims had crossed mobsters in business deals or were suspected of cooperating with authorities, the FBI alleges. But one victim had no known dealings with organized crime. In that instance, Eppolito and Caracappa, who authorities say were paid by the mob to locate a mobster who had been targeted for death, came up with the address of a Brooklyn man who happened to have the same name as the target. He was gunned down on Christmas Day 1986 . . . by mistake. All of it, say Mafia experts, points to a mob in disarray, an organization in which honor and loyalty have been replaced by greed and stupidity.

The days of the "soft-spoken godfathers" are over, said George Weissinger, a former federal immigration agent and parole officer who is now an associate professor of criminal justice at Briarcliffe College in Bethpage, New York. John J. Gotti, who died of cancer in 2002, exuded flash and glitter, atypical of the low-profile Cosa Nostra bosses who for years ruled the underworld with quiet efficiency, Weissinger noted. During Gotti's bloody, flamboyant reign as boss of the Gambino crime family, form always won out over substance. That's his legacy. And it has been embraced by those, like his son, who have come after him.

"These guys have seen too many movies," said Howard Abadinsky, a nationally known mob expert and author who teaches criminal justice at St. John's University. "They've forgotten where the line is between reality and fantasy." The current "Junior" Gotti trial is a case in point, he added.

Curtis Sliwa was supposedly targeted because of things he had been saying on his talk-radio show about the mob in general and the elder Gotti in particular.

"I called John Gotti Sr. America's number one drug dealer," Sliwa, a notorious self-promoter, said from the witness stand last week as he dramatically recounted his June 1992 kidnapping and shooting.

That the mob was even listening to a bombastic morning talk-radio host says a lot about the state of organized crime, said Abadinsky. That Gotti and his son allegedly reacted in such a high-profile way (Sliwa was kidnapped in a stolen cab by two mobsters who were supposed to beat him up but instead shot him) boldly demonstrates the look-at-me-I'm-a-gangster management style that has brought the organization down, Abadinsky added.

Hiring cops to carry out hits, as the indictments allege, is another example. Experts in organized crime say the mob has always used "dirty" cops as a source of information, paying them for tips about where an investigation was heading or who might be cooperating. Louis Eppolito—whose father, uncle and grandfather were members of the Gambino crime family—and Stephen Caracappa allegedly began that way. But their involvement soon escalated to active participation in murders, authorities contend.

In one case, Eppolito and Caracappa allegedly "arrested" a suspected mob informant, threw him into the trunk of their car and delivered him to a Lucchese crime family boss, who beat and tortured the man to death. In another, the two are accused of pulling over a target in what seemed to be a routine police auto stop. Caracappa then allegedly walked up to the driver's side of the vehicle and shot his victim in the head. Both detectives had retired to Las Vegas when they were indicted earlier this year.

Eppolito, who cowrote a book, *Mafia Cop*, on his life as a "hero cop" with a mob family background, was trying to get into acting and screenwriting when he headed west in the early 1990s. He was living in a gated community with a home and a lifestyle that seemed far beyond the reach of a retired detective on a pension.

"This stuff is . . . not the norm," said Fred Martens, the former executive director of the Pennsylvania Crime Commission. Martens, an expert on organized crime who now works for a New York City corporate investigation company, argues that the whole Gotti experience—the hair-trigger tempers, the lack of discipline and the quest for the spotlight—has been an "aberration." The mob, he admits, still exists and is still making money in gambling, loan-sharking, labor racketeering and extortion. But there are those in the organization who have become "reality TV gangsters," he remarked with a laugh. "*Growing Up Gotti*? What's that all about?"

There is a segment of the underworld that is convinced John J. Gotti is rolling over in his grave because of the antics of his daughter, Victoria, and the weekly pouting and posturing of his three maxi-gelled teenage grandsons on that reality TV show. Yet as federal authorities build new cases against the organization, life continues to imitate art.

Wiretaps in a racketeering investigation of another Gambino family crew earlier this year led to the arrests in April of the three Westchester County doctors. All three, the government alleges, supplied boxes of prescription drug samples to Gregory DePalma, a 73-year-old mob *capo* who, on one FBI tape, scoffed at the idea that he personally needed any sexual stimulants. He was reportedly giving the Viagra and other drugs to friends and associates. On another tape, one of the doctors said of the Viagra he was supplying DePalma: "That stuff, that stuff, you know, is like gold." The doctor then asked DePalma whether he could be considered the mob's medical "consigliere."

Two hours before the start of Monday's session in the "Junior" Gotti trial, spectators began to gather in the hallway outside the 26th-floor courtroom. Everyone knew that Sliwa was expected on the stand, and seats would be at a premium. Francine Greene, a widowed Manhattanite from the Upper West Side, was one of the first to arrive. She said she was a frequent visitor to the trial and found it entertaining.

There was the testimony about murders, kidnappings, shootings and extortions that offered a real-life look at the world of organized crime. There were colorful witnesses with names that Greene thought "sounded like a Starbucks menu: Cappuccino, Macchiato, Frappuccino." And there were family members (Junior Gotti's mother, brother, cousins, aunts and uncles filling two rows in the courtroom almost every day) who dressed and acted like extras from a gangster movie.

"It's like *The Sopranos*," Greene said. "Only better."

NEW YORK, NEW YORK

MARCH 12, 2006

The Sopranos swings back into action tonight when HBO launches the long-awaited sixth season of its multifaceted mob melodrama. But whatever the writers have come up with this year for Tony, Paulie Walnuts and the rest of the crew, it will be hard to match the real-life story lines from three federal courtrooms here. You want murder and mayhem? You got it. Corruption? It's covered. Infidelity? Not a problem.

Start with Vincent "Vinny Gorgeous" Basciano, a Bonanno family boss on trial on charges of murder and racketeering. Vinny—he of the expensive suits and soft Ferragamo loafers—once sought the OK to whack a fellow mobster by complaining, "I have a problem living in the same world with this guy."

The trial, now heading into its fourth week in federal court in Brooklyn, has included testimony from a handful of mob informants, including a former underboss who admitted his involvement in 13 gangland murders. His name is Salvatore "Handsome Sal" Vitale. Handsome Sal versus Vinny Gorgeous. Top that, HBO. Then there are Louis Eppolito and Stephen Caracappa, two highly decorated former New York City police detectives who are defendants in a racketeering case set to open tomorrow in the same federal courthouse as the Basciano trial. In one of the most sensational allegations of corruption in the history of the NYPD, Eppolito and Caracappa are charged with moonlighting as hit men for Luchese crime family boss Anthony "Gaspipe" Casso while "on the job." Talk about problems with authority figures. The Mafia cops scenario would have Tony Soprano on his therapist's couch for months.

And finally, there is John A. "Junior" Gotti, son of the late Dapper Don and brother of reality TV series "star" Victoria Gotti. "Junior" Gotti was being retried in a racketeering case that included the 1992 kidnapping and assault of Curtis Sliwa, radio personality and Guardian Angels founder. The motive, say prosecutors: Sliwa had been bad-mouthing the senior Gotti on his morning radio show. A jury in that high-profile case deliberated for less than a day before declaring Friday afternoon that it was hopelessly deadlocked. The resulting mistrial set up the possibility of yet a third trial. The logjam came after five weeks of testimony in a case that ended with a similar hung jury last year.

This year's retrial—call it an encore presentation—included many of the same witnesses telling basically the same story. But Michael "Mikey Scars" DiLeonardo added a new twist when he offered some 20-year-old gossip about John J. Gotti, the Dapper Don who died in prison four years ago. It was common knowledge in many mob circles, "Mikey Scars" said, that Gotti had a daughter with his secret mistress, the wife of a Gambino crime family soldier.

The allegations fueled a tabloid frenzy. Suddenly, the phrase "going to the mattresses" had a whole new meaning. And just as suddenly, the alleged kidnapping of Sliwa—the crime at the heart of a case that could have landed "Junior" Gotti in jail for the next 30 years—became a footnote in newspaper stories around the world. "The Godfather and his 'Mob Love Child'" blared one headline in an Australian paper. "Dirty Don's Cosy Nostra Shocks Mob," screamed another. How are they going to match that at the Bada Bing?

"Truth and fiction, it's a very thin line," said Pete Randazzo, a New York City cabdriver who took a day off last Wednesday to try to get a seat for closing arguments at the Gotti trial. Wearing sunglasses and a black leather jacket over a white turtleneck and jeans, Randazzo said he came to court with a buddy who was "a friend of the family." Enough said. They were on line by 8:30 a.m. at the federal courthouse in Lower Manhattan to score two of the limited seats reserved for the public. Then there was Gigi DiMurro, a financial analyst from Hoboken who said she had been coming to Manhattan each day for the trial.

"I got a nice boss," DiMurro remarked, explaining her free time. "I make him a lot of money." The would-be fan, who opted to wait in the hallway, claimed the younger Gotti, 42, was the victim of a prosecutorial vendetta.

"If he had a different last name, he wouldn't be there," she said. And all the gossip about a love child is irrelevant, added DiMurro, who was incensed by a *New York Post* story that showed a picture of the 19-year-old girl the elder Gotti allegedly fathered.

"They said she had his eyebrows," she scoffed. "Go up to Elizabeth Arden and you could have anybody's eyebrows."

While the Gotti case was wrapping up, the jurors in the Basciano trial were being regaled with Vitale's tales from the underworld. "Handsome Sal" talked of hits and misses, of mob protocol and of some of the guys he had done business with over the years, such as "Louie Ha Ha," "Joey Shakes," "Nicky Mouth" and "Jimmy the General." Vitale, 58, also offered the kind of insider information that turns up in the scripts of popular mob television shows. For example, he said it was stupid to try to do a hit inside a car. Of his 13 homicides, only one took place that way and it was a mess. Sal said he was the driver and the target was in the passenger seat next to him. The shooter, as planned, sat in the back seat.

"After the first shot, [the victim] grabbed the steering wheel and tried to put his foot on the gas pedal," Vitale said. Only after a second shot, with blood splattering on the dashboard, was Sal able to regain control of the car.

"It could've caused an accident," he added.

Through it all, Basciano, 46, and his co-defendant, Patrick "Patty from the Bronx" DeFilippo, 67, appeared unfazed. Basciano, whose nickname comes from a time when he owned a beauty salon called Hello Gorgeous, is cut from the same mold as the late John Gotti. His silver-gray hair is always neatly coiffed. His suits fit perfectly. And despite the fact that he has been in jail for more than a year, he has a tan that others spend weeks in the Bahamas trying to perfect.

Clearly at ease, Basciano's dimpled face breaks frequently into a smile as he plays to his audience, offering nods, winks and shrugs to friends, family members, reporters—and on Tuesday, an attractive young blonde—who show up in the courtroom. DeFilippo, in a conservative pin-striped suit, looks dour in comparison. The two defendants sit at opposite ends of the defense table and seldom interact. While it's not part of the case, there is clearly a reason for that. When Basciano was secretly taped complaining that he couldn't "live in the same world" with a certain wiseguy, the wiseguy in question was "Patty from the Bronx."

The plot to kill DeFilippo is part of a bigger racketeering indictment still pending against Basciano in which he also is charged with planning to kill Assistant U.S. Attorney Gregory Andres, the prosecutor in the current case. Targeting prosecutors, like targeting the families of witnesses, has turned the Mafia into "an evil way of life," Vitale said. Before he became a cooperator, Vinny told the jury, he had a discussion with other mob members about what ought to be done to stem the tide of mob informants. Mob leader Anthony Spero, Vitale recalled, offered a simple solution: "We gotta kill their wives, their kids and their dogs."

That cold and brutal underworld life will be a major theme in the third big mob case that begins this week when Eppolito, 57, and Caracappa, 64, go on trial. The case, which has already spawned four book deals and at least one film project, is expected to draw capacity crowds and has led the judge to relocate to a larger courtroom.

Among other things, the two former detectives are charged with using their badges to kidnap one victim and deliver him to "Gaspipe" Casso for assassination, killing another mobster after pulling him over for a "traffic stop" and providing the wrong address for a third Casso target that led to an innocent man being murdered. All of it is untrue, claim Eppolito, Caracappa and their high-profile lawyers, Bruce Cutler and Edward Hayes.

Playing defense has long been a part of Eppolito's life. He spent years defending his honor and integrity after the police brass learned that his father, grandfather and uncle were members of the Gambino crime family. In fact, the onetime hero detective cowrote *Mafia Cop*, a book in which he claimed he was forced to resign in a sins-of-the-father vendetta. Published in 1992, the book was subtitled *The Story of an Honest Cop Whose Family Was the Mob*. The trial that begins this week could force a major rewrite.

FRANK SINATRA AND THE MOB:
AN APPRECIATION

MAY 18, 1998

Shortly before the first casino opened in Atlantic City back in 1978, a local mobster went into the bar business. The guy was named Saul Kane. He had been a bail bondsman and later he went to jail for dealing drugs. But when he was on top of his game, he was known in certain circles as the Meyer Lansky of the Boardwalk, a major moneymaker and confidant of soon-to-be mob boss Nicodemo "Little Nicky" Scarfo. Kane opened a joint on Pacific Avenue a few blocks from the Resorts International Casino-Hotel. He called the place the My Way Lounge. The interior was plastered with photos of Frank Sinatra, and the jukebox was jammed with Sinatra tunes. Soon all the local wiseguys and wannabes started hanging out there.

Kane would run ads in the paper touting his bar and tweaking the cops: "Come meet the Mob at the My Way." Frank Sinatra never set foot inside the place, but what did it matter? It was another link, however tenuous, between the greatest saloon singer of all time and one of the most exclusive men's clubs in America.

Sinatra and the mob. Fact or fiction? Probably a little of both.

First, a disclaimer. There are those who get upset at any discussion of the "associations" Frank Sinatra had during his career as a singer and movie star. Just because his name ends in a vowel, they say, people want to claim he's a mobster, a Mafioso, a wiseguy. That's not what it says here. What it says here is that over the course of his long and storied career, Frank Sinatra crossed paths with guys who never had to work a nine-to-five job, guys who cheated and stole and lied to get ahead, guys who knew where the bodies were buried. And they weren't all politicians. Sinatra, on the public record at least, never said much about this. But his associations were fairly well-documented and frequently attracted law enforcement attention.

Where to start? How about the trip he took to Havana in 1947 with one Joseph "Joey Fish" Fischetti? Sinatra apparently was just along for the ride, but Fischetti and nearly a dozen other top American mobsters had business in Cuba. They met there with Charles "Lucky" Luciano, who had been deported to Italy and was angling to get back into the United States to solidify his control of La Cosa Nostra in America.

Or how about Sinatra's partnership interest in the Berkshire Downs Racetrack with, among others, New England mob boss Raymond Patriarca? Or how about how he decided to give up his Nevada gaming license rather than fight charges that might have exposed his ties to Chicago Mafia don Sam (Momo) Giancana? The Giancana incident, perhaps more than any other, epitomizes the complex and titillating nature of Sinatra's oft-cited "connections." And while some in law enforcement say it was just the tip of the iceberg, a glimpse of a more sinister association, for those in the entertainer's camp it demonstrated the price Sinatra was willing to pay when it came to friendship and loyalty.

So it was that in 1963, Sinatra gave up his interest in the Cal-Neva gaming lodge in Lake Tahoe, where he had allowed Giancana to stay as a guest even though he was on the state gaming authority's "black list" and banned from all Nevada casinos. Giancana was reportedly visiting his girlfriend, Phyllis McGuire, who was performing with her sister at the casino. The affair, which attracted a lot of media attention, was one of a series of incidents that led to a split with President John F. Kennedy, for whom Sinatra had raised serious campaign money in 1960. But while the president and his attorney-general brother, Robert, decided they had to sever all ties with Sinatra, goodfellas such as Giancana never forgot. According to a book co-authored by his brother and nephew, Giancana used to complain about the entertainers who got a leg up in the business from a "family member," then forgot about it when they made it big. Sinatra, said Giancana in the book *Double Cross*, wasn't that way.

"He's too good for those bums in Hollywood," Giancana told his brother. Sinatra, he said in what is the highest form of underworld praise, was "a real stand-up guy."

Giancana, who himself moved in many circles, went on to share a mistress with John Kennedy, a woman named Judith Exner who had met the president through Sinatra. The singer had also had a brief fling with the flashy brunette. Strange bedfellows indeed.

Several years later, Sinatra again found himself in the middle of a big Mafia media flap when he performed at a fund-raiser at the Westchester Premier Dinner Theater in Tarrytown, New York. The feds eventually charged that the theater was the target of a mob operation in which New York boss of bosses Carlo Gambino and several of his top associates pocketed in excess of $400,000.

The fund-raiser was just one of several alleged mob scams that had the theater as a backdrop. It's mentioned only because of an infamous photo taken backstage after Sinatra's performance. Ol' Blue Eyes is in the center of the picture surrounded by eight serious fans, all of whom showed up on organizational charts in the FBI's New York office. Among them were Paul Castellano, Aladena "Jimmy the Weasel" Fratianno and, smiling benevolently with his eyes closed as the camera flashed, Carlo Gambino. The boss of bosses. Just one of the guys. Rubbing elbows with the star. Go figure.

That Sinatra had a special place in the hearts of certain nefarious underworld characters is without dispute. Those who knew him and those who wanted to, like the guys down at the My Way Lounge, apparently held the skinny kid from Hoboken in the highest regard. He epitomized what these guys wanted to be. Think of the image: a cigarette dangling from his lips in some smoky bar, suit jacket thrown over the back of his chair, tie loosened, a scotch in one hand, a beautiful woman in the other. The existential macho man.

Sinatra's mob associations have been detailed in dozens of organized crime books, from *Double Cross* and Fratianno's tell-all, *The Last Mafioso*, to Stephen Fox's *Blood and Power* and Jay R. Nash's *World Encyclopedia of Organized Crime*. Everybody who writes about the mob, it seems, has a Sinatra story to tell. The post-performance party at the Westchester Dinner Theater is one of the most repeated. Another, told in several versions, deals with Willie Moretti, the North Jersey gangster who either discovered Sinatra or gave the young singer's career a boost when he really needed it.

Moretti, the story goes, was the guy who helped Sinatra get out of what was thought to be an iron-clad contract with bandleader Tommy Dorsey. Sinatra wanted out so he could pursue a career on his own, but Dorsey wasn't about to give up control over the crooner. Enter Moretti, who "negotiated" a deal with Dorsey one night in the dressing room of a club where the band was performing. Moretti put a gun in Dorsey's mouth, according to various accounts of the incident, and told the bandleader he had two choices. Either he, Dorsey, would sign an agreement releasing Sinatra from his contract, or he, Moretti, would pull the trigger. It was an offer that Dorsey "couldn't refuse." Later Mario Puzo in *The Godfather* would borrow some of the details, add a horse's head, and create the signature phrase of perhaps the most widely read piece of Mafia fiction ever written.

Over the course of nearly 70 years in the spotlight, Frank Sinatra, wittingly or unwittingly, provided wiseguys, politicians and writers with a piece of himself. The attraction is obvious. He was the best at what he did, a one-of-a-kind. No one interpreted a lyric in quite the same way. And when he stood on stage or sat in a recording studio, no one was his equal. *Sine qua non*, said the Romans long ago. That's what they were going for in the My Way Lounge down on Pacific Avenue. Even wiseguys have heroes.